LIVING ABROAD WITH UNCLE SAM

FOREIGN SERVICE DAYS

BY

HELEN WEINLAND

ISBN: 1-4140-0182-7 (Paperback)

Library of Congress Control Number: 2003112395

This book is printed on acid free paper.

Printed in the United States of America
Bloomington, IN

Cover drawing © Isaac Robbins

1stBooks — rev. 10/09/03

Acknowledgements

It will become apparent in the pages that follow that I do not regard my career in the Foreign Service with unalloyed pleasure and approbation. Nevertheless, during the twenty years I served in the Department of State, I met a body of people who must be almost unequalled in intelligence, good humor, and a spirit of service to our country. Many of them became friends for life; others may be less good at staying in touch but gave me many happy hours of comradeship while we served together. I extend my thanks to all of them for making these twenty years of my life so enjoyable.

During the writing of this book, a number of persons encouraged me first to keep writing and second to persevere in publication. These people include my mother Virginia Weinland, my sister Margaret Weinland, David Duke, the late George Brockway, Doris Grumbach, and Ted Smith. My friends Luise Erdmann and Emily Chaney went beyond encouragement to making editorial and copyediting suggestions that have proved invaluable. As is usual with writers making these acknowledgements, however, I hasten to say that all faults in construction, all infelicitous sentences, and all failure to answer the question, "What was it *really* like?" are mine and mine alone.

Table of Contents

Introduction: Getting Started

When I am asked why I became a diplomat, "unemployment" is the first word that springs to mind. It is as accurate a response as any. I never set out to become a diplomat. When I joined the Foreign Service, I was astounded to find that several of my classmates had dreamed of such a career. Some had even gone through the lengthy exam process several times.

I was in a difficult situation in the fall of 1972. I had taught history for three years at Ohio State University on a nonrenewable contract. My Ph.D. dissertation—on a narrow slice of nineteenth-century British history—was not finished, although most of the research and much of a first draft were. Even with some teaching experience, I found the demand for British history professors was shrinking—as was, indeed, the university job market in general.

When I began to consider how to use my skills in government or business, a friend suggested I take the Foreign Service exam. Given the first Saturday of every December, it is not unlike a college SAT, a type of exam I had last taken ten years earlier. Suddenly I found myself confronted with math problems I had easily solved in my junior year of high school. Sitting toward the back of a brightly lit exam room, I was completely unable to remember how to set up equations to deal with bathtubs filling and draining at different rates or two trains rushing toward each other across the American prairie. In the end, although I did poorly on the quantitative work, my writing skills and "general knowledge" were enough to qualify me for the next step

By the end of that December I officially had abandoned the Ph.D. and by April had scouted around to see where I might be able to find work. The Foreign Service entry process was so long and unsure, I certainly could not count on it. A day or two before Easter 1973, I set out from Columbus in my Volkswagen Bug, bound for Washington, D.C., where a friend had offered me a free room during my job hunt. A few hours down the road, the Bug obligingly threw a rod and self-destructed on Interstate 70 near St. Clairsville, Ohio.

I fell into the hands of a shady car mechanic who offered me a "rebuilt" engine for the car that could only be installed on the Monday after Easter. I spent a miserable weekend in a Holiday Inn, completely immobile and worrying about the various bills I was running up. The completed job was a rip-off failure as I found out driving at 40 mph over the western Pennsylvania mountains. The car would go no faster, and I limped into my friend Harriet's house at about 2:30 am.

A day and a half later, as one member of the Foreign Service interviewing team led me down the hall for my interview, he asked routinely, "Did you have any trouble getting here?" I roared with laughter, which happily got me off to a good start with the panel. In fact, I had been so undone by the trip that the interview seemed but a minor event in a horrible week; whether I passed was a matter of no great concern.

Almost a year later, in March 1974, I stood with my Foreign Service entering class to take the oath of office. Richard Nixon was still the president of the United States and Henry Kissinger was secretary of state. The hostilities in Vietnam were theoretically over for the United States, but one of my classmates was assigned as an aide to our ambassador in Saigon, only to be evacuated from the roof of the embassy a year or so later by a United States military helicopter. Two of our diplomats in Khartoum, Sudan, had recently been abducted and murdered, and in a month or two our ambassador to Cyprus would be killed in Nicosia. In the years to come, I would lose friends and colleagues to causes as varied as an accident in an armored personnel carrier in Sarajevo, a case of cerebral malaria in Dar-es-Salaam, Tanzania, and the Rwandan genocide.

When I entered the Foreign Service, these dangers were of no particular concern to me. My biggest worry centered on the difficulties of extended periods of life overseas. For many people, the romance of "all that traveling" is the appeal of the diplomatic life; they imagine it as a kind of extended vacation, filling boxes of slides to show the folks back home, and sampling exotic foods.

I had already lived overseas several times, once for an academic year in Edinburgh, Scotland, and another for two months in France where virtually no one spoke English. I found those experiences rewarding—one of my closest friends remains the French "sister" from that summer—but I also knew there were times when I would long for conversation with someone who shared my mother tongue, who automatically understood my sense of humor, and who recognized American values. I was uncertain whether an entire career of overseas tours would be too arduous, particularly for a single person without a domestic partner.

In fact, the general condition of the diplomat overseas is otherness. The diplomat observes from the sidelines, not even usually as a referee or a fan. I may have known this instinctively as I hesitated to accept the offer to join the Foreign Service. I came to see it as a professional requirement after I signed up. This did not mean that I renounced my ability or right to draw moral conclusions about what I was observing. Under certain circumstances, I could express these conclusions, but in classified form, hidden from my fellow citizens and the citizens of my various host countries. It was my job to understand as accurately as possible what was going on, but I could not participate in events. I knew from the start that this would be, for me, the most difficult part of overseas service.

There were factors on the plus side of the ledger as well. My father spent much of his career in international business so we had frequent guests from overseas in our house, and early on I had listened to people struggling to speak English with me. I carried my curiosity about their languages, children, and countries into adulthood. Recently, a close friend from college, an ethnic Indian woman raised in eastern Africa, told me she had found our home the most comfortable place she ever visited in the United States; our family had accepted her completely naturally. That openness to others was a bonus to me in my Foreign Service life.

My job search in Washington, begun in April 1973, resulted by August in a job, one I even liked. My boss there confirmed my suspicion, however, that I was not on a career track. The lack of employment with any future remained a powerful incentive. After weighing the pros and cons, I decided to accept the offer of the Foreign Service.

I joined the entering class in March 1974. A five-week course introduced us to the bare bones of our new profession. I was then temporarily assigned to the office handling Philippine affairs. I quickly realized that government service, specifically State Department service, was a different culture from that of the university. Early on, I was handed a cable from Manila announcing a visit to Washington by a member of the embassy staff; he requested hotel reservations and an appointment or two. I took care of the requests and wrote a return cable with the information; my secretary, who was as new to the State Department as I was, typed it and put it in the outgoing basket. A more senior secretary spotted it and told me, rather sternly, that I had neglected to get the proper "clearances." "What's to clear?" was my reaction; the man asked for some perfectly straightforward help and I was accommodating him. It would be years before I became senior enough in the State

Department to provide the final clearance to my own cables. I was now a bureaucrat, and a pretty minor one.

A little later, the ambassador to the Philippines, William Sullivan, returned to Washington for two weeks of discussions about our policy there. Sullivan later became much better known as our ambassador during the Iranian Revolution, but in 1974 he was already intimidating. A few days into his visit, I was asked to coordinate his schedule of appointments; the job involved confirming each call, making sure cars were available, and adding and changing dates as required. Piece of cake, I thought. It seemed so simple I couldn't understand why I was asked to do this secretarial job.

A major glitch arose, however. I assumed one appointment would last almost an hour, but the person receiving the ambassador had allowed only fifteen minutes. I learned of my mistake only shortly before the ambassador was to leave the building, and I ran up the stairs to tell him. Sullivan and I were about the same height, and he stared at me levelly with his blue eyes as he asked, "How is it that an appointment that was to last an hour is now just fifteen minutes long?" I was mortified, panic-stricken; four weeks in the Foreign Service and I had already blown it. I stared back and said, "Because I made a mistake." Amazingly, Sullivan had no easy comeback, and after a dreadful moment of silence he said, "At least that is an honest answer."

I learned some useful lessons from this encounter. One, happily, reinforced my belief that it was better to tell the truth when I made a mistake. Another, limited to this new culture, was that many ambassadors take themselves extremely seriously and require their subordinates to insulate them from the normal lapses of daily life. Finally, I had my first encounter with the fanatical attention to detail required of a State Department employee when planning schedules, "scenarios," for visiting firemen, writing press releases, or performing staff work. No Foreign Service officer who aspires to continued employment and promotion can ignore the last two of those principles; the first one admits of more fudging.

Standing to take an oath, promising to "defend and uphold the Constitution of the United States against all enemies, foreign and domestic," and swearing to do it all "so help me God" are serious commitments. I may not have consciously prepared for my new career, but I was determined to do well at it.

I find it interesting as I reflect on my first days at the State Department to realize I was at the same time making another commitment. When I joined the Foreign Service, I was living on upper Wisconsin Avenue, in a block of apartments directly across the street from the National Cathedral. The cathedral was then still under construction, but it was already a tourist attraction: the stained glass and stonework were worth more than a glance. One weekend some cousins were visiting, and we wandered across the street on Sunday morning to take a look. A service was in progress, and we were politely asked to sit down. Dean Francis Sayre was preaching, and he had quite a bit to say about the current hot subject in Washington, Nixon's behavior in the White House.

I was intrigued enough by that first, almost accidental visit to return for a full service the next week. When I was thirteen years old, I had chosen to join the Episcopal Church and had been confirmed. Active all the way through college, I lapsed in graduate school. Like many others, I found religious observance irrelevant to the rest of my life. My circle of friends and colleagues did not include many who followed any faith; on the contrary, it included a number who had many reasons for putting all that behind.

National Cathedral is the seat of the Episcopal Bishop of the Diocese of Washington, so the services and music were familiar to me. I found myself drawn back to the fold, partly against my will, partly feeling that I was returning to a well loved home. As I recognize the renewed commitment, I realize that it was a welcome support when I was also committing myself to a new career that would be difficult at times. Returning to the church as a mature adult was a decision I made gratefully. It became a source of strength and purpose in the years ahead.

In the Foreign Service I found that quite a large number of my colleagues were religiously observant. I am not at all cynical about this phenomenon; I don't brush it off as a social convention within the profession, even if the diplomatic service is generally thought of as convention-bound. My colleagues followed a wide range of religious traditions—Roman Catholic, Baptist, Episcopal, Jewish, Baha'i—with serious conviction. I know we found religious observance an important part of our commitment to public service.

I gradually adopted habits and attitudes that supported my professional commitment. Some of these grew out of the need to work with classified material and to protect its integrity. It is easy to get somewhat obsessive and silly about secrecy. Too casual an approach to classification and the protection of government secrets, however, can bring security violations and a whole lot of trouble on your head.

The height of silliness came one evening in Lagos, Nigeria, as I was leaving the embassy, perhaps an hour after it closed. To leave after hours required going past the Marine security guard at the front entrance and signing out in the log. I was carrying my purse and briefcase, as well as a "burn bag," filled with a dozen eggs from the embassy snack bar. A "burn bag" is nothing more than a paper grocery store sack on which is printed in large black letters, "BURN."

We were expected to place all classified paper we discarded into such a bag; it was then disposed of in a large shredder or incinerator. A burn bag is also an excellent container for carrying loose eggs.

"Ma'am," said the Marine guard, "I can't let you leave the building with that burn bag."

I thought he was joking. I showed him it held nothing more than a dozen naked eggs. He was not joking. I had to leave the nice square-bottomed bag back in my office and substitute a plain manila envelope for the eggs.

There is no appealing to the Marine security guard. Knowing that the guards will come through the office at night and often go through anything on top of or inside your desk, looking for a security violation, made me fanatically careful about how I treated classified material. People who had trouble remembering safe combinations often tried to disguise them and keep them somewhere handy—on the backs of blotters or in desktop calendars; they were almost always discovered. It was highly advisable to learn never to place classified material anywhere but in one area of the desk and then to place everything in that area in the safe every night. We even had to remove all typewriter ribbons at the end of the day and place them in the safe as well.

These habits carried over to how I handled my personal papers. I was careful about what I wrote home, not naming the people I spoke with or policies under consideration. I kept no diary or journal. Stationed in Czechoslovakia, I learned not to leave any personal paper in my apartment. If I went out at night, I carried my address book and personal calendar in my evening purse. I kept all my financial papers and personal correspondence at the office, taking them home only if I was going to work on them that evening or weekend. I shredded all personal documents there and later, too, in Kaduna, Nigeria. In Kaduna the problem was not so much hostile intelligence services as the possibility that account numbers would be retrieved from the household trash to be used in fraud schemes. One consulate employee learned that his friends' addresses, collected from his trash, were culled for scam letter targets.

I don't, therefore, have much documentary help in writing this book. My reports were almost always classified in whole or in part. Presumably they are somewhere in the archives of the Department of State, but retrieving them and requesting declassification are next to impossible. I was, of course, not permitted to take anything with me, either from post to post or into retirement.

Perhaps forced by this lack of documentation, I find that what I am interested in writing is a commentary on what it was like in the Foreign Service, being involved at a working level in some of the big events of the last quarter century and making my own judgment about what we did. And I find my reservoir of memory is full to overflowing. Two decades censoring myself have reinforced the dam.

I have reached that point in life when we all begin to wonder what it was for. What did it mean to give twenty years of my life to the Foreign Service? Did I give up too much of myself to loyal service in this hierarchical, command-driven organization? Did I enjoy it? Did I do it well? Was it worth doing well?

On February 28, 1999, I found myself at the Camden Conference, an annual gathering of international affairs aficianados held in a small town on the coast of Maine. The subject was Sub-Saharan Africa, and we enjoyed a day and a half of stimulating presentations. The International Monetary Fund and World Bank came into almost every discussion, and the structural adjustment programs they designed for and imposed on many African countries were, for the most part, bitterly criticized. In the final panel, a man in the audience introduced himself as someone who had worked for the World Bank for thirty years and had spent his last ten years designing these programs. He was wryly amusing in describing how he felt, hearing his work come under such general criticism, and wanted to know what, exactly, had gone wrong with these programs.

His question was fielded by a woman who directed African programs for the UN Development Program. She opened by remarking that she could imagine herself in a few years' time, retired, defending what she had done in her current position. Much of the audience knew what she meant. It is easy to be a Monday-morning quarterback. If we are honest, most of us know as we look back that we would have done things a good deal differently had we known what the outcomes would be. In the case of foreign affairs, we may argue strongly for an approach or a position that turns out to be misguided or just plain wrong. But, as the panelist at the Camden Conference stated, "I try to do the best I can with the knowledge available."

What follows is a record of how I tried to do that.

I: Posts

Learning on the Job

I arrived in Zurich, my first overseas post, ten days before Christmas 1974, and immediately succumbed to a flu bug I'd picked up during a stop in England. The misery of having the flu at Christmas in a strange city, living in a hotel, is a reality of Foreign Service life best forgotten. The manager of the Hotel Im Park, my home for the first three months in Zurich, personified the lovable side of the Germanic character as she brought little Christmas decorations and special soups to my room, clucking over my bad luck. One of the horrible side effects of my flu was an inability to control my emotions; these encounters always left me in tears and her exclaiming with ever-mounting sympathy over my plight. When my fever subsided and I could sit in a chair, I read *War and Peace* from start to finish. That magnificent novel always takes me back to that hotel room and the sense of being cast adrift.

Back on my feet, I was able to indulge in a favorite activity on weekends, discovering a new city on foot. I read maps well and enjoy urban walking, and Zurich is a lovely city to poke around in. It stands at the lower end of Zurich Lake where it flows into the Limmat River. A short distance down the Limmat, the river is joined by another, the Sihl. The land around the lake and rivers is hilly, so streets climb up and over ridges or hug the contours along the rivers. Zurich was always a manufacturing and commercial town, so there are old buildings and plenty of history. The medieval guilds controlled economic life from about 1500 and still wield social clout. The largest ones built magnificent guildhalls (*Zunfthäuser*) in the seventeenth and eighteenth centuries, many of which house elegant restaurants today. The cathedral (*Grossmünster*), originally a Catholic church erected on the site where the city's saints, Felix, Regula, and Exuperantius, were martyred, was made Protestant under the Reformation of Ulrich Zwingli; the pulpit was moved front and center to replace the altar. The more I lived in Zurich and spoke with the Swiss about its history, the more fun it was to walk it into my pedal memory.

My job, at the bottom of the totem pole of the five American officers stationed there, was serving as the junior of two officers in the consular section. A little explanation of Foreign Service structure would probably be helpful. The office in Zurich was a consulate general, what is called a "constituent post," under the United States embassy in Bern, the Swiss capital city. Embassies are always in the capital of a country and are the home of the American ambassador. Consulates or consulates general (bigger and better consulates) are under the authority of the ambassador, but can in some cases be bigger than many embassies. The consulate general in Frankfurt, Germany, for example, is quite large.

I served under three ambassadors in Switzerland. I arrived at the end of the tenure of Shelby Cullom Davis, a political appointee who used his position for expansive entertainment. He was well known among the business elite of the country and performed effectively, given the nature of our relations with Switzerland. Even as I was living in the hotel, the Swiss papers were full of stories of the confirmation hearings of the new ambassador, Peter Dominick. A characteristic grammatical construction in German and difficult for Americans to learn, places an entire adjectival phrase between the article and the noun; it can be used for ironic effect and was in the Dominick hearings. Every morning the poor man was described as "the recently defeated for reelection former Republican senator from Colorado Peter Dominick." The hearings were a disaster, full of frequent misspeakings, such as, "Switzerland is a neutral country, but neutral on our side." Asked to name the four official languages of the Alpine paradise, Dominick came up with French, German, Rumanian, and English, garbling Romansch and leaving Italian out altogether. Dominick did not last long; he arrived in bad health and found himself unable to carry out his duties. Nothing I could ever say convinced my Swiss friends that he left because of a crippling back disease; they were sure it was due to his confirmation statements. Finally, Nathaniel Davis, a career officer, was assigned. Davis was a solid professional, but he met more opposition than usual in Switzerland due to a previous tour as ambassador to Chile during the coup against Allende.

Under the direction of the ambassador and his deputy chief of mission (DCM), the core functions of an embassy—and generally a consulate as well—are carried out by four sections: consular, political, economic, and administrative. In the bigger embassies, these sections are headed by fairly senior officers who carry the title counselor. The political and economic sections do most of an

4

embassy's reporting to Washington about events in the foreign country, in particular, developments that could affect American foreign policy in that country or region. Officers in these sections also build close relationships with relevant officials in the host country, in order to have channels for reporting American attitudes toward the country, to ask for their support of various United States initiatives, and in general to have a way to exert American influence where necessary and proper. The work of political and economic officers is open and aboveboard ("overt"). Their reporting is often classified to protect the frankness with which they may discuss members of the host government and their opinions or the recommendations they may make about the significance of the information for United States policy. They are not CIA agents or spies, nor does their work involve cloak-and-dagger sneaking about.

The administrative section takes care of all the resources of the embassy—financial, human, and physical—to permit it to carry out the embassy's function. The security officer is a member of the administrative section, as is the all-important general services officer, to whom all others turn for transportation, housing, shipping, customs clearance, and virtually everything that smoothes the way and makes life in our short two- and three-year bursts manageable and pleasant. A good administrative counselor will have close relationships with the police and with all the local businesses such as hotels, real estate, airlines, telephone and other utilities, and shipping offices that might be helpful.

The consular section, where I found myself in Zurich, has the dual job of providing services and protections to American citizens overseas and assisting foreign travelers to the United States, primarily with visas, both immigrant and non-immigrant. We did not issue immigrant visas in Zurich, but while I was there the number of non-immigrant visas increased to something like 20,000 a year, all issued by me and the two Foreign Service Nationals (FSNs: the term for citizens of the host country hired to work in our overseas posts) assigned to my section.

I discovered that one of the best things about consular work was that, so long as I didn't name the individuals, I could dine out for the rest of my life on the stories I collected. There is no limit to the fixes people get themselves into, the outrageous things they say to a consular officer, the scams they try to pull, the tragedies, the heroics, the triumphs.

One of the sweetest stories from my days in Zurich concerns a fiancé visa I issued. Fiancé visas are similar to immigrant visas, for they are issued to foreign citizens traveling to the United States to marry an American and settle here. Not yet married, the fiancés do not qualify for immigrant visas, but once married, they can adjust

5

their status to that of permanent resident without undue fuss. These visas are initiated by filing a petition with the office where the person will apply. The petition is filled out by the intended American spouse and, among other things, recounts how the acquaintance with the applicant began and how long it has existed. We are trying to make sure a bona fide relationship exists.

One day a woman appeared at our visa window, explaining in heavily accented German that she wanted to apply for a fiancée visa. She appeared to be in her sixties, so hers was already an unusual case, since most of those headed for wedded bliss in the United States were far younger. My assistant found the petition and brought it in to me. The future husband of our applicant was a naturalized United States citizen, and theirs was a poignant story. They were both of Eastern European origin, Hungarian or Rumanian as I recall, and first met in the 1930s when performing with their respective families in circuses. The solidly built, gray-haired lady at the window had been a trapeze artist; her fiancé had been in another kind of act. They fell in love, but their families, particularly hers, were unwilling to let them break up the acts and refused to let them marry. Then World War II separated them: she and her family found refuge in Switzerland, and his emigrated to the United States. With these upheavals, they lost track of each other, but neither married in the intervening time. Chance brought them back together, and now they decided to consummate the forty-year courtship.

After reading the petition, I went to the window to speak with the applicant. She really was a blushing bride. We gave her all the papers and information she needed to complete her application, and some weeks later, when all the background checks and medical reports were done, she came back to pick up the visa. I tipped off the consul general, who dropped into the office to congratulate her; my assistant presented her with a little bouquet of wildflowers collected from a meadow on the way to work. We all got quite teary and emotional.

Moments like this were rare, however. Most of the time I issued visas for "temporary visitors for business/pleasure" which is the most common visa by far. At the height of tourist season, the applications came in by the boxload from travel agencies, and I learned fairly quickly to review most of them in less than a minute. The rate of problem cases was, in fact, so low, as in many countries around the world, that the requirement for citizens from such places to have visas was dropped entirely. (Visa regulations may have changed again since the events of 9/11.)

The essential qualification for a visitor's visa was that the person intended a short trip to the United States, with no purpose of settling there or earning any money during the visit. Residence and job both had to be firmly established abroad. Almost always I was quite adamant on this essential point, but in at least two instances I winked at it.

The first time was when a young woman came to the consulate directly from the airport. She was carrying a tiny baby girl and all the paraphernalia that goes with babies—diaper bag, bottles, and tiny clothing. The woman was an American citizen, not married, and a dental assistant somewhere in the southwestern United States. Her baby had been born in Sri Lanka and had a passport from that country. The mother had traveled to Sri Lanka to collect her baby, whom she was adopting through an agency. In the 1970s, this procedure was not so common as it is today, nor was it so common for single parents. Everything had taken longer than the mother had planned for, and she was late getting back to the United States and her job. She had all the adoption documentation, but she lacked the one thing she needed for the final leg of her journey—the baby's visa. The airline refused to let her board without it, for the airline had to pay a hefty fine for carrying someone to the United States without a visa.

My conversation with the young mother was in my boss's office. We asked her to step out for a minute, and we looked at each other. The proscribed solution was to direct the mother to Bern, where all the steps for getting the baby the proper visa would take many more days or weeks than the mother could afford. The humane thing to do, with a warning to the mother that the Immigration and Naturalization Service (INS) might still refuse her entry to the United States, was to issue the baby a visitor's visa so the poor mother could get her home to America where support and a job were waiting. Which is what we did.

The second time I blinked occurred when a middle-aged woman with an authentic midwestern American accent turned up at the visa window. During the interview, it developed that she had lived almost her entire life in the United States. Born in Switzerland, she was the illegitimate child of a mother who subsequently married a man, not her father, a few years after her birth. All three then emigrated to the United States. The father and mother were subsequently naturalized on the father's application; since the woman had never been legally adopted by the man she considered her father, she could not be naturalized—although she assumed she had been. She finished her education, married, had children, and lived a normal, middle-class American life, voting in elections and raising her family. Finally, when all the children had grown up, she and her husband decided to return to the land of her birth and have a holiday in Switzerland. They bought three-week excursion tickets, then applied for passports. The woman was stunned to learn she was not eligible for a United States passport and had only enough time to apply for a Swiss one before the trip. She knew she needed a visa to reenter the United States and called in at my office in the midst of sightseeing. I shouldn't have issued the visa, but in all conscience I could see no point in sending them to Bern to start the immigrant visa process, which would last well beyond the date of their return flight. Again, I warned her she might have trouble getting admitted by the INS, and I begged her to start getting herself naturalized properly when she got home. But I did issue her a "temporary visitor" visa.

When I was in Zurich, the most common problem among Swiss nationals involved young people who had arranged for *au pair* employment with American families (girls) or farmwork (boys). I certainly understood why recent school graduates would want to experience this kind of year in America, but it was, unfortunately, illegal at that time.

I could spot these applications easily: the applicants were all about 18 or 19 years old, announced a three-to-six month stay, and gave as a location in the United States the name and address of people who appeared to be unrelated to them. In such cases I asked the applicant to come in for an interview. When I asked how they knew the people in the United States, they would say they were friends of friends or something along that line. I then would ask if they had correspondence from these people inviting them to stay. I was always amazed when they handed me letters in which the mother of the family where the girl was going to work as a nanny coached her on what to say to me at the interview. "Don't tell the visa officer you are going to work for me. Just say we are family friends and you are coming for a visit."

Since these interviews frequently took place within a day or two of the applicant's intended departure—after she had bought her ticket, had a big send-off party, and made all her farewells—it was not a happy scene when I denied the visa. Frequently, the youngster's parents got involved. I remember clearly one enraged father, a well-known wealthy businessman, who threw his tax returns down on my desk. "Do you think I can't afford to support my daughter?" he stormed. "I can understand you have to have these rules for the less civilized people of the world, but after all we are Swiss!"

At these times, I realized that the visa window is the last place to gain an affectionate attitude toward the people of any host country. You can laugh it off later or chalk it up to experience, but I found it unnerving at the time

Another, more difficult, reason for visa refusals was a criminal record in the applicant's background. This was not so uncommon as one might think. Generally, however, the record was an old one—a relatively innocuous theft that crossed the line of a misdemeanor, a past crime that had been followed by a period of incarceration and a blameless life afterward. Financial fraud was also fairly common. In such cases, after looking at the court record and speaking with the individual, I requested a waiver from our immigration authorities, which was usually granted for non-immigrant visas.

One case, however, sticks in my mind. The application first came in from a travel agency. The person indicated the existence of a criminal record, so I asked to see the court documents. When the record was presented, it seemed so extraordinary that I asked our best translator to confirm my interpretation. Our applicant had been the director of a youth home and, in this capacity, had engaged in repeated acts of sexual abuse of the young people in his charge, either by himself or by requiring them to have sex with his wife while he watched. The record read like a pornographic novel.

At the interview, I asked him to tell me why I would want to request a waiver of his ineligibility. He showed no remorse at all, saying that at the time these events occurred, he had been taking some medication that caused him to act as he did. When I said I was not prepared to waive his ineligibility for a United States visa, he became quite irritated but eventually left the office.

Subsequently, the travel agent called, demanding to know why the visa had not been issued. I replied that I could not discuss my reasons; they were a confidential matter between the applicant and me. The travel agent became even angrier than the applicant, blustering, "Is it just that old business?" I refused to get into a discussion with her. She then snapped, "It's easier to get a visa for the Soviet Union than for the United States. I think I'll direct my business there instead of to the United States from now on!" I politely said that was up to her and disconnected.

Infrequently, we denied a visa because the applicant turned out to be an American citizen. Swiss and American nationality laws were so completely different that many Swiss did not know they were American citizens by their birth on American soil. Under Swiss law, nationality is passed only through birth to a Swiss father; the place of birth is irrelevant. In fact, Swiss passports do not record the place of birth but the place of origin, which cites the father's original fixed home. With the development of international business after World War II and the much greater movement of people for temporary work assignments, there was a significant increase of Swiss employees and their families traveling for a Swiss firm to an office in the United States for several years. Quite a number of them had children during these stays; they were, of course, Swiss under Swiss law but, under

United States law, they were also American citizens and could not change that fact prior to their eighteenth birthday.

When these young people applied for visas and named an American birthplace, we informed them of their dual nationality and directed them to the American passport section. Although they were often bewildered, most complied without difficulty. In a few situations, however, their parents raised difficulties. One was if the applicant were male and might have to register for the military draft during his stay in the United States. In another case, the father of the applicant heard the news of his son's nationality and exclaimed, "But he can't even speak English!" I had to tell him that this was true of many American citizens.

As I said, our office did not issue immigration visas, since the process for them is much more complicated and relatively few were issued in Switzerland. One day, however, the consul general called me to his office, where I found the Russian author Alexander Solzhenitsyn seated on the sofa. My boss said Solzhenitsyn had decided to immigrate, with his entire family, to the United States. It was important to the writer to keep this plan confidential, and he hoped that the visa could be processed in Zurich without his having to travel to Bern. I checked with my counterpart in Bern, with whom I regularly spoke, and we agreed that the preliminary work could be done in Zurich. Justice Stevens, the visa officer at the embassy, would come to Zurich on the final day to put the visas together and issue them officially. (Immigrant visas consist of a packet of documents, not just a stamp in the passport like nonimmigrant visas.)

Solzhenitsyn had no trouble qualifying for an immigration visa; he was independently wealthy and could support himself and his family on his earnings. The real problem was that he and all his family (his wife, the son of his wife's first marriage, the three sons of their own marriage, and his wife's mother) had all been expelled from the Soviet Union with little notice and had virtually none of the paper documentation most of us drag behind us all our lives—birth, baptism, and marriage certificates, divorce decrees, and the like. Over the next few months, all the paper had to be recreated through a series of interviews and affidavits, each of which had to be sworn and notarized in front of me. Solzhenitsyn spoke German and a tiny bit of English; his wife, as I recall, spoke much better English. His mother-in-law spoke only Russian. Thus at any one interview, in order to create, say, the mother-in-law's birth records, she had to appear at the office with someone who could translate, and the interview had to proceed between Solzhenitsyn's heavily accented German and Russian.

One useful lesson I took from this experience was not to exercise my ironic sense of humor in the midst of all the multilingual action with a man who seemed not given to lightheartedness. At one point I was interviewing his mother-in-law, who had, at some time in her life, joined the Communist Party in the Soviet Union. For nonimmigrant visas this was not generally a difficult problem, but it could be disqualifying in the application for an immigrant visa unless the applicant could document at least five years of opposition to the Communist Party after the end of membership. I interviewed the mother-in-law, through Solzhenitsyn, to elicit the scope and extent of her dissident activity before she left the Soviet Union. One aspect of her dissidence was her refusal to denounce Solzhenitsyn himself and publicly criticize his writings, which brought reprisals at her workplace, among other penalties.

Ironically, I asked Solzhenitsyn, "How could your mother-in-law criticize your writings if they were banned and therefore unavailable in the Soviet Union?"

He seemed somewhat annoyed with my stupidity. He explained that, of course, his mother-in-law had read his novels in *samizdat* ("self-publication," usually by typing multiple copies), as many Soviet citizens had. I sighed and reminded myself, "Don't get cute, Helen. Just get it down and play it by the book."

As a souvenir of that time, I have the two volumes of *The Gulag Archipelago,* one inscribed "to Ms. Helen Weinland, with gratitude and sympathy," and the second "to Ms. Helen Weinland, with my warm thanks."

Generally, the only work I did in the Zurich consular section was on visas, but when my supervisor was on vacation I also took care of American citizens. Most of this, like visas, was routine: issuing certificates of birth abroad or new passports to Americans living in Switzerland. Occasionally quirky services arose out of Swiss law, such as the need to write an official letter saying that American citizens can name their children anything they like. This requirement originated in the regulation that a child must be registered in Switzerland with a name officially recognized as such by the Swiss authorities. We had Americans who wanted to name their children Sean or Jennifer, but they had been refused birth certificates until I stated in a letter embossed with the consulate seal that, under United States regulation, it would be permitted. The Swiss authorities could not have comprehended that there is no United States or state regulation on this issue, so I phrased the letter without stating so explicitly. Interestingly, such a rule does give a clue to the pressure toward conformity in Swiss society.

Another fairly common event featured the American traveler who turned up with no money, stranded and a little scared. Most were willing to solve the problem by the book, which involved sending a cable to a relative or friend in the United States, asking that funds be wired expeditiously, and lying low in a hotel until they arrived. Other cases were a little crazier.

One involved a group of three young Americans who were spending that year in England where they were studying theater and acting. They had come to Switzerland on excursion tickets, so they had their return fare, but their flight did not leave for another few days and somehow they were without funds. Imprudence? Robbery? I can't remember. They had been trying to survive on little food, but their hunger was growing. By the time any funds arrived from the United States, the wait for their return flight would be over. I interviewed them and was pretty stern: "How can you expect the American taxpayer to pay for your trip abroad?" and so on. I knew that in the safe there was a small fund, provided by the local Swiss-American Chamber of Commerce, from which I could lend them a modest amount, but I was directed to act as though it were a loan out of my own pocket. The idea was, if people thought it was a personal loan from the consular officer and not from the government, they would be more inclined to pay it back.

All the acting skills the group had been learning in their English drama school were brought to bear on me. Finally I relented and told them that I would personally lend them enough for food and to pay for a room, but it had to be paid back. If they failed to pay it back once they arrived in England (and had access to money there), it would make me even less willing to help future, equally desperate, travelers. We completed a loan agreement, which they all signed, I handed over the money (probably about $20 each) and then received a fulsome paean of praise and thanks. "You've saved our lives," he declared emotionally. "We can never thank you enough." I was quite embarrassed about my subterfuge.

About ten days later, I was walking to lunch with a group from the consulate, including Nikolas Krummenacher, the senior Swiss employee in the American citizen services. I remarked that I was disappointed that I had not been reimbursed for the loan. I really believed the three when they promised they would pay me back. Krummenacher, who had been around a lot longer than I and seen a great deal more of traveling Americans, laughed and remarked on my naiveté. Still, I was surprised and chagrined. Happily, in the next day or two, a letter with a bank draft arrived from England, apologizing for the delay and explaining the foreign transfer had taken time to arrange. I rushed into Krummenacher's office and waved it at him: to give him credit, he was as pleased as I.

A much more difficult case appeared another day when I was filling in for the boss. It involved a sixty-seven-year-old American man and his Danish partner who were stuck in Switzerland. He had been living in Denmark for some time with his companion, when they decided to move to Yugoslavia (this while Tito was still alive and the system thoroughly Communist), where they heard the living was cheaper. After some time, they realized it was not the place for them, and they made it as far back as Zurich when their car broke down. When they came to the consulate, they requested a substantial amount of money to pay for the car repairs, as well as the hotel and meal bills while they were waiting.

I explained to the American citizen that I could help him wire someone in the United States for funds, but he adamantly refused. He insisted that the consulate had to pay all his bills, and I as adamantly insisted it could not. As the case dragged on for some weeks, the American exhibited periods of near violence. One day he came to the consulate and insisted on occupying a chair in the hallway. In plain view of all our visitors, he moaned for ten or fifteen minutes and then rolled off the chair to the floor, groaning loudly. As we moved to help him, he leapt to his feet and rushed into the stair landing, where he entered the elevator and disappeared from sight. He had been checked into a hotel by the Swiss police, who requested that the consulate pay the bills, and I had to explain to them as well that we could not do so. The car remained in the repair shop. Periodically, the American found enough cash for a train trip to Bern, where he tried his luck as well; the consular officials merely gave him enough money to return to Zurich. This practice is known as "moving the problem to the next consular district," and is considered a very unfriendly act among consular officers. At some point early on, the Danish woman decided to leave, particularly after I explained to both of them that she could not qualify for a visa to the United States since they were not married and she had no residence abroad. In the end, our American citizen managed to find the funds, by selling what remained of his car and other assets, to return to the United States.

Equally protracted and unhappy was the case of an American woman who appeared in the consulate one day requesting a list of lawyers so she could sue the Swiss authorities who had "violated her human rights." She was obviously suffering from mental illness, and as the case unfolded, we found she had been traveling from one European city to another. She received Social Security disability payments, but she never remained in one place long enough to change her address and receive her checks. She was occasionally involved in threats of violence to others, for she feared rape and was concerned whenever a male, trying to help her, entered her space. This was what happened in Zurich, where she pulled a knife on someone at the hostel where she was staying. The police took her to a mental health clinic; the next day she talked her way out and came to visit us. Proper treatment might have been available in the United States, but she was completely unwilling to return, and we could not legally force her to do so. She used to come to our waiting room, dressed in a bizarre collection of off-season clothes, and conduct long, angry conversations either with herself or on the phone to various lawyers' offices where she sought help in her suit. It was an intractable situation and was solved for us, but not for her, only when the Swiss refused to renew her permit to stay and she drifted over the border to Austria. We received a cable from the consulate in Salzburg asking what had happened in Switzerland.

One of the most extreme difficulties Americans abroad can present to the consular section is an arrest by the foreign authorities. Generally, in Switzerland, we heard from the authorities about such events a few days after the arrest. In one case, during weekend duty, I was informed of an arrest by a telephone call from the wife of an American citizen in Brussels. She said her husband had been picked up and was being held on charges of financial fraud. I made a series of phone calls and a few days later went to the prosecutor's office to request a permit to visit the prisoner in jail. At the office, while I was speaking with one of the investigators, another was interviewing a man who, I was told, was the brother of the man I was asking about. I asked him if he also was an American citizen and he said, no, just his brother. They were both Kenyan-born ethnic Indians, and only the brother had traveled to the United States and been naturalized.

Armed with my permit, I headed a day or two later to the city jail where my citizen was held. I took a few, rather lurid books we had around the consulate as solace for the prisoner. After I waited some time in a visitor's sitting room, the prison guard took me to an interview room where there were two plate glass windows, each with a very broad counter to separate prisoner from visitor. One such booth was already occupied. I stood on my side of the glass and eventually the prisoner arrived. I thought he looked remarkably like the man I had met at the prosecutor's office. I asked him, "You are an American citizen?" and he replied, "No, that's my brother." I then turned to the guard, and said, "You've brought the wrong Mr. K.! This one is the brother and a Kenyan citizen; the one I want to see must be in his cell." The guard was completely flummoxed. "The wrong one?" After a lengthy wait, I was told the "right" Mr. K. was at the prosecutor's office being questioned. I rounded the circle and returned to the prosecutor where I finally met the American K., who was pleased to see me. He told me his arrest was a mistake, he would soon be out, and it would all be cleared up. Yeah, yeah, I thought to myself; that's what they all say. I asked him if there was anything he needed, and he said he would like a copy of Thoreau's *On Civil Disobedience*, making me quite embarrassed about the westerns I had dropped off at the prison office.

In any case, before I located a copy of the Thoreau book, I had another call from Brussels from Mr. K. telling me he had been released and was very grateful for my visit, which had cheered him up no end. He said he was going to sue the Swiss for false arrest. I could not believe anyone could be successful in such a quixotic venture, but some months later, describing the case to a Swiss lawyer who had stopped by, he said he was the lawyer handling the case, which was in fact quite a strong one.

If processing visas and providing services to American citizens were the bread and butter of life at the consulate in Zurich, the visits of Henry Kissinger were the caviar and champagne. The first was a short and sweet affair, when the secretary of state dropped in on Zurich to have a lunchtime meeting at the Dolder Grand Hotel with the Shah of Iran. I was most impressed by the defensive perimeter the Swiss security people had thrown up around the beautiful, traditional hotel standing in extensive grounds on one of the hills high above Zurich. To get there, I pointed my car straight up hill and put the gas pedal to the floor. Arriving at the drive to the hotel in my red VW Bug, I found the hotel entirely surrounded by accordion barbed wire. I had to go through an identity check that included looking under my hood and in the trunk. Armed guards patrolled the entire perimeter. I was not privy to anything the Secretary and Shah talked about. The only job I had was to be at the hotel in case an extra body was needed for an errand, and it wasn't. Instead, I was included in a sumptuous lunch served to various straphangers in a room where the Secretary's special assistant, the security officer from Bern, and others sat around while the talks went on.

On this occasion, in 1975, Kissinger did not stay overnight nor was his entourage very grand. A year later, during the summer of 1976, we were blessed with the full treatment. Kissinger arranged to meet South African President Vorster in Zurich to discuss solutions to southern African issues, particularly the civil war in Rhodesia (now Zimbabwe). These talks were to last about three days, and Kissinger and his cast of hundreds (by today's standards a modest number) would be housed in the Dolder Grand. An advance team came a few days ahead of time to set up a control room, work out details of the schedule, and instruct the Zurich staff, as well as the Bern administrative section that moved to Zurich en masse, on their duties. A truck full of office equipment and supplies arrived from Bern and the typewriters, copy machines, and supplies were placed in all the offices established in hotel rooms. In Zurich, we had no United States Information Service (USIS) office, so officers were brought in from a number of posts in Germany to run the press side of things. This operation also required office equipment, phone banks, and supplies. All these people had rooms in the Dolder Grand, of course.

One of my jobs was to be a loose liaison with the communications team, also flown in from around Europe. We dealt with relatively little classified information in Zurich and our equipment was primitive. A "can-do" package, amounting to more than a ton of much more sophisticated communications equipment than our slow telex link-up, was also flown in, along with the people to handle the high volume of cable traffic necessary within the vicinity of the Secretary of State. A courier service between the consulate and the hotel for transporting classified documentation was established.

Finally, Henry Kissinger arrived, along with a delegation of high-ranking State Department officers who worked on the substance of the meeting, as well as all the support staff, press, security detail, and others, like Mrs. Kissinger. When the meeting actually started, I effectively moved into the hotel. I was expected to put in fifteen or twenty hour days in the control room or shuttling back and forth between the consulate and the hotel. Moving in and out of the security perimeter of the hotel was quite burdensome, even with United States government ID badges and buttons. When I had time to sleep, I merely borrowed a bed in a room of one of the Washington-based secretaries.

At the end of the visit, my last job was to accompany the communications "can-do" package and its courier to the Zurich airport, setting off at some ungodly hour of the morning. Security regulations require that classified material being transported by airplane be under eye control of a cleared American employee at all times when the aircraft is on the ground. Once the courier had shepherded his tons of equipment through the airport security screening and onto the airplane, he had to take his seat. My job was to stand at planeside, where I had been conveyed by a baggage-handling tractor and trolley, to make sure no one tampered with the equipment until the plane actually took off. The courier had some difficulty persuading the baggage handlers that everything had to go into one luggage compartment, so he could stand in one place at the other end and watch it being unloaded. Once the courier had been swallowed up in the aircraft, the baggage cart drivers decided we could leave. I protested, they insisted. As we drove off, I looked back and saw the baggage handlers shifting some of the equipment from one hold to another. I was thus able to win the argument and go back to stand at the side of the plane until it taxied off.

High-level visits can have their drama, but there is nothing like the worm's eye view to arouse questions about the worth and meaning of all the hype of highly classified communications that have to be read in the middle of the night.

Two or three days after the visit, our political officer went to the Dolder Grand to meet friends for lunch. The manager of the hotel, whom he knew well, came over to greet him. Our officer remarked that the manager must be relieved that the visit had gone so well and that Kissinger and the others had been pleased with the arrangements. The manager looked at him and said, "But Mr. Ginsburg, haven't you heard? They are all coming back next week!"

So much for the secrecy of cables that invariably arrive after the office has closed for the night announcing a visit by the Secretary of State. The Swiss hotel manager knew at least six hours before the first cables began arriving that the whole process had to be geared up again. Since I was the person at the consulate who had to decode classified communications, and since they didn't begin arriving until after business hours, I had to put in several more hours of overtime processing all the cable traffic that no one had to read, in any event, until the next day. All the really important information was passed by completely insecure telephones.

Under the personnel rules of the State Department, I was junior enough at this time to receive pay for overtime. Ordinarily, if I had to go to the office on the weekend when I was on duty or stay an hour or two after normal hours to take care of classified communications or something, I didn't bother to claim it. But two back-to-back Kissinger trips that meant dawn trips to the airport prior to a full day of visa work or processing classified traffic until midnight were something else. I told the consul general I planned to claim the overtime pay; he tried to talk me out of it, appealing to my "professional pride." I disagreed with him and vowed to remember my disagreement whenever I became senior enough to ask people to work overtime hours. In any case, I used most of the pay to buy a plane ticket to Washington to lobby for my next job.

A good consular officer, like a good administrative officer, is a person who likes solving problems. Encountering strange cases of destitution, difficult and dangerous arrest cases, and complicated visa and nationality problems only stimulates the consular officer, who works with the regulations and figures out a way to make everyone happy. One day my supervisor, the consular officer who generally handled American citizen issues, came into my office. His face was purple with suppressed glee. "Here's a visa question for you," he announced, sitting down in my armchair.

A Swiss citizen had just been in his office for some notarial services. This was a man who had his finger in all kinds of strange and fanciful projects. He periodically stopped in the consulate to get papers certified for one or another of them. On his call that morning, he informed my supervisor that he had read about a new practice developed in the United States of freezing corpses so they could be revived when a cure was found for the disease that killed them. His question to my boss, posed with all seriousness, was: if he created a franchise for this service in Switzerland and the frozen corpses had to be shipped to the cryogenic storage center in Berkeley, what kind of visa could the corpses be issued for their "stay" in the United States? After howling with laughter until tears began to run, my boss and I decided there just was not an appropriate visa: the "applicants" would in all likelihood be abandoning their residence to which they intended to return after a temporary stay (the fundamental requirement for a non-immigrant visa) and would be unable to pass the necessary medical checks for an immigrant visa (as they were dead). The good consular officer solves problems of equal complexity but more possibilities for resolution.

I found in Switzerland that I was not a good consular officer. I became irritated with people who created messes and expected me to clean them up. Some of the visa work was fun when it involved helping someone realize his or her plans but most of it was routine drudgery. In addition, as my supervisor pointed out, Switzerland was "wasted" on me. He already had a long career and had served in some fairly difficult spots; Zurich was a good post for someone who had been in one of those, a rest cure for the physically or culturally deprived. Over the rest of my career I came to recognize the truth of his remark.

Switzerland was in many ways an easy place to live. Once I found an apartment and moved in, after three months in the hotel, it was a comfortable home. One great difficulty in locating an apartment was that in Switzerland, only three days a year are generally recognized as ones on which leases lapse and can be signed—the last days of March, June, and September. Because I had arrived in December, very little was on the market. I finally found my apartment only because it was in a newly renovated building. Switzerland was the only post I served in at which I was expected to find my own housing and ship my own furnishings from the United States. In all the others, I occupied government-leased and furnished housing.

Public transportation in Zurich was excellent; food supplies were ample and tasty; the country is by and large safe, clean, and healthy to live in. The mail service is reliable; the telephones work; the water is drinkable. We take these things for granted in the United States, but I was to learn in the coming years they are not universally available.

Even in Switzerland you could run into blank walls. One time I was shopping for food for a dinner party. I planned to make a cold chicken salad (it was an uncharacteristically hot day) and wanted to buy grapes. I stopped at the fruit and vegetable shop. Far more than in the United States, I shopped at specialty stores, at least in those days—the dairy, the baker, the produce vendor, and so on. I looked around the store and then asked the shop assistant for seedless grapes. Her answer was, "Such a thing does not exist." She didn't say, "Seedless grapes? Is there such a thing? How marvelous, but we don't have them here." She just said they didn't exist. I ran into this attitude a lot in Zurich. If the Swiss did something a particular way, it was the only way a person could think to do it. If an alternative were proposed (say, doing away with assigned laundry days in our building), it was ruled impossible without any consideration.

The Swiss live in a small, mountainous country that over the years and centuries has survived by not getting involved more than it has to in the struggles and passions of its neighbors. Living as the people do, cheek by jowl in that small part of the landscape which is amenable to human habitation, the Swiss have worked out intricate rules that they all understand and, for the most part, accept to make their lives possible. An outsider from the wide-open, frontier-shaped United States, I neither knew the rules nor, often, found them reasonable. Nevertheless, when I, usually unwittingly, broke them, the nearest Swiss citizen was sure to inform me of the transgression and make certain I toed the line.

For example, it is an unwritten rule that older Swiss citizens (the age limit is not specifically determined) have the right to go immediately to the head of any line, say in a department store to pay. An older Swiss trying to board a tram will, if the stranger does not yield the place, use an umbrella or other weapon at hand, to force the issue and gain the right to board first. The teenaged daughter of our political officer was slapped in the face by a tram passenger, who thought she was deliberately slouching with her feet in the aisle, nearly tripping up the elderly passenger.

In my apartment house, newly renovated and thus occupied by people who all moved in more or less at the same time, I was introduced to the age-old tradition of the laundry day. Only by degrees did I understand what this was about. In the basement, there were two laundry rooms, each provided with a washing machine and a dryer. In addition there was a space in the basement where one could hang washing from lines. Every six months, a calendar was placed in our mailboxes, assigning two successive days about every three weeks, when we were permitted to use those machines. We were not allowed to do laundry on any other day, nor were we allowed to do laundry at all on Sunday. In all Switzerland,

19

there is a "Polizeiverbot" (an ordinance enforceable by the police) against doing wash on Sundays.

These rules had first come into being in the days when there were no dryers and wash had to be hung on lines in the basement. In the damp winter air of Europe north of the Alps, sheets and towels could take two days to dry. Since space in the basement was limited, and the wash of any one person could fill the room and take two days a-drying, the laundry day was born. For the good of all, the days had to be clearly delimited.

I remarked to a Swiss woman in the building, when we met in the laundry room, that I could not see why we could not agree in our building to move to a first-come, first-served basis, since the apartments were all so small that the largest "family" was a couple. She thought I was mad.

I had a real problem, however, since I did not own enough underwear, sheets, and towels to get from one laundry day to the next. I therefore resorted to what seemed the lesser evil—doing my wash on Sunday. I had the impression I was one of the few churchgoers in the building. Every Sunday morning, I placed my first load in the washer, scampered off to the English-language Anglican church on Promenadeplatz, and returned from services just in time to shift the wash to the dryer and start the second load. I formed a good friendship with the German woman in the building who followed the same schedule with the other set of machines, the two of us nattering away with our illegally operating machines thumping in the background.

One Sunday, like many before, I scurried to the basement, started my load, and went off to church. When I returned, I went down the stairs to continue the routine and came face to face with a couple of Zurich policemen. I experienced panic. They must be there to look into complaints about Sunday washing. I mentally reviewed the terms of my immunity as a foreign diplomat to judge whether that would save me the humiliation of an arrest and fine. Outwardly, I kept my composure, nodded to the cops, and walked toward the laundry rooms. They went the other way.

In the laundry room, I found Ursula, my German co-conspirator. "What are the police doing here?" I hissed at her. She informed me that there had been a break-in the previous night in the storage compartment of one of the other residents (we all had little lockups in the basement), and his entire stock of wine had been stolen along with other things. The police were investigating the theft. I was relieved to learn I was not going to have to explain to the consul general and ambassador why I was in the Zurich city jail.

One time I asked a Swiss friend whether he would report his neighbor to the police if the neighbor hung out wash on Sunday or washed the car on the Sabbath (another no-no). He said, after some deliberation, no, he would not report the neighbor to the police. "I would just think less of him." The ultimate Swiss sanction appeared to be that your neighbors might think ill of you. For this reason you rushed to wash the car on Saturday, you did your wash on any day but Sunday, you did not vacuum in your apartment or take a shower after 10 p.m., and on and on.

One time I asked one of the Swiss women on the consulate staff if she and her husband could come to dinner on a particular evening. She said they couldn't make it. It was one of her laundry days, and she had to wash a lot of sweaters because the season was changing. I cannot imagine permanent residence in a place in which your social life is driven by the assignment of a laundry day.

The obverse side of this coin of conformity is, or was in the mid 1970s, a functioning of community beyond what we know in the United States. If you grow up in Switzerland, and if you know and accept all the rules that govern your life in the community, it can be a comfortable and safe place to live. I was convinced the general acceptance of communal controls was what permitted every adult Swiss male to have a rifle and ammunition in his house without the high rate of slaughter we endure in this country. Every Swiss male until the age of fifty-two is in the active reserves of the Federal army. The purpose of holding the weapons at home was to permit a rapid and universal mobilization of the army should all-out national defense be required; the purpose was not the defense of the home or personally delivered justice, and the Swiss did not use them in this way. The Swiss know and accept the rules, and those who chafe at them frequently find a way to leave the place.

During my assignment in Switzerland, I did not do any official entertaining. I occasionally attended receptions given by the consul general or the political officer and found them horribly boring. At one, I well recall getting stuck in a doorway with two Swiss lawyers. I introduced myself, to one of them for the second or third time. They both spoke excellent English, but asked me if I spoke Swiss German. No, I replied, I could speak *Hochdeutsch* but Swiss German was beyond me. Smiling at this piece of information, they resumed their conversation in Swiss German and permitted me ultimately to shove my way past the doorway bottleneck.

On one rare occasion, the consul general asked me to stand in for him at a function given by an association of American university graduates. The consul general had an exceptionally busy schedule that particular week, and called his host to say he would be unable to make it and I would be the official representative of the consulate. I duly turned up at the event and introduced myself to the president. He took note of my presence, but did not offer to get

21

me a drink, let alone introduce me to the rest of the leadership. When dinner was served, I was not seated at the head table, but sat down with a group of people I had been chatting with. After the meal, the president rose to his feet and welcomed the members. He informed them he had returned from military service too late for a timely invitation to the consul general, who had sent "someone from the consulate" to represent him. I stood and smiled at the crowd. The rest of the painful evening was turned over to a Chinese professor from the local technical university. He showed us his thoroughly amateur slides of his first trip to China since his emigration. "This is the room in my hotel in Beijing," he narrated about a dimly lit view. After about an hour of this torture, but with still another tray of slides ahead of us, the president thanked our speaker for his most interesting presentation. I drove home swearing I would never attend such a function again. My introduction to diplomatic representational entertaining, as it is known, was not auspicious.

If Switzerland is not a place I would want to live, it certainly is a nice place to visit. A particular pleasure I indulged in there as much as possible was hiking in the mountains. The Swiss publish beautifully accurate and large-scale maps of the entire country that include not only roads and towns but also all the hiking trails in the country. Whenever I had company staying with me, I tried to organize a trip and hike somewhere in the mountains. I also traveled a number of times with a Swiss friend who knew how to organize things so that we could move along a route by means of local trains, buses, and various mountain lifts, in addition to serious hiking. It was a wonderful way to see a spectacularly beautiful country.

One weekend in particular I will never forget, when we hiked in the Jura Mountains in the northwest of the country. In the entire central valley of Switzerland, the day was overcast and gloomy, but we took a chair lift up from a train station in the valley. Near the top of the ascent, we broke through the cloud into pure, intense sunlight. From the top of the lift we climbed up to the ridge and turned to the southeast. Across the valley, entirely filled with cloud, was laid out the full range of the Swiss Alps, from east to west, with many of the recognizable peaks like Eiger and Jungfrau. It was an unforgettable sight. Whenever I remember the ennui of visa issuance in Zurich, I also try to remember that epiphany in the mountains.

In Zurich, the mountains were rarely visible and then only when we were having a weather phenomenon known as *Foehn*. A *Foehn* is a warm southerly breeze accompanied by low atmospheric pressure. This wind brought with it a clearing away of all water vapor in the air, so the view in all directions became crystalline. One time, in the winter, I had the impression I could count every needle on the fir trees on the other side of the lake. With *Foehn*, you could look down the lake to the south, and see the first range of Alps in their snow-covered glory.

Some of the effects of *Foehn* were less marvelous. I found that when it moved in during the night, it generally woke me up, presumably because of the sudden drop in pressure. It also seemed to bring every mad person in Zurich into the consulate. I debunked this theory for some time, but eventually came to believe it. I would pass a morning with one wacko after another at my window and then go out to lunch, only to see the mountains looming up over me.

A protracted spell of *Foehn* also seemed to increase the number of Americans who died of heart attacks and strokes. During my tour in Zurich, I had a change of supervisors. In the first week of the new boss's tenure we had three American deaths, for which we had to prepare death certificates and all the papers for shipping the bodies home. As he was processing the third case, he looked up at me and asked, desperately, "Is it always like this?" I told him it was very unusual, but I thought it was probably due to the *Foehn*. He thought I was crazy, but I bet he came to believe it after a time.

I did not find it easy to make friends in Switzerland. There were probably a number of reasons for this, including the demands of my job. I was on friendly terms with all the employees of the consulate and socialized with them. Over the two years I was there I met a few people who invited me to their houses and whom I invited back—an American woman living with a Swiss partner, older couples to whom I had introductions from mutual friends, and an academic who had been told to look me up by a former colleague. This latter contact was my mountain hiking partner. But one day he commented to me, "By the time you leave university, you have all the friends you are going to need for the rest of your life."

I was appalled. "That's crazy," I protested. "You should be making friends all through your life, as you move along and meet new people and new places." But, of course, that is very much what the Swiss generally do not do. The country is so small, and the lives of the Swiss so generally set once they leave school and begin their career pattern, that they do not ever move far away from school friends. It is my impression that a large number don't even bother to change dentists or doctors when they move to a new town. For one thing, when I was there, dentists were in short supply and it was difficult to be accepted as a new patient. One of the Swiss women working at the consulate took a day of leave at one point to travel all the way back to her home in Solothurn (practically all the way across the country) to see her dentist. So the American habit of picking up and leaving people and places, the restlessness and rootlessness that keep us constantly changing and expanding our circle of acquaintance is not a necessity or a desirable pattern to the Swiss like my hiking friend.

This same friend asked me, early on in our acquaintance, to share with him my impressions as a foreigner of the Swiss and their ways. He described himself as interested in my reactions coming from the outside. He wanted to know what in particular I noticed about his homeland. After perhaps a year in the country, I told him that one conclusion I had drawn was about the particular glue that held Switzerland together as a country in spite of its multicultural, multilingual past. Switzerland exists in the form it has today, I argued, by accreting pieces of disintegrating empires along its borders in the fifteenth and sixteenth centuries. It fought wars with much bigger rivals on the frontiers, which it won by always being a sideshow in much bigger conflicts the neighbors were fighting at the same time.

"The Swiss," I told my hiking friend, "stick together because they dislike their neighbors—France, Italy, and Germany—more than they hate each other. However disdainful the Ticinese are of the Zurichers, they would rather be united in the same country with the Zurichers than be Italians living in Italy." I was thinking of an anecdote told me by an American woman who lived in Lugano, a town in the Italian-speaking part of Switzerland, about a visit to her bank. When she asked to see the bank manager, she was informed, "Oh, he's not here today. He's gone to Switzerland." That was how the Italian Swiss in Ticino thought of Zurich—somehow a foreign country. You did have to cross the mountains to get there.

I told my hiking friend this insight of mine about his country. He had, after all, asked me to share such insights with him. He listened to me and then responded, "That's not true." That was the end of the discussion—he, the male, the Swiss, had heard my attempt to describe his country but judged it inaccurate. I didn't share any more conclusions with him for the rest of my stay.

Shortly before my departure from Zurich, I had a party for all my colleagues in the consulate to say goodbye. My apartment was small, and they all crammed in, in party mode. There was food and drink, and I made it clear all drink that was not consumed would be handed out among them since I couldn't take it back to the United States. I was touched they had all brought presents with them, and at some point they handed them to me to open. The first proved to be a lovely crystal wine glass, engraved with my initials. It was filled with something, I forget what, but perhaps a few delicious chocolates. I thanked the giver, and opened the next beautifully wrapped gift. This was a brandy snifter, into which had been placed a pretty, lace-edged handkerchief. "Oh," I remarked, "it's engraved like the other glass." One colleague allowed as how that was an

24

amazing coincidence. I am pretty slow on the uptake. I think I had opened at least four packages before I realized the entire Swiss staff had gone in together to purchase a set of six wine glasses and two snifters. Each had then filled and wrapped them individually. It was an imaginative idea and a treasured gift that has now followed me all over the world.

The Twilight Zone

In January 1977, I began a year's stint in the State
Department's Operations Center. In doing so I moved from
the mole-like perspective of visa work in a relatively insignificant
overseas post to the Olympian view from the top and center of
things. Our working environment reinforced this view, for the chairs
in which "watch officers" sat were large, comfortably upholstered
ones placed on a raised platform from which we could view the room
and, indeed, the world. Across the room from our platform was a
glass wall, behind which was a narrow "viewing corridor." Visitors to
the State Department were occasionally brought there to observe our
work, reinforcing the sense we were rare birds indeed.

The Operations Center is part of the executive staff that
serves the secretary of state and other principal officers of the State
Department. Our job was to process all urgent incoming diplomatic
information, mostly in cables from posts overseas but also from the
press and other sources of fast-breaking news. Work there has
undoubtedly changed beyond recognition with the technological
revolution in communications of the past twenty years, but in 1977
things already seemed to move pretty fast.

Once we received information, we decided who needed to
know it and how quickly. From our desks, consisting partly of
sophisticated telephone consoles, we alerted the offices of the
primary officers in the Department. On any given day we could be
dealing with several fast-breaking stories at a time, ranging from
what could be thought of as "normal" diplomatic issues like the
death of a foreign leader, armed conflict, or a sensitive set of
negotiations all the way to hostage situations involving American
citizens or natural disasters ravaging a foreign country. Frequently
we had to field questions from the press (although these were

generally referred to the press duty officer) or a member of the public trying to learn the fate of someone overseas.

In the case of crises that seemed set to last for days, a special task force was set up, staffed by the geographic bureau covering the country where the crisis occurred. Such a task force might be created for an evacuation of American citizens from political chaos or to resolve a hostage event. The Operations Center included several bedrooms as well as working space for task forces. Once a task force was established, it took over all the work around the crisis even if we watch-standers processed all the cables and knew what was going on.

There were special procedures for airline hijackings (not uncommon in the 1970s), mob violence against United States installations, seizures of foreign ships by the Coast Guard, and deaths of Americans overseas. We often had calls from the local police forces in the Washington area to confirm the diplomatic status of someone picked up for drunken driving. If the person was listed in the diplomatic "Blue Book," he or she could not be arrested, but we might have to provide the police with a telephone number to call to have the person conveyed home. (Occasionally they were so drunk they refused to take a taxi.) I took perverse joy in providing the telephone number of the person's superior at the embassy, hoping to create enough embarrassment that there would be no repeat offense.

In the Operations Center, we were in the center of anything interesting going on in the world. I knew the inside dope on any foreign story in the papers or on TV. I came to see how the Department of State operated from the top down, invaluable information for later on when I needed to know how to get something done efficiently. As we had to coordinate with all the other foreign affairs agencies in the government, from the White House to the Office of the Special Trade Representative, I learned a lot about the coordination of foreign policy across Washington.

Since the world never sleeps, even in those days before CNN and the Internet, the Operations Center was open twenty-four hours a day. We worked in three eight-hour shifts a day. Sleep experts would be horrified to learn that our schedule consisted of two day shifts, two swing shifts, and two midnight shifts, followed by two full days off. By the time of our second midnight shift, it was nearly impossible to stay awake in the middle of the night unless there was plenty of stimulating work.

I found it increasingly difficult as the year went on to sleep after the midnight shifts. I arrived home at about nine in the morning and went straight to bed, only to wake up two or three hours later. As anyone knows who works the midnight shift, it is difficult to tell workmen and neighbors not to make noise during the

27

"working day." One particularly awful period coincided with the decision of the neighbor whose apartment was under mine to drill holes in the cement ceiling of his balcony for hanging flower baskets. No earplugs on earth could block out the sound of that drill; it seemed a giant sadistic dentist had moved into my living room.

It was also difficult to explain to friends that I did not have free time when they did. Weekends had no meaning during that year. While it was pleasant to be able to shop and do other errands during the middle of weekdays, it was impossible to have a normal social life.

Most disconcerting, however, was my increasing sense of living in a haze. As sleep deprivation built up on me, I felt less and less connection to life away from the Operations Center. Luckily the normal tour of duty in the Operations Center was only twelve months; I do not think I could have survived it much longer, fascinating as it was.

I gave an enormous party about two months after I finished my work there and began to live a life of daylight work, weekends, and eight hours of sleep a night. I felt it was necessary to announce to the world that I had emerged from my cocoon and was again a real person, available for excursions and dinner dates.

A Love Affair Begins

The first encounter with Africa is always dramatic. It looks so completely different from America or Europe, even from the air. In large parts of the continent, the earth is red, a rare color in the temperate zones of the northern hemisphere. The vegetation along the equator is dominated by intensely green, fleshy, wide-leaved plants. As the airplane loses altitude for its final approach, the traveler can see corrugated metal roofs winking in the sunlight, small cultivated fields around every modest house, and the dense, low-rise, mud-brick, sprawling human settlements that generally ring the modern center of an African city.

I first traveled to Africa—Nigeria—during the year and a half I was assigned to the Nigeria Desk in the Department of State in Washington. Every country in the world has a "desk officer," that is, an employee assigned in Washington whose function is to monitor and guide all our relations with the country in question. This person can be viewed as a kind of funnel—all decisions and policies affecting the country, whether developed at the Pentagon or Department of Commerce or Peace Corps or any other Washington agency flow through that person and require his or her "clearance" in State Department parlance. Cable messages and other reporting flowing back from that country pass over the desk even if action is required from some other office or department of the Executive branch.

Some countries are too small to warrant an exclusive desk officer, and others are big enough to call for more than one. That was the case of Nigeria in January 1978 when I reported to the Office of West African Affairs and became one of three officers whose responsibility was handling Nigeria. My particular responsibility was for consular and political issues. One of the best perks of a desk officer is the opportunity to travel to the country covered for

29

"familiarization." At least this was the case until budget constraints severely cut travel funds.

In the spring of 1978, I landed at the airport in Lagos on my first trip to Africa. One of the first things I noticed was a group of poorly dressed laborers huddled underneath a plane next to which my PanAm 707 parked. Why on earth, I wondered, were all those men hunkered underneath an airplane. I quickly learned—for the shade it provided. The African sun is brutal; it is directly overhead in Nigeria, which is quite close to the equator. The difference in temperature between sun and shade is palpable, and even a short spell in the direct sun can cause a pounding headache. Anyone working outdoors quickly learns to take advantage of any shade available, and that includes baggage handlers waiting for the next international flight to land.

I spent the next three weeks falling in love with Nigeria. I traveled extensively, to the east and the oil platforms just off shore where the coast of Africa swings from its east-west orientation south to the Cape of Good Hope. I visited the former regional capitals of Enugu, Ibadan, and Kaduna; I stopped in Port Harcourt, the center of the oil business, source of about ninety percent of Nigeria's foreign exchange earnings. I visited Sokoto in the far northwest corner of the country, seat of the Sultan of Sokoto, the nominal leader of all Nigeria's Moslems, about half of the country's population. I departed Nigeria from its second international airport in Kano, the largest city in the north, still ringed with the mud-brick wall built for the defense of the city hundreds of years before.

I met lots of Nigerians—government officials, business people, academics, traditional rulers, and market people. I was offered kola nut, the traditional offering of welcome to the guest, in a chief's house in eastern Nigeria. I learned the hard way not to eat the entire lobe of the kola nut in one mouthful—it is dry and can also be very strongly flavored, something like chewing and swallowing peppery chalk. I was offered "minerals," the African term for soft drinks. In one government guesthouse I was given a stew made from meat that the embassy officer and I could not identify (and weren't sure we wanted to). At the palace of the Sultan of Sokoto, to which I was accompanying the Consul General from Kaduna, whose job I would have thirteen years later, we were met with praise singers and court musicians playing the *kankanki*, the traditional long trumpets of the northern Nigerian court. I also stepped out of a helicopter on the top of an oil platform in the Bight of Benin and realized I was two hundred feet above the ocean on a flimsy edifice that appeared to be built from erector set pieces. In that same helicopter, I traveled with the embassy officer responsible for reporting on petroleum matters along the Nigerian coast from the oil rigs to Port Harcourt. Along the way, we saw the fishing villages of the Niger River delta, inaccessible by road; canoes made from dugout logs were pulled up on the sand by the fishermen who lived there.

As I said, I fell in love with the place. I traveled back to Washington determined to return to Nigeria for a full two-year tour and, after some wangling, managed to do just that. In August 1979, I arrived as a new political officer. My major reporting responsibilities were both functional (the new legislature, one of the major political parties) and regional (the northern part of the country).

Official American interest in Nigeria was high. President Jimmy Carter had visited the country the previous year. A seemingly successful transition from military rule to civilian, democratic government was underway. Nigeria was home to roughly one in four of all Africans living south of the Sahara and produced a fairly large proportion of the sweet crude oil from which United States refineries made the gasoline that propelled American cars. Nigeria appeared to be a promising place for American investment and trade.

I set out to learn the territory as quickly as possible. This meant reading the daily newspapers, meeting as wide a group of people as possible, and getting the feel of the place. This last job can be accomplished in conversations with drivers and servants, visiting the market and shopping for food or crafts, and trying so far as possible to get into the daily life of the country.

Meeting people, making "contacts" as it is called in the business, was challenging at the time I arrived because the government was changing over. Simply looking up people listed by my predecessor, a fairly common way to start, was not going to do the trick. Once the legislature arrived in town, it was still not easy. The outgoing military government constructed housing for members of the National Assembly, following the general African practice of providing housing for government officials. However, the Honorable Members took one look at the efficiency-size apartments they were expected to inhabit that, in addition to the cramped spaces, were also miles away from the center of town, and rebelled. Some enterprising senators and representatives goaded on the civil servants appointed to take care of their welfare and cruised around town looking at other accommodation. They discovered five large apartment houses on Victoria Island, the premier area for new housing construction at that time, and announced this would do them just fine. Those buildings had been constructed for civil servants, but no matter, said the legislators. The civil servants could live somewhere else. And thus, after a few months of bunking out of town and several traffic jams' distance away from the National Assembly building, the legislators took possession of the Victoria

Island apartments. This was convenient for me, since they were now just down the road from the embassy and conveniently close to my own apartment from which I felt it perfectly safe to drive myself in the evening. Where the civil servants ended up, I hate to think, for modern living space in Lagos was not easy to come by.

I began looking up the various legislative party leaders in both houses. They did not have offices at the legislative buildings, or any kind of telephone service for which there was a directory, so finding them and introducing myself was a job that took a number of trips to the legislative chambers and their housing. Even getting a list of their apartment numbers took a bit of wangling. Compounding the difficulty was the fact that they were all new and frequently did not know each other at the start, so members could not point out to me people I hoped to meet.

There were five political parties, each with a strong base in one part of the country but generally with members elected from other regions. In addition, the outgoing military regime had created new states by splitting up the former four regions, so that there were now nineteen states. I tried to get to know at least one or two legislators from each. The members were themselves for the most part anxious to meet me, since they were not entirely certain about the finer points of the political system in which they now played an important role. Nigeria's previous democratic government (1960-66) had given a great deal of power to the regions; the federal government as well as the regional ones had followed the British parliamentary system. This system had last functioned thirteen years before when it was ended by military coup. The new constitution incorporated many features of American political life—a presidential executive, separation of powers, checks and balances, far more emphasis on the work of committees in the legislature, to name a few. Its new practitioners understood the general outlines, but had many questions about the detail. My colleagues at the American embassy and I became instant experts on the Nigerian system of government.

Over the two years I was stationed in Lagos, my routine evolved. Once or twice a week I drove down to the National Assembly building, often to attend a debate in one of the houses on an issue I found important or interesting. The building itself dated from the previous regime, so the seating in the two chambers was similar to the British parliament, with two ranks of facing benches. A table in the center of the chamber divided the two ranks. A rack at the end of the table provided for the mace, placed after the President of the Senate or the Speaker of the House made his entry at the beginning of the session.

Gradually I came to recognize most of the members. More important, they came to recognize me. Most visits to the assembly meant not only attending a session, but also encountering a large number of members in the lobby or on the grounds. This was the opportunity for me to stop and chat, ask about various pieces of legislation under consideration, quiz them about what was going on in their respective parties, and generally get up to date on what was happening politically. From their side they had a chance to ask about the American political system, ask for printed materials or assistance with projected travel to the United States, and occasionally request help with their private business ventures.

Inevitably they also asked me about visas—for themselves there were generally no problems, but for their relatives (an elastic concept in Africa where a brother or uncle is quite often simply someone you have grown up with in the same village), friends, relatives of friends, friends of relatives, there were often difficulties. Occasionally I could help, at least to the extent of getting a second hearing for a person who had been refused a visa. Sometimes I came up against a complete refusal by the consular officers to look sympathetically at a case. In fairness to the consular officers, the Lagos visa section was a high-stress, intensely difficult place to work; the incidence of fraud was among the highest in the world, and the press of numbers limited the time for each case.

One consular officer was particularly hard-nosed. Generally I found this amusing, although sometimes I was thoroughly annoyed by it. She was known widely in Lagos, partly because she was a favorite of the just-departed Ambassador, who often had her over to play tennis with local dignitaries. She was adept at singling out the most senior Nigerian present in a room and playing up to him throughout a party or other social event. But she was implacable on the visa line. She believed nothing anyone told her; she usually refused to reconsider a case. More than once I found myself in the lobby of the embassy dealing with a friend asking for reconsideration of a refusal and, at the same time, inquiring about the well-being of the visa officer who was refusing help. I never gave her away, nor did I criticize a decision of the visa section to a Nigerian, even a good friend; but there were times when, convinced the case was a good one, I wanted to pirate one of the visa machines and print the visas in my own office.

One visa case, directly involving a member of the Assembly, was quite troubling. It surfaced when we were processing the visas of a group of legislators traveling to observe the United States government in action. The routine checks on all the applications turned up a serious disqualifying history on this one legislator, what was called a "Category I" refusal. Such a refusal usually meant something in the person's background disqualified him or her permanently from an immigration visa and required a waiver of the ineligibility for even a visitor's visa. In this particular case, the reason for the refusal suggested activity aimed at subverting or overthrowing the United States Government, a reason that was almost never waived for obvious reasons. The "evidence" for this disqualification was obscure, buried in surveillance files of one of the United States intelligence or counter-intelligence agencies. What was more infuriating was that the "evidence" was considered so sensitive, I could not see any more than a general summary of it, so that I could not ask the legislator how he had accumulated such a record and then, possibly, have it removed from the record or at least waived for a visitor's visa.

We did manage, with frantic activity, to have the disqualification waived for the particular trip the legislators were taking. But the record remained in the file. When I returned to Nigeria, over ten years later, this person looked me up and said he was still hampered by the record, since he wanted to travel to the United States on business and kept running into his past history. The end of the Cold War had, happily, made it easier by the 1990s to demand a fuller account from the FBI in this case about the reason for ineligibility. The person's "subversive" activity appeared to be participation, while he was a student in the United States in the early 1960s, in demonstrations against some United States policies in Africa, particularly United States animosity against some of the early African independence leaders like Nkrumah and Lumumba. Presumably, the FBI had infiltrated whatever student group organized the demonstrations and must have placed notations of this kind not only in the Nigerian legislator's file but quite a number of others. Due to his persistence in demanding a clearing of his name, my support, and that of my visa officer in the 1990s, we had the record permanently expunged.

In addition to the lobby gossip sessions during my calls at the National Assembly, I usually stopped in the office of the Clerk to the National Assembly and the mailroom there. Debates of both houses were printed in "Hansard" reports (another holdover from British days, since Hansard was the nineteenth-century British publisher who produced the parliamentary records). After some discussion about how I might get hold of these reports, the clerk agreed I could have my own pigeonhole at the Assembly buildings. This was better than trusting the mails to deliver them in any expeditious time.

I thus became a familiar figure at the National Assembly complex during my two years in Lagos. To some, I was probably too familiar. I remember one time I attended a debate in the Senate and was accosted by a man who followed me out when I left. He asked who I was, although he refused to identify himself. I am certain he was a member of the National Security Organization, the equivalent of the FBI, who somehow saw me as a foreign spy, although of course I had been sitting in a public gallery listening to a public debate. Most likely, my frequent visits there had been noted, as well as my extensive friendships with the members, providing grist for the mill of the unimaginative mind of the security police.

Reading Nigeria's daily newspapers was another way of keeping abreast of events. In 1979, Nigeria's press was vibrant and independent, which is not saying that the standards of its journalists were universally high. Nigeria's journalists only partially understood the mechanics of checking sources and making sure of the merits of the story. Many papers carried stories similar to our own *National Enquirer*, a favorite theme being a man's loss of genitals through the workings of witchcraft invoked by an enemy. For some reason, this story had particular appeal in Benin City, a large town in the south central part of the country, and variants of it appeared with some regularity. One interesting paper was *Punch*, published in the southwestern stronghold of the Yoruba ethnic group in Ibadan. *Punch* was filled with good editorial comment and pretty good reporting, but it also subscribed to a European service that provided the daily "page three girl" photo. What I found most fascinating was that these teasing, nearly pornographic photos featured a lot of bare bottom that was clearly more objectionable to Nigerians than, say, bare breasts would be. On most days, someone took a marking pen and drew black panties, usually with rather crude "lace" decoration, on the photo before it was printed in the paper.

Nigerian public opinion on balance was favorable toward the United States, but lying under the admiration and friendliness was occasional suspicion and resentment, perhaps born of envy. These feelings were most common among educated, urban elites. They were understandable, given the particular form the colonial experience took in Africa and the attitudes the Social Darwinian-influenced colonial occupiers had exhibited toward the African populations. American actions in Africa from the days of independence were also ambivalent, combining development aid and lots of scholarship money with, for example, a continued sympathy toward the apartheid regime in South Africa in 1979. As an American diplomat serving in Africa, I learned to recognize the blunt expressions of African ambivalence for what they were and tried not to rise to them.

The Nigerian press was one place where these less friendly feelings surfaced. Often hair-raisingly inaccurate stories and

35

editorials would appear about events in the United States or American intentions toward Nigeria. Most of it I just shrugged off, although it could be irritating to have to counter it if my Nigerian friends brought it up and appeared to believe it.

One morning a fellow political officer and I were working through our respective piles of newspapers as work got underway. I can no longer remember what the papers were reporting that morning, but we began to read the editorial comments to each other through our open office doors, putting increasingly dramatic emphasis and inflection into our reading. Our voices swelled in volume as the editorials became wilder and more rife with anti-American sentiment. Suddenly, through the door that connected the political section suite with the front office where the ambassador worked, the ambassador himself erupted. Our noise had reached him and he was upset.

"What are you two carrying on about?" he demanded to know. "Can't you keep your voices down?"

"Don and I are just reading the morning papers to each other," I replied, wondering how to explain why we found it so funny and why it was necessary to do this at top volume. This was, of course, the ambassador's next question.

As a response, my colleague picked up one of his papers and read an excerpt to the ambassador. "What," yelled the ambassador. "Let me see that!" He took the paper out of my colleague's hands, scanned the editorial, and exclaimed, "That's outrageous!" He was now on our side, no longer concentrating on our adolescent behavior and rowdiness but on the editorial writer's flight of fancy.

Another time, there were two or three days of press comment that I found particularly uncomfortable. Ronald Reagan had recently been inaugurated, and Chester Crocker was selected as Assistant Secretary of State for African Affairs. Crocker took his first swing through the region and stopped in Lagos for a few days. One event on his calendar was a visit to the National Assembly that I arranged and at which it was decided he should meet with the combined committees on foreign affairs of the House and Senate. The format and arrangement of the room was similar to that of a hearing room in the United States Capitol—a horseshoe arrangement of seats for the Assembly members and a desk facing them for Crocker, me, and several other Americans.

The meeting began with a statement from the senator chairing the event, who stood during his remarks to Crocker while he welcomed the Assistant Secretary and expressed his committee's concerns. Crocker then replied with an outline of American perspectives. Unfortunately, he remained seated during his remarks—a perfectly natural thing for an American accustomed to appearing before a congressional committee. It was, however, not proper according to African and Nigerian norms, particularly after the chairperson of the committee had stood to address Crocker. Several members present, from the most radical of the five political parties as I recall, complained to reporters that Crocker had insulted the chair and the National Assembly.

Nothing I could say to my contacts in the National Assembly for the next days could dissuade them from believing Crocker had intentionally snubbed them. I tried to explain that a witness before an American congressional committee would remain seated while making his prepared statement. Nothing doing. We just had to ride out the negative press comment that ultimately faded from view. But I was upset that I had not spotted the problem and nudged Crocker to stand up to make his statement.

Another responsibility that resulted from my contacts with the National Assembly was proposing legislators as guests at various functions at the ambassador's residence. Official entertainment is an important part of diplomatic life overseas, helping to build friendly relationships in a social setting that can bear fruit if you need help in a hurry. If a person has been a guest at the ambassador's home, or at yours, you feel less awkward asking for assistance putting together a schedule for a visitor from Washington or requesting an appointment for a *démarche* (that is, asking his government to support an American position on an issue or explaining why the United States government has taken a particular stance).

Thus, before most ambassadorial parties, I was asked to propose a number of legislators for inclusion on the guest list. I tried generally to balance them by party and by region of the country. That was the easy part. The difficulty was getting Nigerians to commit themselves to turning up and then doing so. It is not part of the Nigerian culture to respond to an invitation with anything more than a promise to "try to be there." Northern Moslems added the traditional "Insha'allah," meaning "God willing." And anything could derail a Nigerian's plan to attend a party—the death of a family member or family member of a friend, a sudden decision to take a trip out of town or out of the country, a visitor from the home village who showed up unexpectedly. This latter event could also mean the invitee would bring his guest along with him, so the host could just as easily end up with more rather than fewer guests than planned on.

My problem was that Sue Low, the ambassador's wife, began her entertaining program in Lagos with the idea she could give seated dinner parties and know in advance who would be coming, whether they would bring wives or not, and that they would reply to her invitations. My job was to get those replies and check back a day or two before the party to remind the guests. But there just was no way to be certain. Someone could say at noon he was looking forward to the party, and then at 7 pm fail to turn up. The only reasonable solution to this was to give buffet dinners only and not try to seat people according to any protocol-derived plan. Gradually we all arrived at this conclusion, but it created tension in my relationship with the ambassador's wife when "my" guests did not turn up.

Another issue in Lagos was the weather. Although there was a rainy season, there could be rain any time of the year. Generally if the ambassador were throwing a buffet with seating at a number of small tables on the unroofed patio outside, the plan could be thrown off by a freak storm. One night I remember showing up for an ambassadorial function (early, as the embassy workers were expected to do) to find Mrs. Low fretting about the look of the sky.

"Well, Mrs. Low," I said, "you could try pouring a libation to the gods, as Kay [my boss, the political counselor] always does. She has never had a party rained out. All you do is take a new bottle of gin, open it up, and pour about half of it out over the threshold while asking for fine weather for the party."

Mrs. Low looked at me as though I had taken leave of my senses.

"You don't really believe all that nonsense, do you Helen?" she asked. Mrs. Low had two master's degrees in economics.

"Well, all I know is that Kay does it and has never had a party rained out. It can't hurt to try."

I guess Mrs. Low was worried about how it would look to claim a half bottle of gin on her entertainment voucher for "libation to the gods." She didn't pour the libation, but the gods sure poured on her party that night.

Ambassador Steve Low and his wife were entertaining people to travel with. They were low-key so far as their personal self-importance was concerned, unlike some other ambassadors I served under. They were prepared to put up with the uncertainties and glitches of travel up-country, for you could never be certain letters and messages setting things up had arrived at their destination and been acted on. They enjoyed getting out of Lagos. They loved Africa, having spent a good part of their career there, and they were flexible and easy on the road.

I remember one trip to the northern and "middle-belt" area of Nigeria, the middle belt being roughly the area around the great "Y" formed by the Niger and Benue Rivers that flow together in the center of the country. A stop was scheduled in Minna, a small town in the newly created Niger State. Like all new state capitals, the infrastructure was shaky—hotels and restaurants were in short supply, state office buildings were under construction but not completed, and the state civil service was just being patched together.

I had been told a state protocol officer would meet us on the edge of town and escort us to the secretariat of the state government. Our party of five arrived in Minna in the chauffeured Chevrolet van belonging to the consulate in Kaduna. I had my eyes peeled for the promised protocol officer, but could not spot him. Therefore, we proceeded to the protocol office. The chief of protocol was concerned at this unceremonial arrival, and cars were dispatched to find the officer he assured us had been posted to give us the proper escort.

It turned out we were traveling in a vehicle that did not meet the Nigerian standards for transporting eminent individuals like the ambassador of the United States. Our protocol officer had been expecting a large Mercedes sedan. I explained the ambassador had a Cadillac in Lagos that could never be trusted to the open Nigerian road. Furthermore, no American ambassador would be permitted to have a foreign car like a Mercedes. Our protocol man was not completely convinced.

He took us to our overnight accommodation, small bungalows constructed for the foreign employees of an Italian construction company that had finished its contract and turned the compound over to the Niger State Government. Ambassador and Mrs. Low were housed in one of the cottages, and the other three of us were in another. The rest of the party set off to explore the town and visit the market while I worked out the details of the visit with the protocol chief.

He said the ambassador and Mrs. Low would eat in their bungalow while we three grunts would eat in ours. I demurred and said we would prefer all to eat together. My protocol man was horrified at the idea, but finally yielded to my persuasion. Thus, when the others turned up, Mrs. Low had a chat with the cook at their bungalow about the menu and they agreed a roasted chicken would be nice.

We had to wait quite a while. I suspect the cook first went out to purchase the chicken and had to slaughter and pluck it before he put it in the oven. Eventually, however, a roasted chicken was placed on the table before the ambassador. African chickens are pretty small and don't have the large meaty breasts we are accustomed to in America. This chicken was no exception. It probably weighed no more than a two or three pounds. There were five of us, making the division of the chicken something of a problem. The carving implement provided to the ambassador was a

39

cheap, stainless steel table knife designed for spreading butter on the morning toast.

Ambassadors have many talents, and Steve Low was no exception. He carved that chicken into the cleanest, most even strips of meat, doling out exact shares to each of the five of us. It was a meal I have never forgotten, punctuated by a great deal of laughter. Our protocol officer would have been astounded.

At the end of that same trip, we were returning to Lagos and stopped in the town of Oyo, north of Ibadan, for a call on one of the major traditional Yoruba kings, the Alafin of Oyo. By this time, I had made a number of these calls and was familiar with the protocol. The Alafin was seated at the upper end of a long audience hall at his palace, occupying an elaborate throne-like chair. The ambassador was escorted to the over-stuffed upholstered chair to the right of the Alafin, the first in a row of chairs along that side of the room. Members of the Alafin's court were across the room in a similar row of chairs.

As a relative low-ranker, I was seated someway down the row on our side of the room. While the ambassador and the Alafin chatted, there continued to be much coming and going among the Nigerians present. I was suddenly horrified to see a man lying flat on his face in front of where I sat. I thought he had fainted and that he surely needed medical assistance. I was on the verge of springing from my seat to organize help when I noticed he appeared to be speaking, addressing the floor under his nose. He then rose from the floor and went to sit on the other side of the room.

We Americans were not required, when approaching Nigerian royalty, to observe court protocol. But a Nigerian entering the audience chamber of the Alafin is required to prostrate himself while greeting the monarch. Traditions governing these practices differ from one part of the country to another. In the Yoruba-dominated southwest, prostration is required and practiced at the courts of the "obas," the generic name for Yoruba kings.

At the very end of that trip, driving from Oyo into Ibadan, we were met along the road by a police escort that was to take us to our hotel in Ibadan. Ibadan is a large, congested city, so we were glad to have the assistance of the escort in plunging through the rush-hour traffic at the end of the working day. I have never seen anything like that police motorcyclist. He rode his motorcycle at a healthy clip, probably about thirty miles an hour, through solidly compacted traffic, standing up on his pedals and seemingly steering the bike with his knees like a rodeo horseman. With his arms he waved the cars and trucks to the sides of the road, pounding on vehicles and gesticulating wildly. Our driver had to follow unhesitatingly behind the cowboy, maintaining close contact with him. Behind us, of course, came as many Nigerians as could catch our slipstream before it closed in our wake. Some experiences of diplomatic life are not to be missed.

After every such trip, the embassy generally sent a trip report to Washington and neighboring posts, giving a general view of life and opinion outside the capital. Such trip reports are one of many forms of political writing. Others include the MemCon or Memorandum of Conversation, generally recounting one particular conversation with a key contact, spot reports on particular issues of importance to Washington policy makers, and major studies mandated by the embassy's annual reporting plan.

The reporting plan evolves from consultations among the major agencies in Washington that depend on embassy reporting (State, Central Intelligence Agency, Defense, Commerce, sometimes Treasury and others). The desk officer at State coordinates the exercise, asking the embassy what it believes will be the major issues in the year ahead and asking the Washington agencies what they most want to know. At a certain point, a list of required reports is drawn up, with realistic due dates. At the embassy, each is assigned to a particular officer who plans his or her work around making contacts and collecting the necessary information.

During the time I was in Lagos, one of my major responsibilities under the plan was following the progress the country was making in its transition to civilian, democratic rule. I also did almost all the spot reporting on legislative matters, noting bills that might have particular impact on American policy like minimum wage, budget matters, and foreign policy issues. It was during this time that I learned to draft directly on a typewriter (this was prior to the computerization of the State Department, the United States, and the world).

I remember the process as a physical sensation. After collecting the relevant Hansard reports and usually after a final visit to the National Assembly complex where I checked in with party leaders and committee chairpersons, I returned to the embassy. Often I took an hour or so to revive from the exhaustion of the tropical heat and humidity; the air-conditioning of the embassy slowly returned my mind to drafting-level acuity. My typewriter was on a table placed in front of the office window, which looked out at the conjunction of Five Cowrie Creek and the Lagos harbor. Often I could see large ships anchored in the harbor; the newly built elevated highway that runs along the edge of the harbor shoreline and, unfortunately, blocks the view of the water from the downtown streets and buildings, always presented something interesting to look at. Finally, cooled off and sharpened up, I started typing, trying to draft my telegram in one sitting before going home for the evening.

41

As I have always liked writing, I found this part of the job pure enjoyment.

One time I was immersed in this process when I glanced out the window to see a column of dark smoke rising from the direction of the harbor. I telephoned to the Air Force and Navy attaché whose office was directly below mine.

"Peter," I said, "look out the window and tell me what all that smoke is about." He told me it was very likely a ship in the harbor "blowing its stack." In any case, he told me, it was nothing much. Somewhat later, when the smoke did not abate, he set off in his car to track it down. There was a serious fire on the oil-saturated land near a major oil tank farm facility, on the mainland but near the bridges to the Lagos islands. The fire had caught hold from a cooking fire of an itinerant woman, and took several days to put out. At its height, it threatened the oil distribution system for most of Lagos.

Visitors from Washington are a frequent phenomenon at Foreign Service posts overseas, the more pleasant the post, the more frequent the visits. Lagos was not a particularly easy city in which to be a hotel resident; even the Holiday Inn there at the time, newly built and with modern amenities, could have power outages and water cutoffs. Nevertheless, Jimmy Carter's visit in 1978 and the transition to the civilian government in 1979 put Nigeria on the traveling Washingtonian's map. We had several congressional delegations (Codels) including one headed by then House Majority Leader Jim Wright and, in 1980, Vice President Walter Mondale.

Mondale's trip to Africa in 1980 came during the build-up to the 1980 election and was a thinly disguised attempt to solidify the African-American vote for President Carter. The Vice President was preceded by the normal advance team that arrived two weeks ahead of Mondale. The new wrinkle in this advance trip was that the job had been contracted outside normal civil service offices to a private firm. Security was still in the hands of the Secret Service, but work on scheduling, accommodations, and scenarios was the responsibility of several rather pugnacious young men.

The head of the team led off the first meeting with the embassy staff working on the visit by saying they were easy-going, regular guys who were not there to give us any trouble. I have never since trusted anyone who describes himself in that way. They struck almost all of us at the embassy as very unprofessional, with no experience dealing with foreign government officials.

In particular, I remember a scheduled call on the Nigerian chief of protocol to discuss Mondale's call on the Nigerian president. The advance man who was to make this call met me dressed in a net sport shirt, open at the neck, with gold chains entangled in his chest hair. The outfit was completed with slacks and equally casual footgear. Nigerians are very particular about dress, and high-ranking government officials always wore business suits or expensive national dress. I told the Mondale advance man the meeting would go better if he would change to a business suit with a tie. "Shit," was his delicate response, although he did ultimately change into something slightly less objectionable. His attitude was typical of a lot of Americans—Africa is hot and tropical, is it not? Doesn't this mean it is like Miami Beach, and one should dress as if for a beach vacation?

Like the episode some months later with Chester Crocker, it is easy for visiting Americans to step on foreign sensibilities. Avoiding such incidents is something Foreign Service officers learn with experience. It seems to me the American attitude has gradually become one of taking pride in an almost total lack of sensitivity and manners, reinforced by a belief that if foreigners don't like it, they can get lost. This attitude underlay Jesse Helms' attitude to foreign affairs and ultimately spawns the resistance and opposition the United States encounters around the world when it tries to bring other nations to support our positions.

Living in Lagos presented its particular challenges. As a fairly low-ranking member of the embassy staff and a single person, I was assigned to an apartment in a six-apartment building on Ikoyi Island, one of several islands on which the city of Lagos is built. Ikoyi was developed before Victoria Island, and the buildings were older and more pleasantly landscaped than those on Victoria, which were generally only a few years old, if that. The grounds of my apartment building backed up on the golf course, and the building itself was at the end of a short cul-de-sac, so it was a quiet place to live.

Generally, a Westerner living in Africa hires one or more servants to take care of the house, shopping, laundry, and food preparation. Some decide to do without it, preferring privacy to convenience, but I opted for convenience and, after a short time, hired Innocent Ogbonna to be my "cook-steward." As a single person with a three-room apartment, I found one person completely adequate. Innocent came from eastern Nigeria; he was Ibo, the large ethnic group that had led the secession of Biafra from Nigeria in 1967. When that war broke out, he was working as a parts warehouse stockman for one of the big oil companies in Port Harcourt. After the Nigerian Civil War, Ibos were not at all welcome in Port Harcourt, which had suffered badly in the war. Innocent, therefore, moved to Lagos, leaving his wife and six children behind in Okigbo, their hometown. The children were able to attend good schools there, which they would not have been able to do in Lagos.

My employment agreement with Innocent gave him one paid trip home a year, and sufficient time off for a good visit. Additionally, one time during the two years I was in Lagos, Mrs. Ogbonna joined Innocent with their youngest child, an engaging little boy of about five named Sylvester; by the time she left, after some months, child number seven was on the way.

Although most Americans find the employment of servants, particularly full-time, live-in personnel, somewhat exotic, it is a routine part of life in Africa. Most Africans of any means at all have helpers in their homes, whether they are hired outsiders as Innocent was to me, or, in the case of people of more modest means, relatives from the village who take care of children and perform simple chores in the kitchen. The preparation of most African food is so labor-intensive that one woman working alone would find it difficult to provide for a family.

Innocent took care of all the normal cleaning, shopping, and cooking, as well as all the entertaining I did at home. For the most part, this consisted of fairly small dinner parties, never more than ten or twelve guests, for which Innocent prepared and served all the food. I found that he was a fairly good cook, but had trouble making things all come out at the time I wanted to sit down at the table. Thus for every dinner party, he and I discussed the menu. He made a list of ingredients that needed to be purchased and, provided with the money, visited the shops and market to procure them. In addition to providing recipes for him to follow, I also prepared a fairly detailed time line ("6:45: put carrots in water; 6:50: pour water and light candles"), so generally we came out right.

Although Innocent did most food shopping for me, I sometimes came home with produce from a Sunday excursion to Bar Beach. Bar Beach was a long, white sand beach on the outer shore of Victoria Island, open to the sea. The Eko Holiday Inn was located just off the beach. Up the beach, closer to town, was an area used in the mid 1970s for firing squad executions, first of persons implicated in an attempted coup and subsequently of armed robbers, an increasing plague in Nigeria. (Fortunately, the public executions had been halted by the time I arrived in Lagos.) The stretch that ran between the Eko and the former execution spot was a pleasant place to go for a little sun, a paddle in the surf, and some shopping.

The first encounter in a beach trip came as I wedged my silver Honda Civic in among all the other cars parked along the beach road. As soon as I got out of the car, a number of young boys approached, all clamoring for the privilege of "guarding" it. The drill was to cut one out of the pack, pointing to him, and saying, "What is your name?" Once he told me, I then said, "Okay, Peter (or whatever), you may watch my car. And if I return and find everything in order I will give you fifty kobo [just under a dollar at the current rate of exchange]." When I did return to the car, Peter was always there, I handed over the coin, and all was fine. We were told that if we did not hire a "Peter," we could easily find the car gone or the tires slashed; fifty kobo was a cheap form of insurance.

(Some years later, when I was stationed in Kigali, Rwanda, I tried this same procedure. The difficulty in Kigali was that the young boys clamored at me not only when I arrived and needed to hire one of them for the job, but also at the other end of the transaction. Once, returning to my car, I was besieged by a crowd of youngsters. I jumped in, rolled down the window, and handed the payment to the boy I thought was the one I had picked out. He ran off with the coin, but left behind a few kids, one of whom started crying and sobbed, "Mais, Madame, c'était moi." I looked at him closely and realized he was right, so I had to pay twice on that occasion.)

On Bar Beach, if I sat on a blanket on the beach, the traders soon found me. Some of what they offered was interesting stuff— trader beads on raffia ropes, intricate carvings of thorn wood that illustrated scenes of Nigerian life, tie-dyed fabrics and simple dresses and dashiki-style shirts, and sometimes even what appeared to be antique masks and bronze statues. Purchase of art objects, however, was more reliably made from a trader visiting at home, for over time we could build up a relationship of trust and be more certain about what it was we were buying. One of the more common thorn carving scenes, one I never bought, was called "Bar Beach," showing one person tied to a stake and a firing squad aiming rifles at him. A visit to Bar Beach always preceded a trip back to the States for gifts to take friends and family. There were also fruit and vegetable sellers. Thus, I generally drove back from Bar Beach with an additional layer of sunburn, some carvings and beads, pineapple and oranges.

Commercial transactions like these, and those in an organized market, were always conducted by bargaining. One time, when traveling in the Middle Belt with the consul general in Kaduna, we decided to buy some fruit to eat in the car. In downtown Jos, we saw a woman with a headpan full of oranges and bargained with her over the price, agreeing finally on a dozen for one naira. We opened the back door of the van and she tossed in twelve oranges, and then continued tossing more. "No, no," we said, "a dozen for one naira."

"Two dozen, two naira," she said.

"No," we countered, "we only want a dozen. One dozen, one naira."

"You take two dozen, two naira." We finally convinced her she was going to get only one naira and that we wanted only one dozen oranges, all the four of us traveling together could eat. She began to remove oranges from our back seat, first the excess oranges and then the first dozen. Piling them all back in her headpan, she stalked off. I cannot account for this failed transaction, except to think she had two dozen oranges and wanted to offload them all so she could get a new supply from the market.

Life on Kingsway Close was never dull. There were only four properties on our little dirt road. The first house in from the main drag belonged to Senator Joseph Tarka. Tarka was one of the major players in the independence struggle of the 1950s, and the only one of that group who was still an elected politician in the 1979 class of elected officials. (Another, Obafemi Awolowo, had run for president but been defeated.) Tarka came from the Middle Belt and belonged to the Tiv ethnic group, one of the larger minority tribes from the Middle Belt. Tarka ran for the Senate from Benue State and was elected, only to come down shortly afterwards with the cancer that killed him.

I never met Senator Tarka and was only vaguely aware of his residence on the road until his death. At that point, we all became aware of the wake-keeping, which went on for almost an entire week and produced parking and traffic jams that made it almost impossible to move up and down our road. Paying respect in this way to someone who has died and visiting with the family is exceptionally important in Nigeria, indeed in all Africa. For the entire period of time between Tarka's death and his funeral in the Benue State capital of Makurdi, supporters and mourners came to the house to sit in the rows of chairs outside. And the American diplomats resident at 4 Kingsway Close picked their way home through the large automobiles parked along both sides of our narrow lane.

Although our little street was a dirt road leading nowhere, it opened from Kingsway, one of the major thoroughfares on Ikoyi Island, which bisected the island from north to south and led directly to the Falomo bridge connecting to Victoria Island, the embassy, and the open sea. The corner of Kingsway and Kingsway Close, therefore, was a prime area for traders. When I arrived, a woman had already staked out our corner as her location. She sold small items that could be carried in an enamel pan on her head— matches, a few bunches of bananas, sweets, and so on.

Trade was brisk, and she soon had capital enough to build a small booth on the corner to provide shelter from sun and rain. She expanded her inventory to include tinned goods and, most important, liquor that was smuggled and therefore free of import duty. We diplomats were able to import our booze legally through our embassy commissary system, but for all the Westerners working for aid agencies and businesses, not to mention Nigerians, outlets like this one were a godsend. Trade was intense, particularly at holiday times. Obviously, it attracted the attention of the police, and periodically the place was raided. At least one of these raids took place just before Christmas. I suspected its major motive was to provide the police with the necessary liquor for their holiday parties. It generally took the booth-keeper the better part of a week to build her inventory back and open up again.

As one year turned into the second, business kept expanding. The first booth grew into a second, and then a third. Liquor was not only sold but also consumed. Electricity was added along with a television set for the patrons of the bar. A friend, a prominent Nigerian accountant, lived on Kingsway in a compound that bordered on the back of the booths. Running into him one day at a reception, I noted that our trader-lady had added electricity to her amenities. "Not any longer," replied Arthur. He told me he, too, had noted the light bulbs and television at the booths. He had looked upward to discover where the power came from and was horrified to see the booth-keeper had tapped directly into the city transmission wire with no proper step-down transformer in between. Since this was the line that also served his house, he had asked the local Nigerian Electric Power Authority (always called NEPA) to look at the hookup. Informed that the jerry-rigged electricity supply risked not only frying the trader in her booth but also burning down his house with all its contents, Arthur had gotten NEPA to cut off the booth power.

I do not know where the trader woman got her liquor, but it was undoubtedly smuggled. The topography of Lagos is a smuggler's paradise, with islands, creeks, and inlets that permit small watercraft to operate undetected. The American embassy stood on Eleke Crescent, a street bordering Five Cowrie Creek, which separated Ikoyi and Victoria Islands. One day I was driving to work and ran into a mammoth traffic jam on Eleke Crescent. There were cars and small pickups every which way and a large crowd of people that included a number of young men in swimming trunks or underpants. There were also several men in the water itself.

At the embassy I learned that a smuggler's dugout canoe had been chased up the creek by a police patrol boat. The canoe, loaded to the gunnels with smuggled liquor, overturned, while the paddlers were arrested by the police. News of the event spread quickly, and the crowd along Eleke Crescent gathered to see if any of the booze could be recovered from the bottom of the creek. I suspect our trader-lady was selling the stuff by the next day.

NEPA was one of the more important institutions in our daily life in Lagos. Power outages were constant, unpredictable, and of uncertain length. By the time I arrived, the situation had become so difficult and affected the quality of life of embassy personnel to such an extent that all housing units had been provided with standby generators. The care and feeding of these machines, particularly in a multi-unit building like mine, became the source of some friction.

Our generator was powerful enough to run all the essentials—lighting, water pumps, refrigerators, and freezers. It was not powerful enough to run all the air-conditioning units in all the apartments. It did not kick in automatically when the public power went off, but needed to be turned on manually. Thus, one of us would run around the entire building, after waiting to see if NEPA would come back after a short wait, and tell all the other inhabitants that we would turn on the generator. This meant all air-conditioners should be turned off—something that several inhabitants either did not understand or simply refused to do. An additional problem was that the power to the building came in three phases, one for each floor, and one phase could go out without the others. Thus, running the generator for one of the floors meant the inhabitants on the others had to do without their full power for the greater good of all. Finally, the only way to tell that NEPA was back for all was to check a light bulb by the back door of each unit that bypassed the generator circuit; when the light bulb came back on, the generator could be turned off.

It was difficult to persuade all members of our little band that we should check the fuel level of the generator before flipping the switch. Running the machine dry was a dire thing to do, but convincing people that it should be avoided was one of the more difficult diplomatic jobs I ever had to perform. I learned many skills in the Foreign Service, and generator operation and maintenance was one of the unanticipated.

Telephone service and communications in general in Lagos were a matter of chance. I had a working telephone in my apartment, the only one in the building. For some reason, the number that responded to dialing was not the one on record with the telephone company, so I was not billed for the service for most of my tenure in Lagos. Nevertheless, the phone worked almost without pause through the entire two years. At one point, it did go out of service. The outage occurred at a time when I was arranging for a United States congressional visit to Lagos. One person I hoped to involve in the schedule was the leader of the largest party in the Senate. He told me he would telephone to confirm some part of the plans. When I informed him my home telephone was not working, he asked for the number and location of the apartment. The phone was fixed the next day, for the senator was chairman of the Communications Committee.

Hardly any Nigerian telephones worked without failing at some point, and most subscribers did not have a friend in high places. For those who could afford it, the solution to on again/off again telephones, was to install two or more lines in a house or office. After some time, my address book was filled with alternative telephone numbers written in margins, spilling over into the next entry, scribbled everywhere.

For the embassy, two-way radio was a more certain form of communication. At that time our embassy in Lagos was a large one, and radio sets were not issued to every American stationed there. Routinely they were carried by the administrative personnel who might be called on to solve emergencies at residences, by security personnel including Marine guards, in most of the vehicles, and so on. One radio was issued to whoever was serving a particular week as the duty officer of the embassy, to permit the Marine standing watch at the embassy to contact him or her. All radio terminals were identified by numerical call-signs, which I quickly came to recognize.

One time a Nigerian friend dropped in for a chat when I was serving as duty officer and had the radio in my living room. The radio suddenly came to life, as "6-2" was trying to contact "6-4." Repeated calls for "6-4" were issued, but "6-4" did not respond. My guest finally said to me, "What on earth is going on?"

"Oh," I replied, "one of the Marine guards at the Marine house is trying to find his driver. The driver is probably having his dinner and isn't in his automobile."

My guest was relieved to learn that the United States was not about to go to war.

Being on duty was a standard obligation for Foreign Service officers overseas. Duty rotated through the roster of all commissioned officers, excluding a few at the top (who could, in any case, be considered to be always on duty). In Lagos at the time, consular officers served on a separate duty rotation, which relieved all others of the most common problem that could come up out of hours or over the weekend—an American in distress.

Duty came up rarely in Lagos, because of the large number of personnel. In Zurich I had duty every five weeks, but in Lagos it came up only about four or five times in all. The bane of the duty officer's existence there was the "Niact Immediate" cable. "Niact" is short for "Night Action," and was originally devised for cables calling for action that could not wait for daylight working hours. An obvious problem for an agency many of whose offices and workers are in different time zones is conveying important information and requests for help when Washington is working and Lagos, for example, is not. Thus, the Niact Immediate.

In Lagos, and in most American diplomatic posts, when a Niact Immediate arrived, the first thing that happened was an alarm alerting the Marine guard at the main guard post. The guard called in a communications officer, whose job it was to go into the secure communications area and process the cable. To avoid a situation in which the communicator would not pass along the cable until daylight, he or she was required without exception to notify the duty officer. And so it was that the radio or telephone would come to life at one or two in the morning, announcing a Niact. In most cases, of course, the cable was not only Night Action, but also classified, which meant it could not be read over the telephone. I would drag on my clothes, stagger out to the garage and get in my car, drive over to the embassy to read a cable which virtually never had to be acted on until daylight, and reverse the process back to my bed.

I had to do this several times in Lagos. A colleague in the political section had the great misfortune to draw the duty during the week between Christmas and New Year 1979, when the Soviet Union invaded Afghanistan. I got duty a few weeks later and read his entries in the duty officer log. He didn't have an uninterrupted night that entire week. He had to go to the embassy to read seven Niact Immediates and four "Flash" cables, "Flash" being the precedence reserved for information that has to be transmitted faster than the speed of light.

I look back on my time in Lagos as a time when culture clashes could produce ridiculous encounters. As one example among many, I recall a time when I went to the local state liaison office for Kano in Lagos to make arrangements for the visit of our deputy chief of mission (DCM—the second ranked officer in the embassy after the ambassador) to that state. Liaison offices were necessary since communications with places outside Lagos were difficult to impossible. In theory, these offices had regular radio and courier contact with the state capitals and could make arrangements for diplomats traveling there. In practice, the theory had major flaws. Nevertheless, diplomats were expected to get approval from the state governments, by way of the liaison offices, for official trips outside Lagos.

Thus, one hot, muggy morning I found myself at the Kano State Liaison Office, which turned out to be a collection of one-story buildings in a fairly large compound. It was difficult to see where the office itself was located. Thus, I addressed myself to the only human I saw around, a sleepy looking gentleman whose chair was tipped back against the wall of one of the buildings.

"Can you tell me where the liaison office is?" I asked him. I assumed he was some kind of compound guard.

He tipped forward on to all four legs, opened his eyes, looked at me, and replied, "You could at least say 'good morning' before you ask me a question!"

He was right. You do not begin conversations in Nigeria, or anywhere in Africa for that matter, without first greeting the interlocutor and asking after his or her health, if not that of the entire family. So, I backed up, greeted him, and repeated my question. This time he waved his hand toward the relevant building.

I walked in the door of the office and found a lovely creature sitting at the receptionist's desk. She was fashionably dressed, with manicured nails and well arranged hair. Having learned my lesson from the guard, I greeted her, asked after her health, and then asked if the head of the office were in and if I could see him.

Her desk was set in the waiting room to face the door, with a space for visitors' chairs to the right, and a blank wall to the left. The lovely creature turned toward the blank wall and, in a loud and penetrating voice, said,

"Mr. Ogundipo! There is someone here from the American embassy to see you!"

Much to my surprise, a male voice responded from the other side of the wall, "I am busy now. Tell them to have a seat."

The lovely creature then turned back to me and told me, as if I had not heard any of the exchange, "Mr. Ogundipo is busy at the moment. Please have a seat and wait for him."

I did as I was asked and sat down in one of the visitors' chairs. It soon became apparent why Mr. Ogundipo could not see me immediately. A furious argument was in train between him and some of the employees—drivers, guards—of the office, who wanted higher pay and better working conditions. It made for fascinating eavesdropping.

At a certain point during the wait, the lovely creature turned again to the wall to remind Mr. Ogundipo I was waiting. His reply floated out loud and clear—he was still busy.

When I finally was permitted to enter Mr. Ogundipo's office, I had to run the gauntlet of drivers and guards who continued to occupy their ground. My business with Mr. Ogundipo was conducted in front of this crowd of spectators, not an uncommon occurrence in Nigeria.

By the time I concluded my call and climbed back in the embassy car, I was close to hysteria. All of us at the embassy had encounters like this every day; sharing them with each other was one of our greatest amusements. And my laughter at least came from a deep affection for Nigerians and admiration for their coping mechanisms. When there is no functioning intercom, just talk to the wall. And don't forget manners—greetings before requests.

Nigerian men are, as a group, quite self-assured about their sexuality. They know they are sexy, they flaunt it, and it can be fun up to a point to deal with it. I would not say that the legislators who

51

were my regular beat always made passes, but a number of them did. Generally, I deflected them simply by failing to notice in any way that a pass had been made. And the legislators were gentlemen enough not to press the matter.

On one occasion, however, the issue escalated to absurd proportions. One of the legislators asked if he could drop by one evening. I had the distinct impression that I would find it uncomfortable to be alone in the apartment with him, and I arranged for another female political officer who lived upstairs to happen by. The final complication in the evening was that it was the same night on which I was cooking a turkey for the annual Marine Corps Ball, which takes place in early November on the anniversary of the founding of the Marine Corps. Various members of the embassy staff had taken home hams and turkeys to cook for the buffet. The turkey I had signed up for was roasting away in the oven when Fola knocked at the door.

For the next hour of Fola's visit, I was offering him and my fellow officer hospitality while making periodic visits to the kitchen to baste the turkey. Fola would follow me into the kitchen, as I dealt with the bird, to try to take my hand and press his suit; on other occasions he remained in the living room and flirted with Susan. She and I exchanged notes following his departure, when he finally realized, I guess, he was having no luck with either one of us.

After two years in Lagos, I was ready to return to Washington. I had been assigned to study the Czech language for a year, prior to a two-year posting in Prague. I was ready to leave in a way—the difficulties and dangers of life in Nigeria had accumulated to a point at which I wanted a break. But I left with real reluctance as well. I had made a number of friends among the Nigerians, particularly in the National Assembly; I had been privileged to see the transition to civilian government somewhat from the inside and had come to appreciate the difficulty of that process.

And, in fact, the process proved too difficult to sustain. For many reasons, the civilian government could not maintain its hold on power. At New Year 1984, the government of President Shehu Shagari, recently reelected to a second term, was toppled by a military coup, led by Mohammed Buhari.

In Darkest Commiedom

From Lagos I was assigned to Prague, again as a political officer. Before traveling there, I had to learn Czech, the first Slavic language I ever studied. One of the policies of the American Foreign Service about which I am most proud is the insistence on language training. There is some grumbling that staff members, as opposed to officers, do not receive enough language instruction, which is true. It is also the case that the colonial languages (English or French) are the ones required at African posts, except in countries (say, Tanzania) that have adopted an official African language. Nevertheless, language training is an important part of an assignment.

For me, learning Czech was not a pleasure. It was, in fact, pretty terrible. Czech is much harder than French or German, the two languages I already knew. It has many more inflections for nouns, and the adjective endings are not the same as the noun endings. The objects of pronouns fall into several different cases. There are two verbs for each one in English, and there is not always a clear relationship between the two forms. Czech is difficult to pronounce, at least for the beginning student. I could go on.

The worst thing about studying a difficult language like Czech was that for about five months of the ten I spent in language school, I was unable to say anything at all interesting or sophisticated in the language. Although I was forty years old, I was speaking on the level of a three-year old. Even worse, the instructors often treated us students like three-year-olds, practically passing out lollipops when we got an adjective to agree with a noun.

I also confirmed what I already suspected—that I could only make myself study the language until I could communicate with limited facility. I was not driven to master Czech (or French or German) to full fluency. I can converse one-on-one in all three

53

languages; I can read the morning newspaper. But I cannot easily understand group conversation around a dinner table, nor can I read novels and genuinely literary writing with any speed or sense of enjoyment. I simply cannot make myself work at the language hard enough to reach that level. Many American diplomats love mastering a language and are completely fluent in one or more foreign languages.

Armed, then, with my barely serviceable Czech, I left for Prague in July 1982.

I cannot adequately describe the impact the physical beauty of Prague exerted on me and, indeed, on most first-time visitors. Prague is a city that escaped the urban redevelopment Paris underwent in the nineteenth century, attractive as much of that is. It was not an imperial capital like Berlin or Vienna, with the nineteenth century accouterments built there. It also was not badly bombed during World War II, and what bombs did fall did not touch the central part of the city. Thus, much of the city center dates from no later than the eighteenth-century rococo. There are streets and streets of baroque and rococo buildings. Downtown, twentieth-century buildings are frequently showpieces of the Art Nouveau and Art Deco periods. The Vltava River (Moldau in German) flows through the center of town, crossed in several places by beautiful old bridges. Hills rise on both sides of the river, one crowned with the castle. Wherever I looked, there was something that knocked me out.

The American embassy is in the former Schoenborn Palace. The oldest part of the building is the fourteenth-century cellar in one section, with a long, brick barrel ceiling and a functioning well at one end. Above ground, the embassy is actually three formerly adjacent houses remodeled into a large city mansion, one section each from the renaissance, baroque, and rococo architectural periods. Entering through the center gate, the baroque one, I found the courtyard beyond giving over to a beautiful divided stone staircase. A series of stepped gardens rises up the hill behind the embassy to the third garden, with a terraced orchard and a glorietta or little garden house all the way at the top. While I was in Prague, the American flag flew from this glorietta and was visible from many vantage points in the city, including the office window of the head of state in the castle.

Quite a number of people assigned to the embassy had apartments in this building. I was fortunate to live off campus, in an apartment building up the hill behind the castle. The apartment was probably built just before World War II, and had eighteen-foot ceilings and correspondingly high, double windows. From the windows in the large living room, I could look through a space between the buildings across a neighborhood park to the tower of the cathedral, standing in the castle precincts. This apartment was one of the favorite homes in my life.

Although I was a political officer in Prague, as I had been in Lagos, the work was entirely different. Czechoslovakia in 1982 was firmly within the Soviet sphere of influence, behind the Iron Curtain, with a government hostile to ours. Czech officials did not meet freely with NATO country diplomats; I could not just drop in on them or telephone for an appointment. The ambassador was able to call on ministers in the government as appropriate; the deputy chief of mission (DCM) also had relatively easy access to officials in the Foreign Ministry and others. I don't believe even they had access to Communist Party officers in their party roles, although, of course, many top officials in the Party also had government positions.

One time, a counterpart in the British embassy, a first secretary in the political section, informed a number of us that he had submitted a list of ten persons on whom he wished to pay calls, the formal procedure we were expected to follow when we wanted to see someone. His list included the completely standard range of contacts for a political officer—newspaper editor, university professor, a few cultural figures, a religious leader, and some mid-level government types. He left his post a year later without having seen more than one or two of those listed. The Foreign Ministry protocol office to which he submitted the list just did not see any reason for a first secretary at the British embassy to pay calls on such people.

I had a similar experience one of the few times I actually tried to call on a government official. Our embassy had received an instruction from Washington, one sent to every embassy around the world, to discuss the upcoming International Year of Youth being organized under United Nations auspices. I was given the job of tracking down the relevant working-level person in the Czech government, making an appointment, and talking with him/her about Czech participation in the event. I asked the Czech employee in our embassy who took care of making our appointments to find out who this person might be and to get me a date. It took her quite some time to track down the right official, and, in all, about six months actually to get an appointment that he kept. It went on so long it became a joke, but an instructive one. In fact, the meeting was so bland and uninformative, that the build-up to it was far more interesting.

One result of the closed nature of the Czechoslovak government was that we were forced to write more reports based on newspaper reading than I believe is a good practice. Reading a Communist-era Czech newspaper was an art in itself, since of course the truly interesting news never made the paper. What did make the front page were items like the periodic visits of Gus Hall, head of the American Communist Party and perennial presidential candidate, whose calls on the Czech Communist Party leaders were treated as those of a head of state. Occasionally stories on peace movement activities could render clues about Czech foreign policy. A certain amount of biographical information could also be gleaned from the pages of *Rudé Pravo,* the Prague daily rag, and a few other papers.

Another result of the closed-door policy was that in Prague I had much more interaction with other members of the diplomatic corps than at any of my other posts. As a junior member of the political section, I was included in the Secretaries Club, a group of about ten or twelve mid-ranking diplomats of non-Communist embassies. In addition to several members from NATO embassies, the club also invited officers from the Egyptian, Japanese, Austrian, and a few other missions to join. Once a month we met for an elaborate lunch and talked over events at the top of the news. The non-NATO embassies often had better access to Czech officials than we did, even if they were no friendlier toward them. We also benefited from our Japanese colleague's nearly perfect facility in Czech; during a previous posting to Czechoslovakia he had done nothing but study the language, and he understood it very well indeed. He had a similar command of English, the language of our get-togethers, so he was a valued colleague. We all had little notepads at our places at the table; I loved watching my Egyptian and Japanese friends making their notes in Arabic and Japanese, while I spoke in English. I returned from the two- and three-hour lunches filled with information, but useless for the rest of the day from too much food and wine. Nothing got written until the next morning.

Yet another result of the official attitude toward Western diplomats was that we tended to meet frequently with "non-official" Czechs and dissidents. Early in my posting, I was detailed as note-taker to the ambassador, who had decided to call on the leader of every officially recognized religious organization in the country. The communist government of Czechoslovakia adhered to the line that religion was old-fashioned superstition. True communists believed religion would fade away and had tried to force it to fade away in the 1950s as they were consolidating their hold on power. By the 1980s, seventeen religious organizations were permitted to exist, carefully monitored by the government. Aside from a small remnant of the pre-World War II Jewish community, the rest were Christian. Religious groups were the only legal organizations in the country recognizing a source of authority outside the Communist Party, the characteristic that made it so difficult for the Party to decide how to treat it. During my time in Prague, the government had determined that religious organizations could provide useful support for the officially organized "peace movement," a cynically manipulative policy. Writing a long report on religious organizations and their uneasy relationships with the political regime was one of the most interesting assignments I had while in Prague.

The ambassador's calls on religious leaders were to some extent a prelude to a visit to Czechoslovakia by Billy Graham in the fall of 1982. This visit followed a well-publicized mission Graham had conducted in the Soviet Union. It appeared to me, an outside observer, that Graham hoped to extend his influence to the central and eastern European countries under communist domination. To do this he had to walk a narrow line, for the regimes in question clearly wanted to use his visits and public evangelizing to convey respectability to them, implying their regimes permitted freedom of worship. In Czechoslovakia, the authorities wanted Graham to endorse their "peace movement" so far as he might be willing to do so. As this was the period of deployment of NATO medium-range nuclear missiles in Germany and elsewhere in Europe, the peace initiatives of the Warsaw Pact countries were meant to build up public opinion against these deployments. No mention was ever made, of course, of the Soviet deployments of comparable missiles in Czechoslovakia.

Graham's advance party called on us at the embassy. His visit was obviously not sponsored by the American government; we were more than willing, however, to share our views on the state of religion in Czechoslovakia. We tried to point out the kinds of pitfalls the regime might set up for Graham, particularly efforts to get him to endorse their positions on Cold War themes. The ambassador also agreed to have a reception at his residence to honor the Graham visit.

I was greatly disturbed at some of what went on during the Graham visit. In my opinion, the evangelist was too willing to participate in events set up by the regime, too willing to sign on to peace movement positions. One stop on his itinerary was a visit to Lidice, a small town that had been obliterated by the Nazis in retaliation for the assassination of Nazi Governor Heydrich. The town's site had been made into a memorial with photo exhibits and plaques supporting the end of war and oppression. The exhibits in 1982 were one-sided, pointing out the numbers killed in Hiroshima, for example, but not mentioning the Gulag. Graham came close to endorsing the anti-West tilt of the exhibits there. During another appearance, one sponsored by the government and not the church, Graham made a statement that ran in Czech as stating there was "a freedom to worship" in Czechoslovakia, a remark that was discouraging, to say the least, to Czechoslovak Christians practicing their faith under the regime's hostility. At the ambassador's reception I asked a Methodist leader if he had attended any of the Graham preaching services and what he thought. He tactfully answered that the Graham "style" was not one most Czechs had seen before. True enough—the anecdotal, emotional flavor of American revival preaching is worlds apart from the intellectual, closely argued sermons of Czech Protestant tradition, even the Baptists.

For me, the most egregious sight of the Graham visit came at his departure. I was in the VIP waiting room at the airport where Graham, with his party, his Baptist hosts, and the Czech government Director of Religious Affairs were gathered to take leave. It appeared to me Graham spent far more time speaking with the Director of Religious Affairs than with his co-religionists. This particular man had held that office for over twenty-five years and had, among other things, presided over the savage repression of the churches in the 1950s. When it came time to board the plane, Graham gave this man a big, seemingly affectionate hug of farewell. Possibly in his mind he thought this was appropriate as a sign of the infinite forgiveness Christ teaches us to exercise. Knowing what I did about the official (which we had passed on to the Graham staffers), I was disgusted. It smacked too much of playing up to the person who had the power to permit him to come back.

Those churches permitted officially to exist had to work cautiously, except for those known to have embraced the communist regime with some enthusiasm. I went often to a Baptist congregation while I was in Prague. The pastor had the attitude that most honest ministers had—in order to provide pastoral ministry to the followers, he had to cooperate with the authorities but only to the minimal point necessary to keep his license to practice his ministry. His sermons were intensely intellectual, a different tradition from most Baptist preaching in the United States, but they did not touch on political or social themes. Once a month or so he had to meet with his minder in the Office of Religious Affairs and show that official, not a believer, his sermons and other records. I also attended a Catholic church from time to time when I needed a little ritual. The first few I tried out were nearly empty. It was only when the Catholic wife of my German counterpart told me where the "good" priest was, one known not to be enthusiastic in toeing the government line, that I found a Catholic church full to overflowing.

Although churches were permitted to hold Sunday services and some meetings for Bible study and fellowship, the full range of pastoral activities we expect in America were not permitted. Hospital and prison visiting, social service and missionary activity were ruled out. Nor were churches permitted to perform weddings or burials,

58

except as an adjunct to the civil ceremonies for such events. All funerals were conducted at state-owned crematoria, and the family could only request a pastor to come there to deliver a Biblical reading or prayers for the dead.

A person known to be religiously observant was excluded from any career path that would guarantee reaching the top of a profession. A person had to become a member of the Communist Party as he or she rose through the ranks at work, and party members could not be religiously observant, baptize their children, or otherwise publicly exhibit a belief in God.

The ambassador did not call on any clergy who were part of the underground churches existing among both Catholics and Protestants. We knew these organizations were there and were a vibrant part of the religious scene, but for an American diplomat to attend services or in any way try to contact the members would have been highly dangerous for those who led or took part in their services. The congregations assembled in private homes and were cared for, liturgically and pastorally, by clergy whose licenses to work had been revoked.

Another part of our unofficial contacts centered on the dissident community in Czechoslovakia. The signatories to Charter 77 were the most visible part of this group, which numbered about two thousand in the entire country. Charter 77 was a document issued in January 1977 by a group of like-minded persons, drawn from three roughly defined groups: former Communists who had left the Party or been thrown out in the early 1970s during the normalization after the Soviet invasion; intellectuals and artists who had never joined the Party; and various religious ministers and lay persons. The Charter was drawn up a little over a year after the adoption of the Helsinki Final Accords, signed on to by NATO and Warsaw Pact members alike, that, among other things, required signatory nations to respect the human and civil rights of their citizens. Charter 77 called on the Czechoslovak government to honor its adherence to the Helsinki Accords and grant its citizens rights such as free speech, a free press, freedom of movement, and so forth.

When I reached Czechoslovakia in summer 1982, the authorities had been trying their best for five years to stamp out support for the Charter. Generally, as soon as a person signed the Charter and had his or her name disseminated as a signatory, he or she was dismissed from the job, subjected to other sanctions such as having children denied entry into good schools or university, and, occasionally, arrested. These measures failed to deter a fairly steady number of persons from continuing to sign the Charter. The total number within Czechoslovakia did not change much, however, as some yielded to pressure and emigrated every year. Each year as well, the Charter group selected three spokespersons, one from each major category of signatories. Those three persons came under particularly heavy pressure of surveillance, short detentions, and other cat-and-mouse games intended to throw them off stride. One reason to have three spokespersons at all times was to guarantee continuity if one were detained or arrested.

In 1982, the most internationally famous Charter signatory in jail was Václav Havel, serving the fourth year of a five-year term. Havel was a writer and playwright by profession. He had never been a party member; his bourgeois family background would have prevented it even if his temperament and beliefs had not been anathema to the Party. Havel was released from prison in early 1983 after he became extremely ill and the regime grew frightened he might die on them in jail. Somewhat later, another Charter signatory known to the DCM expressed the interest of some of the dissidents in having periodic get-togethers with people at the American embassy. I was chosen to host these evenings, since my apartment was away from the embassy, out in a residential area of the city. I was also low enough in rank that contact with dissidents would not be seen as overly provocative by the regime. Thus began the most interesting and deeply affecting part of my assignment to Prague.

Our policy was to permit the group to do its own inviting, so anyone at my apartment was there at the group's choice, knowing what the risks might be. I met a number of people who were not in sympathy with the regime, and were even Charter signatories, who did not wish to come to the bigger gatherings because they did not always know all the people there. I also organized evenings for these people if they wished, to which they might bring one or two others of their own choosing. Distrust was intense under such a political regime, and each person determined the degree of comfort and risk he or she was willing to accept.

The wisdom of this procedure was pointed up by an incident at the very last party I threw for these friends. One person who had frequently attended our get-togethers told the political counselor that he had just accepted the job as AP stringer in Prague, a position long held by a woman who was retiring. We knew his predecessor, who had the normal embassy contacts for a stringer working for an American press organization, but we always had to assume she could continue in the job only by reporting to the secret police. Thus, we believed the new appointment meant the man in question had made some compromises with the authorities. Quite possibly they included reporting on the little salon conducted in my apartment. We never knew for sure about any of this; we just had to assume for the safety of everyone. The possibility that some such person might be numbered among my guests kept away others who might have wished to come.

At the first such gathering we set the pattern followed for the rest of the time I was in Prague. We announced we would show a video of a film that had not been permitted distribution within Czechoslovakia; the conveners agreed on the title ahead of time. I prepared large amounts of appetizer-like foods. Well before the announced time, my doorbell rang. Standing in the hallway was a person I knew only by name and reputation, Father Václav Malý, a Catholic priest whose license to practice as a priest had been suspended a number of years before when he signed Charter 77. He had been jailed for a time and was now free, working as a stoker in a heating plant that served a number of apartment buildings.

Václav Malý came in and stood in the kitchen chatting while I finished putting the food and drink together. Gradually the others arrived as well—I can't recall exactly who was there that first evening, but Václav Havel came as he frequently did in the ensuing year, along with his brother Ivan; Jiří Dienstbier, a former Communist and journalist by profession; Anna Šabatová, another journalist and wife of Petr Uhl who was in prison during my entire time in Prague; possibly Václav Benda, a mathematician and devout Catholic layman. There were about twenty in all, as well as my immediate boss, the political counselor, and his wife.

The evenings were valuable for us, giving us entree to persons who did not endorse the government. Often they passed to us the documents the Charter 77 people prepared on numerous subjects as varied as economic policy, environmental issues, and continued detentions of persons condemned only for speaking out on matters the government did not want aired. The most accurate list of political prisoners was issued periodically by Charter 77. Occasionally, proposed Charter documents were passed around among my guests for comment and editing by other members of the group.

The evenings at my apartment were probably even more important for the dissidents. It was a place they could gather in a group, discuss problems of general interest and interact with persons of like mind. It gave them access to culture beyond that officially sanctioned by the government. We showed a wide range of videos (*Hair* and *Ragtime*, both made by Czech exile Miloš Forman; *Dr. Strangelove*; *Sophie's Choice*; and many others). We also placed out on tables copies of books published abroad by Czech writers living in exile or still within the country but not permitted to publish at home. Issues of *The International Herald Tribune*, *Newsweek*, *Time*, and other American publications were also favorites; almost all the publications displayed had a way of disappearing by the end of the evening, tucked into women's handbags or men's coat pockets. We diplomats assumed they would be widely circulated once they "walked" out of my apartment.

One time, a couple I was friendly with brought a friend to see *Sophie's Choice*. My friends were horrified to see a person they had brought to my home simply pick up some newspapers and magazines off the hall table and tuck them inside her coat while we were saying goodbye. I had to indicate, mostly by smiles and gestures, that the periodicals were placed there for that purpose. The "thief" was later to become the first Czech Ambassador to the United States following the regime's change.

Most important, the meetings we had with the Chartists, as well as others they most likely had with other Western diplomats, permitted them to realize they were not alone and forgotten. The Czech government attempted to increase their isolation and make them feel the world beyond the western border had forgotten them. Meeting at my apartment allowed them to overcome their depression and feelings that no one really cared.

The Czech authorities, of course, were aware that such gatherings were taking place at my apartment. It was surely bugged, and street surveillance recorded those coming into the building. By 1982, the authorities appeared to have decided that the numbers of Charter signatories were not growing at a dangerous pace. Permitting some access to Western diplomats was probably less risky than preventing it with detentions and other harsh measures. I once asked Václav Malý if he didn't occasionally get called in and interrogated about his contacts with us. He laughed it off. "Of course," he said, "but I am in so much trouble for other things, this doesn't add much to it."

I did not talk with my fellow diplomats from other countries about my contacts with dissidents, nor did they discuss theirs with me. While we might share information we had gained from them, it was just safer all the way around not to speak too openly of such gatherings.

What a number of us Westerners did do as a body was attend, or try to attend, any trials of political detainees we could learn about. I did this a number of times, and in no case did we succeed in gaining entry to the "public" courtroom. One time, I remember, the trial was held in Prague. Our little clump of court attenders gathered: the Canadian, the German, the British, the Austrian, me, and possibly several others. In addition to us, there were also a few members of the dissident community who were there for the same purpose. We stood around the central staircase in the building, asking one of the policemen standing at the intersection of side corridors where the trial was to take place and how we might gain entrance. Our British colleague was informed by one of the policemen that the trial was to be in a courtroom opening right off the hallway where we were standing. There was no room for us, said the policeman, although he made the mistake of saying this when the door was opened briefly and we could see the room was completely empty. The location of the room was also a mistake, for the prisoner, a man named Jiří Wolf, had to be escorted past us into the courtroom for his trial. This permitted his Czech friends to call out their encouragement briefly and also permitted him to see us, obviously Westerners by our clothes and shoes. We were told later that our attendance had given him quite a boost in morale, although the guilty verdict and a harsh sentence were foregone conclusions.

Contact with the dissidents served a concrete reporting purpose. Under congressional mandate, similar to ones in other NATO countries, we were required to report every six months on the compliance of the Czech government with the accords signed at Helsinki. There were several "baskets" of issues, one of which was human and civil rights. Others included facility of business contacts, security concerns including pre-notification of military exercises, and various consular issues such as reunification of families. Prior to filing these reports, I convened diplomats from all the other NATO embassies. We traded all the information we had about obstruction of our businessmen, new political detainees, visa problems, and such issues. These reports were additional to the required annual report to Congress on human rights observance, the draft of which I also prepared.

I remain firmly convinced that these reports, well publicized in the Western press, were a constant thorn in the side of the Czechoslovak authorities and served to moderate their behavior toward their dissident community. More generally, I believe the Helsinki Accords and continued Western insistence on meeting the requirements of all baskets were a major contribution to the dramatic events of 1989.

Czech authorities fretted at our contact with dissidents. At one embassy reception, a Czechoslovak official asked our DCM why we bothered ourselves about the dissidents, a negligible bunch he suggested. "Why do you waste your time talking with such people?" The DCM answered that since Czechoslovak officials generally wouldn't meet with us, we had to talk to somebody!

Up to this point, it might seem the Czechoslovak Government in 1982, although unfriendly and cranky toward Americans, was not all that bad. The further away we move from the era of monolithic Communism in eastern and central Europe, the more difficult it is to remember that the Cold War had particular malign realities.

During the time I was in Prague, Czechoslovakia was still completely mired in the Warsaw Pact world, occupied by the Soviet Army and controlled thoroughly by the Communist government, including its secret police and informers. We Americans had to work in an environment in which we were constantly under surveillance, either openly or covertly. We had to assume our phones, apartments, and cars were tapped and bugged. Although I worked in a part of the embassy that in theory was free of taps and bugs, we had to operate as though it were not. There were only a few places where we could speak with freedom.

Everywhere I went in Prague and Czechoslovakia I was followed, or I had to assume I was if I could not actually see it. Generally, I could spot the surveillance cars whenever I drove away from the embassy or my apartment; people sat in the park outside my front door at least until darkness, ready to call up the cars when I went out. (One friend tipped me off to the fact that they generally broke off the surveillance at about 8:00 pm, if I didn't go out before that; if, in fact, I wanted to call on somebody without my tail I generally waited until then, although of course it was foolish to assume they were not there if I could not see the obvious ones.)

Most of us at the embassy had surveillance, and for some it was more intense than others. For me it was not so heavy as it was for our military attaché and for the attachés of other NATO embassies. Our military attaché most of the time I was in Prague was Bob Piper, an Air Force colonel with a great sense of humor. The humor was a necessary weapon when he got stopped and detained for being in some place the Czechs thought he ought not to be. Bob's job was partly to travel about the countryside probing for areas where there might be missile sites or other military installations the Czechs did not want him to see. One of their favorite forms of harassment was to permit him to drive down a country road from which they removed the "no entry" signs, replace the signs behind him, and then detain him and whomever else he might be traveling with (occasionally his British counterpart). The military police then notified the Foreign Ministry protocol office, which in turn phoned the embassy. Someone from the embassy accompanied a protocol officer to the location where the attachés were detained, and everyone then engaged in a minuet of protest, outrage, and, ultimately, dismissal.

The military attachés were generally used to this game and, while it was never fun, I assumed they learned enough from it to make it worthwhile. After the fact, it could provide laughs.

One time, however, the Czechs misjudged. They had become increasingly irritated at the junior officer in our USIS office, who had a number of friends among the dissident community whom she saw with some frequency. USIS was also a threat to the Communists, since it ran a popular library, showed well-attended films, and mounted a number of interesting exhibitions and shows. Cultural information and exchange is threatening to totalitarian governments, and USIS was a thorn in the side of the Prague commissars.

Alice came under increasingly heavy surveillance, which irritated and outraged her. Then she went to West Germany, a trip of three hours to the border where we western diplomats had to go through a wearisome series of controls by the Czechs. Alice spent a night or two in Weiden, Germany, shopping and venting the tensions of life behind the Iron Curtain, and then returned to the border crossing to travel back to Prague. She sensed something was wrong when the Czech immigration and customs officers brought a sniffer dog up to her car. The dog indicated there was something in the car, which the customs officers demanded to search.

International diplomatic law generally rules out the search of a diplomat's car, under the rubric of immunity. Alice refused the request of the customs officers to look in her car and a standoff began, lasting several hours. They refused to let her return to Germany or proceed to Prague. Finally, she placed a call to the embassy and the chief of the consular section drove to the border to see what was going on. He and Alice ultimately agreed the customs officers could conduct a search of her car. A brick of marijuana was discovered in the spare tire compartment, wrapped in newspaper. All these proceedings were photographed by the Czechs. Alice hotly denied having placed the marijuana in the car, protested the entire incident, and ultimately was allowed to finish her trip home to Prague.

Our ambassador fully believed Alice and supported her story that the dope had been planted in her car, either in Prague prior to her departure or by Czech agents in Germany while she was in Weiden. The Czechs called for her withdrawal from the country without actually "PNGing" her (i.e. declaring her *persona non grata*, an unwanted person). Had they done that, the American embassy would have had no recourse but to withdraw her. Instead, the Czechs hoped the embassy would doubt her story enough to pull her out, which the embassy refused to do.

After a standoff of several weeks, during which the Czechs made life more and more difficult, the United States government decided to take action. It closed the Czech airlines office in Chicago and threatened to close the Czech trade office in New York. The point made was, "You have more to lose at this game than we do. Drop these stupid charges and your harassment, or you will end up with a lot fewer resources in our country." The Czechs finally blinked, and Alice was permitted to finish the final two months of her tour.

I never was subjected to the kind of confrontation Bob and Alice encountered. As we used to say among ourselves, I never got the "Tatra" treatment. The Czechoslovak auto industry manufactured several types of cars, the Škoda for the ordinary car owner, and the Tatra, a much bigger sedan, for officials. Alice and Bob, as well as some other Western diplomats and military attachés, were surveilled by Tatras. These heavier cars occasionally tried to do things like force the diplomat off the road, box in his or her car, or follow at a dangerously close distance. My surveillance cars were always Škodas or Soviet built Laďas and never did anything more than follow me, in packs of three at a time, dropping back and handing me off to the next, circling around and picking me up again.

Of course we were often amused by the surveillance, although I usually felt irritated and harassed as well. One time, on Labor Day when the American embassy was on holiday and the Czechs were not, I set off for the center of town to shop for presents to take home on an approaching vacation. Because of center-city parking difficulties, I headed off on foot for the Metro station when I left my building, walking briskly up a small side street. One of the surveillance cars, standing by to pick me up, was parked in the street. As I walked past, the driver ducked down behind a handy newspaper. Just as I boarded the train, I saw one of "my" team jump on to the next car, and when I emerged from the station into Václavské náměstí (Wenceslas Square), a follow-car was standing on the street outside.

First I went into a record store. In Prague shops, the procedure was that as many clients could enter, as shopping baskets were available at the entrance. Any overflow had to wait until a basket was turned in. Since it was a working day, neither my shadow nor I had to wait. I spent the next twenty minutes or so selecting records for my nephews and watching the shadow trying to look absorbed in the racks of recordings.

At my next stop, I ran into an embassy friend who told me of some attractive garnet jewelry at a shop in a labyrinthine building called the Lucerna. She tried to explain exactly where the shop was, but I kept going down dead-end corridors in Lucerna, turning around to find myself face to face with my pursuit. He kept taking off and putting on his jacket and, one time, changing his shirt entirely. I'm certain he thought I was trying to lose him and became ever more frantic. I never did find the jewelry store; perhaps I should have asked my shadow if he knew where it was.

Another time I went to the theater with a Czech friend who had received permission from the authorities to emigrate. Generally I did not go out publicly with any dissident friends. In this case I judged it would be acceptable, since he was about to leave the country in a few weeks anyway. We drove in my car to the theater, which was located on the outskirts of the city. We were early so we went into a neighboring coffee shop while we waited. Surveillance had caught up with us, and one of the followers stood with his hip wedged right up to the corner of the table where we were sitting. I assumed he had some taping device in his pocket, but we had nothing of moment for him to carry back to his lab for analysis. There is nothing like a hostile hip to dampen even the most innocuous conversation. After the performance was over, we left the theater and, driving away, I could see we had at least twice the normal number of surveillance cars on our tail. My friend consequently decided he should disembark at a Metro station, since he was living against regulations in an apartment without registration. When we met some months later in London, he told me he was followed for three days after our outing.

Wherever we were in Prague, we had to assume we were observed, listened to, followed, and photographed. Some of the cameras were ingeniously hidden in pocketbooks (for women) or the old-fashioned, accordion-style briefcases (for men). I became adept at spotting them in crowds out on the streets; the pursuers would turn the cameras at rather awkward angles to shoot me buying souvenirs on the Charles Bridge or walking up the street. Men also carried small, leather purses in which they had two-way radios, with wire antennas, with which they could communicate to a surveillance officer on an adjacent street. What possible use all this was, I cannot tell. Except for my contacts with the dissident community, about which the authorities were well aware, my life in Prague was an open book.

General embassy policy about contacts with Czechoslovak citizens dictated that the initiative had to come from the Czech side. It is safe to say that by 1982, virtually no one in Czechoslovakia believed in or supported the Communist Party any longer, except possibly for the thin layer of top party and government officials. I have my suspicions that even they only subscribed to Party ideology because of the perquisites it brought them—large houses and cars, support from Moscow, authority and power.

Beside these faithful, then, stood the rest of the population. Some joined the Party and went through the motions, because this was the only way to achieve promotion in their professions, have the right to travel abroad, send children to university, and enjoy other benefits. At the other end of the spectrum stood the dissidents, who publicly called on their government to adhere to the international standards of the Helsinki Accords. In between was the great mass of people, generally sympathizing with the dissidents but unwilling to take the public step of signing the Charter. These people were disposed to be friendly toward the United States but knew that any overt steps toward contacts with American diplomats could bring unwelcome consequences. We had to respect their fears and hesitations, for they were founded in reality.

Even the hesitant citizens of Czechoslovakia could break out of their isolation with enough motivation. In 1983 or 1984, the USIS office mounted an exhibition on astronauts and American space exploration. The items on show included an astronaut suit and "space food," great stuff for kids to see. The public space in which the exhibit was held was the cramped USIS library on the ground floor of the main embassy building. Across the street from the entrance gate was a police observation post from which the cops on duty photographed anyone entering the building. In spite of the intimidating circumstances, the line of people patiently waiting to view the exhibit stretched all the way down the street; during the ten days the exhibit was on, thousands of Czech visitors waited to see the astronaut suit and photos from the moon.

An even more dramatic expression of defiance of the regime took place every May at the anniversary of V-E day. The official Communist history of World War II in Czechoslovakia stated that liberation was achieved with assistance only from the Soviet armies. This version ignored the truth, which was that the United States Third Army under General Patton liberated a large crescent of territory in the western part of the country, advancing more than fifty miles into Czechoslovakia. Quite a large number of towns in this area erected monuments and plaques after the war, commemorating the United States' contribution to their liberation. Some of these plaques were removed during the Vietnam War, but we knew where the remaining ones were and where many of the missing ones had been as well. There were about seventeen or eighteen such sites.

On the selected weekend, the American ambassador, accompanied by a contingent of embassy personnel and the military attachés in uniform, traveled to each place, laid a large wreath, and made some remarks recalling the contribution of our troops to the freedom of Czechoslovakia in 1945. The schedule of these appearances was announced repeatedly a few weeks before the weekend over Voice of America. In 1983, I went on the tour of sites, which took two days. It was an unbelievably emotional experience. In some places, in spite of intimidation from the Czech authorities, there were hundreds of Czech citizens with their entire families. The presence of surveillance police photographing the crowd was obvious. In one town square, where the plaque had been removed, loud music was played over the public loudspeakers to drown out the ambassador's remarks. At another spot, a father told me vehemently that he was determined his son would know the truth of

68

the liberation and America's contribution. People brought old photographs, showing General Patton at his headquarters or themselves with American soldiers. I spent both days photographing the crowds, many members of which wanted to be filmed standing next to our uniformed attachés; much of the rest of the time I spent weeping while people told me their memories of the liberation and the arrival of the American forces.

On Easter Monday in 1983, I was in my apartment on a holiday reading or catching up with correspondence when the doorbell rang. I found an unknown woman standing at the door holding an enormous bouquet of daffodils. She asked after a previous inhabitant of the apartment, a man who had headed the consular section some years before. I told her he no longer lived there but had been transferred to Vienna. I affirmed that I was a member of the American embassy staff. She thrust the daffodils at me and said, "These are for you." "But I don't know you," I spluttered. "What are they for?" "For friendship," she answered, and abruptly turned and walked down the stairs. I stood there staring after her, thinking too late I should have asked her in for tea or something. I have always believed her gesture was one the overwhelming majority of Czechs would have made, except for the terrible fear on which the authority of the state depended. Attending the wreathlaying ceremonies was another, when large numbers did defy the state.

Springtime was also the time when the Czech authorities organized what was meant to be a spontaneous celebration of the workers of the country, the traditional May Day celebration. Any genuinely popular support of this event had long since evaporated. The first May I was in Prague, I walked over to the wide area on the cliff overlooking the Vltava River called Letna where the May Day parade took place. Prague was divided in ten districts, and as the parade was forming up, participants were asked to gather at the large signs with their district's number. They had generally been recruited by the party organizers at their places of work. A respectable number turned out, thanks to whatever pressures had been brought to bear. The same organizing principle that devolved down through local groups guaranteed that each window in apartment buildings was festooned with small flags mounted in brackets, the Czech flag and the Soviet flag. These little brackets were attached to each outward facing window at my apartment, and I was tempted on those occasions when flags were in order, to fly little American flags.

Once the marchers had gathered at the collecting spots, the music began and each city district marched off. Participants were handed posters, many of which inveighed against American nuclear weapons. Some groups in the parade represented specific factories, while other marchers were just undifferentiated residents of that part of Prague. I have never seen the May Day parade in Moscow, but happily in Prague the occasion was not one used for the display of military hardware. The route took the marchers past a grandstand erected on the outside of the city's soccer stadium on which were ranked all the leading members of the Communist Party, beginning with General Secretary Gustav Husák and proceeding on down to characters I could not identify.

The parade was in one sense pleasant, for family groups marched together and there was no attempt at strict regimentation or discipline. Toward the end, after all ten districts of the city had passed, various clubs and organizations took part carrying paraphernalia representing the group's activities. I remember one group carrying elaborate model airplanes; the most dramatic was some kind of falconry club that carried their hooded birds on their wrists. One curious aspect of this whole scene was the fact that there were few onlookers, except for the Party functionaries in the grandstand and, down below, my surveillance and me. As the groups reached the end of the route they simply broke ranks and headed off for family picnics and trips to the country cottage, having had their names checked off on the block warden's attendance sheet. I learned from acquaintances that people would do almost anything to get out of participating in the parade. I heard of one case in which a wife had taken pity on the organizer at her place of work, who was having trouble filling his quota, and had agreed to march; her husband was so furious he hit her when she got home.

People in Czechoslovakia had interestingly wild ideas about the United States. They did not believe very much of what they read in the local press, even if it were based on truth. One day I went to my Czech lesson in the embassy. Paní Olmerová, my teacher, began to discuss an article that appeared that morning in *Rudé Právo* about the costs of American health care. Translated into Czech currency, the price tag for cancer treatment, horrifying even to an American, seemed to Paní Olmerová a ridiculous lie. I told her the figures were accurate, but what the article did not state was that most Americans had health insurance that covered the costs. Even those without insurance, I told her (somewhat optimistically), received treatment somehow or other. She was so disposed to disbelieve everything in the Communist press and to believe everything about the United States was perfect heaven that I do not think I convinced her the story was technically true.

The ordinary Czech had very little sense of reality about even the size of the United States. Shortly after I arrived in Czechoslovakia, I took a short trip to Košice, a city far to the east of

Prague in Slovakia. I had some time before catching my return plane, so I stopped in at the local museum. I was asked to sign the guest book when I entered, so I put my name and "American Embassy, Prague." A young employee of the museum then chased me down about three rooms into the exhibit and asked breathlessly, "Are you from America?" When I answered yes, he then asked, "Do you know my aunt? She lives in Bridgeport." I had to disappoint him.

The government of Czechoslovakia was certainly aware of the ordinary Czech's affection for the United States. The major offensive against it was carried on through the officially sponsored peace movement. It is, of course, difficult to oppose "peace," but the support of most Czech citizens for the organized conferences and rallies was hedged or minimal. They knew the regime was controlling the movement and that it did not draw on the passion of private citizens to ensure a more peaceful world for their children. It was designed, rather, to represent a world of Manichaean duality, posing the Warsaw Pact nations as the forces for peace and brotherhood against the evil of NATO countries.

The regime did all it could, nevertheless, to mobilize the population to call for peace and an end to nuclear weapons. This drive came at the time American cruise missiles were being deployed in Western Europe and President Reagan was speaking of the "evil empire." The Czech government, of course, never publicly acknowledged that Soviet medium-range missiles were deployed on their territory.

Enrolling the officially recognized church organizations was one means the government used to try to broaden support for their peace movement. In the case of the Protestant denominations, this was done with a declaration of sympathy from the national headquarters of each denomination. With the Catholics, however, individual priests and bishops were asked to join an organization called "Pacem in Terris." Quite a number did, seeing it as a harmless act that subscribed generally to Christian principles. Shortly before I arrived in 1982, however, Pope John Paul II (a native of neighboring Poland, a biographic fact threatening to the Czech authorities) issued an encyclical instructing members of the Catholic clergy not to participate in political activity. This instruction was aimed in the first instance against the liberation theologians and activists of Latin America. Czech Archbishop Tomášek, however, who resisted joining or instructing his clergy to join Pacem in Terris, wrote a letter to the pope requesting clarification of whether Pacem in Terris could be considered a political movement covered by the encyclical. The pope judged it was, opening the way for the Archbishop to tell the Catholic clergy not to join the Communist peace movement. Resistance along these lines continued until the "Velvet Revolution," the bloodless end to Communist rule, in November 1989. By this time well over half the bishoprics in Czechoslovakia were empty since the government refused to permit the pope's nominees to take their offices.

Although Ronald Reagan was anathema to the Communist authorities in Czechoslovakia, he was admired by the population at large. One dissident friend told me that a late Reagan movie was given a short run in a movie theater in Prague. In this film, Reagan played, uncharacteristically, a bad guy. Every time he appeared on the screen, nevertheless, the audience cheered; when he was shot at the end, the theater erupted with booing. I kept looking for the film to be shown again but never saw it listed in the guide.

Life in Prague had many pleasures. Music is an important tradition in the city, and symphony and opera performances were frequent and good. It was a little jarring to hear the opening lines of *The Marriage of Figaro,* and realize the opera was going to be performed in Czech. Generally all operas were, with the exception of *Don Giovanni,* which had premiered in Prague in Italian and was always performed in its original language. Another exception was during the spring music festival known as Prague Spring. I went to a performance of *Rusalka,* a Dvořák opera written in Czech. It started off predictably enough in Czech, but at some point in the lead soprano's first big aria, I realized she was singing German. She was an international star, Bulgarian by birth, and usually performed the opera in Germany and in German. The opera wound on, bilingually, to its conclusion some two or three hours later.

Once I got over the initial hesitations of speaking Czech, I gained some fluency in everyday interactions. My greatest problems came when I addressed a stranger on the street in Czech, perhaps asking directions to some shop or other. Hearing that I had a foreign accent, the Czech would answer me in German, assumed to be the language of all persons with accents. For me, who also spoke German, this had the distressing effect of closing down all synapses in the brain, rendering me speechless altogether.

One utterly confusing encounter came at the end of a musical performance of a Christmas Mass by Ryba, a Czech composer, performed all over the city by professional and amateur groups during the Christmas season. My Canadian diplomatic counterpart was an excellent amateur cellist and was in an orchestra performing the Mass one year. A friend and I went to the concert, held in a turn-of-the-century building, full of Mucha wall murals, originally built to house an organization called the Hlahol. This was a word I had not encountered; I could see from looking around the auditorium that Smetana and Dvořák, the great composers of the nineteenth-century Czech revival, were part of the tradition of the Hlahol, but I still did not know what the word meant. After the concert ended, I turned to the older woman sitting on one side of me and asked, "Pardon me, can you tell me what 'Hlahol' means." She began to tell me Hlahol was a musical society founded by Smetana, taken over by Dvořák, and so on and so forth. I tried with the best "conversation management devices" taught us in our language training to say, "I understood you to say this, but I still do not understand what 'Hlahol' means." She then turned to her husband and told him to go quickly and find some friend of theirs who could speak German. The husband scurried off. I thanked her for her concern but said German was not my mother tongue; rather English was since I was American. She then dispatched another courier to find a friend who could speak English. Just at this point the German speaker arrived and, although he had no teeth at all in his upper front jaw, proceeded so far as I could tell through the hand he held over his mouth, to relate the same story the lady had told me. Then the English speaker arrived, and went through the same drill in my own language. The problem was solved only with the arrival of the Canadian cellist, who informed me that Hlahol means "a joyful noise." The initial mistake was mine; I should have asked the question, "What does *the word* 'hlahol' mean?"

Going to concerts had other perils as well for those from America. It was absolutely mandatory to check coats at the coatroom. Ushers were completely unyielding on this point and would not permit us to take our seats until we were coatless. Because the lines were hopelessly long at the end of the performance, most of us left our coats in the car, assuming we were parked close enough not to freeze to death on the dash from car to theater. Taking our seats, we were required to face the people we were pushing past, the opposite of the normal American habit of shoving our buns in peoples' faces. And, finally, there was the tradition of the halftime promenade in the lobby. If we retired to the lobby, we could not just chat in clumps as we do in American concert halls. A line of concertgoers formed up and proceeded to trace a stately circle around the edge of the lobby until the bells summoned us back to our seats. This practice allowed us to greet anyone we might happen to know, comment to our companions on the dress of other opera-goers, and engage in light gossip.

Many evenings were filled with entertaining other members of the diplomatic corps. After some time in Prague I realized if I accepted all dinner party invitations, I would find myself out at all hours every weeknight. Since phoned invitations were delivered a month in advance of the date, it was difficult sometimes to regret with any conviction.

One reason for such advance planning was that we had to arrange for a cook and wait staff, and then figure out how to procure the food the cook and we agreed would be prepared. There was a regular group of waiters the diplomatic corps hired for these occasions. Gradually they came to be as familiar as the hosts and other guests. They were paid in "units," as was the cook. A unit was either a carton of western cigarettes (we got Marlboros from the commissary system in Germany) or a bottle of whisky (Johnnie Walker). Each cook got two of each, while the waiters received one/one. These units were permitted as payment for casual labor; we tipped waiters in city restaurants in cigarettes (a pack per couple), we paid the car wash man who came to the embassy three packs per wash, we paid babysitters a pack an hour. I once remarked to my boss's wife that I had a large supply of cigarettes and was afraid they would become stale. She laughed and asked me if I actually thought anybody ever smoked them! I envisioned a carton of Marlboros making endless rounds through the unofficial economy of Czechoslovakia, bribing doctors to treat children, paying off butchers to save good cuts of meat, and so on.

Procuring good meat for dinner parties was arranged through the Czech national who staffed our little commissary store. Dennis (Zdeněk in Czech) had some source of excellent meat; it was probably advisable not to ask too many questions about it. I assume Dennis skimmed our commissary as much as he could get away with and bribed a local butcher. I do know that the filet mignon, duck, and other meats he delivered for my parties were cheap and incredibly delicious.

Other ingredients were more difficult. During the time I was in Prague we built up what we called the "Greengrocer" run to Weiden, the closest German town across the border. All non-Communist diplomats in Prague were permitted to participate in this program, and the number of dinner parties on the circuit always multiplied around the time of the monthly run. Everyone indicated what he or she wanted to order—fruits and vegetables mostly. The day before the run, a consolidated order was phoned to the Weiden greengrocer and early the next morning an embassy truck left for Germany, carrying a Czech driver and an American employee to insure easy passage at the border. Gradually, other services such as dry cleaning were added. The run was always made on a Wednesday, since Wednesday evening our embassy bar, the Dobrý Den (which means hello in Czech) was open to the western diplomatic community. The truck arrived back about six o'clock in the evening, and then a group of volunteers broke the trays of lettuce and carrots, the sacks of potatoes, and bunches of bananas into the amounts ordered by each family. Paper sacks with each name were stacked on the stairs for the owner to claim when he or she emerged from the Dobrý Den.

This process was necessary from our point of view because the supply of fresh foods was uncertain and intermittent at Prague shops. Usually we had to line up for varying lengths of time even to get into the store, and we never knew what would be available. Almost nothing exotic, even oranges and bananas, was on sale except perhaps at Christmas time. We served a big fruit salad at my farewell party for the dissident community, and all the guests marveled at the fact that at one time in one bowl there were fresh pineapple, bananas, grapes, apples, and so on. For a dinner party, therefore, I either had to order through the greengrocer run or go to Weiden myself, taking a day of annual leave from work. (Married officers had a distinct advantage here, as a non-working spouse could make the trip to Weiden and no leave had to be sacrificed.)

Late in the afternoon of the dinner party, the cook and wait staff arrived and got to work. They needed no help from the host or hostess. At my first party, I tried to coach the wait staff on setting the table; the head waiter informed me he knew exactly what he was about and I could go sit down in the living room. At some point during their task, he came to find me and announced they were unable to find the white wine glasses. At these parties it was de rigueur to serve white wine with the appetizer, red wine with the main meal, and champagne at the end, necessitating supplies of crystal stemware I just did not have at that time. I told the waiter I did not have glasses specifically produced for white wine. (Yes, there is a difference between glasses for red and white; in fact there are glasses specifically for Rhine wine and on and on.) They would have to put out extra generic wine glasses for the white wine. I think he was quite disappointed at my low standards. I am ashamed to admit that on my next trip to Germany I purchased a set of white wine glasses.

It was not possible to call on this kind of assistance when I was entertaining dissidents or other unofficial guests. We always had to assume that any household help we had reported to the secret police. The particular headwaiter who was appalled by my lack of white wineglasses had once been found during a Dutch embassy dinner party going through the briefcase of the host. I avoided this problem by never having anything at home the headwaiter or anyone else could be interested in.

I had a wonderful cleaning lady who came three mornings a week. Particularly in the winter, when Prague was heated with soft coal, the house quickly became filthy. Blažena was energetic and enterprising, always suggesting ways to do a job and volunteering to do extra jobs when needed. Occasionally, the way she performed a job could throw me off my stride. After my household shipment arrived, I unpacked all the kitchen equipment on to counter-tops and tables; Blažena put it in the cupboards. Looking for a mixing bowl a few weeks later, I felt total frustration until I recognized her organizing principle was material (glass, plastic, metal) rather than function (bowls, platters, baking pans).

Toward the end of my time in Prague, Blažena's son, who sounded like something of a hard-luck case, became seriously ill. He had a motorcycle accident at some point, and the bone became infected, perhaps with osteomyelitis. He was hospitalized in what Blažena considered a mediocre hospital, and she feared he was not getting the treatment he needed. She therefore made arrangements to see an orthopedist on the staff of a much better hospital and the university medical faculty. I learned of this when she was late one morning and telephoned to say she would tell me what the problem was the next time she came. (She did not trust my phone any more than I did.)

The next time I saw her she was indignant. It all spilled out, even though the bugs in my apartment probably picked up the conversation as efficiently as anything on the telephone would have done. She called on the orthopedist fully expecting she would have to bribe him to make an exception for her son. Usually she made such bribes with the cigarettes or whisky she earned from me and other diplomats for occasional work like sewing, babysitting, or working at parties. In this case, however, the orthopedist demanded a hefty amount of cold cash although, fortunately for her, in normal Czech currency. (There was another form of Czech currency, "Tuzex crowns," that was tied to hard-currency values and was used in stores that imported their goods or sold Czech export goods to tourists. I paid half Blažena's salary in Tuzex crowns.) She paid the bribe, but she was furious.

Corruption and illegal transactions were common everywhere in the Czech communist system. It was quite normal for workers to help themselves to building materials at their work sites for use at their country cottages. So many things could not be procured in shops through open means that an entire parallel economy based on barter or the cigarettes/whisky currency developed. One time the ambassador asked a protocol officer assisting us with a trip whether he were going to attend the Olympics being held in Los Angeles that year. The mid-level government functionary replied that only "rich people, like butchers" could afford such travel. Butchers, the people who supplied Dennis at our little commissary with such tender filet mignon, were placed as well as anyone in the society to extract funds for the luxuries of life like attending the Olympic games.

Only once was a "thank-you" I offered refused. One evening I agreed to take duty for a friend and, as luck would have it, received a call. The wife of the United States Army Corps Commander based in Frankfort was in Prague on a military-sponsored trip for Army wives. Mrs. General had an artificial heart valve and had forgotten to bring her medication. After a series of tedious telephone calls, during which I learned that if she did not take the medication for the three days of her stay she could run into serious problems, I agreed to pick her and her major-wife escort up at their hotel and take them to a clinic especially designated for diplomats and high-ranking Czechs. The doctor on duty there was not, strictly speaking, supposed to treat tourists. After he first urged me to go to an emergency room, he realized he was probably much better placed to help out. All this was lost on Mrs. General, who, accustomed to the complete military cocoon of Frankfort, somehow did not understand she was behind the Iron Curtain and cut off from her support system. Both she and Mrs. Major assumed, incorrectly, all the drugs they knew by proprietary names would be available in Czech pharmacies. The doctor, in fact, ascertained what kind of valve implant she had and then telephoned to colleagues all over Prague to figure out equivalent drugs and dosages to prescribe. I was extremely grateful for his care, and as we were leaving the clinic, I offered him a plastic shopping bag with a bottle of whisky in it. He refused, to my surprise and admiration. There was, of course, no official charge for his help.

I have said that I did not receive the "Tatra level" of surveillance. This did not mean, however, that I was not occasionally the victim of secret police pranks meant to throw us off guard. One night a group of diplomatic friends came over for drinks and a movie. After a good evening, they left toward 11 o'clock. A short time later, a few them were back at my door, telling me my car, parked on the street, was covered with red paint and had some kind of flag placed under the windshield wiper. I went down to the street with them to find a high-quality red enamel paint, impossible to wipe off, was dumped on the roof of the car and had run down over almost every panel. The flag under the windshield wiper was a hand-made representation of the PLO flag. This incident came not too long after the massacres in the PLO refugee camps in Beruit.

The Marine guard on duty at the embassy patched my telephone call to the home of the DCM where the duty officer was spending the evening. The duty officer, hearing my report, exclaimed, "It's the same MO!" It turned out he left his party to find his car in the same shape as mine, about a mile away from my apartment. The DCM told me the police had been called to that car and, as soon as they finished there, he would accompany them to my place. He told me to telephone the military attaché, whom he saw driving down the street a short time before, to alert him to park his car inside his garage. I telephoned that house, only to find the attaché already asleep. Very, very slowly I told him to go check on his car and, when he did, he found it out on the street where he had left it, covered with red paint and, in his case, also splashed all over with an extremely effective paint remover. The police checked all three of our cars, each a mile from the other and the only diplomatic cars so affected, and found no bombs or other worrisome problems.

When we delivered a diplomatic note the next morning to the protocol office at the Foreign Ministry, the protocol chief innocently asked if the DCM or I had any idea who could have done such a terrible thing. Just as innocently we acknowledged we could not imagine. We were, of course, convinced the vandalism had been officially sanctioned. There were PLO members in Prague, but they were under tight wraps on any activity within Czechoslovakia. Whoever had painted our cars had to know the license code to know what numbers United States plates had; they had to know where the three of us, living well separated, would have parked our cars; and they would have had to have access to a quality of paint unavailable on the open market in Prague.

Another "prank" supposedly perpetrated by the PLO occurred during the same period. When the Marines went at early daylight to raise the United States flag over the garden glorietta one day, they found a large, cloth PLO flag flying from the flagpole. Obviously during the night someone entered the garden, surrounded by a simple, easily scaled fence, and hoisted the flag as an embarrassment to the United States.

Officially inspired demonstrations occurred from time to time at the embassy. I recall at least one "spontaneous protest" against United States friendship with Israel and another against United States nuclear policy. When we got word a demonstration was on the way, we closed up the gates, shuttered the ground-floor windows and then watched what was going on from the upper stories. The crowds were always quite small (although photographed by the accompanying TV crew from inside to make it appear like hundreds) and, interestingly, always seemed to have the same voice at the megaphone.

A far more pleasant view from the embassy windows was provided during the filming of the movie "Amadeus" during my stay in Prague. Many ordinary Czechs were interested in this operation, as the director, Miloš Forman, had left Czechoslovakia during the 1968 upheaval; this was the first time he was permitted to return to work in the country of his birth. Since Mozart lived for a period of his life in Prague, which of all European cities has the greatest number of buildings dating from the late eighteenth century, it was a natural background for the film.

Shortly after the crew arrived in town, I was behind the bar in the Dobrý Den on the evening when embassy personnel (rather than the Marines who tended it Friday night) served up the drinks. We did not permit anyone from unfriendly countries to come into the bar and so were expected to make sure who all our patrons were. A strange man sat down on one of the stools and asked for a beer, and I asked him if he were with the film company. When he said yes, I persisted and asked if he were part of the production crew or one of the actors. "Actually," he replied with amusement, "I'm the star." It was Murray Abraham, "Salieri," who proved to be a friendly, approachable person during the weeks the crew was in town. It became a common sight during lunch at the embassy snack bar to find "Mozart" and "Salieri" sharing a table, dressed in their velvet frock coats and buckle shoes. The snack bar was one of the few places they could get a quick lunch. If the filming that day were in the neighborhood, we could count on seeing them, as well as the gaffers and best boys and other mysterious people in the film business.

Two or three scenes in the movie were filmed in front of the embassy itself. The opening sequence is filmed in the French embassy, and I can identify the locations of almost all outside shots in the movie. Several members of the embassy staff were selected as extras for the film, although I am not able to spot any of them in the finished cut. I watched my boss repeatedly walk down a darkened street during one evening's shooting, but still cannot see that sequence in the film.

I loved Prague and was profoundly and permanently affected by my experiences there. I could never take in enough of its beauty. It was the first place in which I came in direct contact with people persecuted for political and cultural activities or with an entire population forced to accommodate itself to a malign, totalitarian regime. I gained an enormous respect for the dissidents who persisted in their principled opposition to their government in spite of the detentions, interrogations, and jail sentences they endured. I was told, and believed, that the act of dissidence was a form of freedom, that having taken the decision to acknowledge one's opposition to a system imposed from the outside, it became possible to regain self-respect and independence. I felt an overwhelming admiration for those who found it possible to take that step. I could not judge those who did not, for whatever reasons; I had never been forced into a similar choice and had no stance from which to judge.

The visual image of Prague implanted on my mind is of a late spring day, when all the fruit trees were in bloom. The uppermost level of the garden behind the embassy was a terraced orchard. The employees' Recreation Association paid every spring to have a gardener come till up a number of large plots in this part of the garden; these were then assigned to anyone who wanted one. I combined forces with our commercial attaché, so we had a double-sized plot, enough, for example, for a sufficient stand of sweet corn for proper pollination. I am an avid weeder, and one of my favorite forms of relaxation during that spring and summer was to spend a Sunday morning or afternoon weeding our plot, usually all by myself. From that high on the hill behind the embassy, I could look straight across a valley in which most of Malá Strana, one section of the city, was built, at the castle and cathedral thrusting up behind the long castle wall that followed the contours of the hill opposite. Later on, in the summer, a brass band gave morning concerts in the castle precincts, and the music floated across the valley. The sight was one of the most beautiful I have ever seen. As I grubbed around in the garden, looking at that lovely view, it was possible to forget all the ugliness of the regime, all the frustrations of working in a hostile environment, and just live in the moment.

On the Roof of Africa

In early July 1984, I stepped off an Air France plane at the airport in Kigali, Rwanda. I was unable to move my head or neck very much. I had spent five frantic and tension-filled weeks between leaving Prague and arriving in Kigali. Three of the five weeks had been spent in Washington, attending a course to learn how to be a deputy chief of mission and calling on various offices within the government with interests in Rwanda. As I was going to be responsible for both the direction of the small Peace Corps contingent within Rwanda and the administration of our modest military assistance program, in addition to my DCM duties, I had a lot to learn in a short time. Ordinarily, both programs would have been administered within country by officers of the Peace Corps and the Defense Department, respectively. In Rwanda, however, they were both tiny, six Peace Corps volunteers, and four military training slots a year. The DCM had inherited their supervision by default. Before I left for Kigali, I also had to take care of a lot of personal business in the United States, including massive amounts of shopping I had been unable to do in Prague.

Two nights before my departure for Africa, I was at dinner with friends of my parents, with whom I was spending the last days of my leave. My neck began to hurt, and by the time I actually boarded the plane I had a completely rigid set of neck and shoulder muscles and was in considerable discomfort. Two long overnight flights in economy class did not help matters. Only intensive massage over the next few weeks from a Belgian-trained Rwandan physical therapist put me back in shape.

Coming in for the landing in Kigali was fascinating. I always enjoy looking at African countries from the air. In this case, what struck me forcibly after my tour in Nigeria was the lack of villages or any kind of concentrated housing. Instead, I saw one tin-roofed

81

compound after another winking in the sunlight, each separated by fields and banana groves around the house.

At the bottom of the airplane ramp stood my new ambassador, John Blane, and all the American embassy staff. Kigali was a small post for an embassy, eight Department of State personnel, the United States Information Service (USIS) director, three or four United States Agency for International Development (USAID) employees, and then quite a number of people hired locally or on USAID contract. There was, of course, also the usual large complement of Foreign Service Nationals (FSN), non-American staff hired locally.

I had met John Blane briefly nine months previously when I had been lobbying for my next post. Only the fact that I made a point of contacting him and meeting him personally gave me the edge over two male candidates. At the time of my appointment, I was one of only three female DCMs at all our embassies worldwide. There were, in fact, more female ambassadors than DCMs. (Ambassadors are permitted to choose their DCMs personally, something in theory they may not do for other officers assigned to their embassies. At that time, most male ambassadors did not feel easy with female DCMs, and most female ambassadors probably believed choosing a female DCM would place "too many women" at the top level of the embassy.)

The ten days after my arrival were amazingly busy. I had to acquire an on-the-ground knowledge of embassy people and procedures and meet our most important Rwandan contacts before the ambassador and his wife Deedee (a USAID officer) took off for six weeks of home leave. I was going to be on my own shortly, running an embassy. A small embassy, to be sure, but I was going to be in charge, *chargé d'affaires ad interim* as it is known in the business.

Within a day or two of my arrival, I accompanied the ambassador to the dedication of a USAID-funded reforestation project in the countryside north of Kigali. Reforestation was an important effort in Rwanda, with its population pressures and widespread use of wood or charcoal for cooking. The dedication was part of an annual period in Rwandan governmental life, known as the *quinzaine de projets* or Project Fortnight. For two weeks, the President of Rwanda traveled to and fro across the countryside, launching development projects. The countries sponsoring such projects were expected to have a presence, and usually this meant the ambassador. Ambassador Blane and I set off in a Toyota Land Cruiser, and I had my first glimpse of the hills northwest of Kigali. I had procured a neck collar from the embassy nurse to support my painful neck during the jolting ride.

The driver knew how to find the town headquarters of the commune where the project was located, but when we arrived there we were told the festivities were in quite another part of the commune. The driver followed the directions he was given and, finally, we arrived at the foot of a steep hill. The ceremony itself, we were told, was on top. The ambassador took a look at his watch and at the grade of the hill (about forty-five degrees); he then took his prepared remarks out of his suit pocket and thrust them at the USAID officer in the car. "Here, Ed," he said. "Go on up there and read this. I'm going back to Kigali." I was disappointed in one way to miss the ceremony, but relieved I did not have to climb that hill in my navy knit dress and open heeled sandals.

The period when I lived in Rwanda was five years before the first stages of the ongoing tragedy in that country. To foreign eyes, all appeared relatively peaceful, although it was peace maintained under an authoritarian, military, one-party regime. Some degree of reconciliation between Hutu and Tutsi appeared to be underway, even if all the top jobs in party and army were reserved for Hutu, mostly the clans from areas in the northwest from which President Juvenal Habyarimana and his strong-minded wife came.

Prior to independence, Rwanda had first been colonized by Germany and then transferred by the League of Nations to Belgian protectorship after World War I. There was still some German influence (a number of Lutheran churches and missionaries, for example) but the country now used French as an official language (at least among government and business officials), was predominantly Catholic, and had large Belgian and French expatriate communities, many of whom had moved there following the upheaval in the Congo in the 1960s. A number of enterprises—the insurance company, the coffee processing company, tea plantations, the brewery—were managed by foreign directors, although they were state-owned. Compared to Nigeria, there was nothing like the depth of well-educated and trained indigenous leaders to run crucial industries; Belgium had not been a benevolent or far-sighted protector preparing Rwanda for independence. Also compared to Nigeria and other African countries, Rwanda almost entirely lacked natural resources to support economic development.

A little over six million people lived in Rwanda, the overwhelming majority of them in farm compounds like those I had overflown on my way in to the airport. Kigali was a small town, and there were only a few other settlements that could aspire to be called even that. Subsistence agriculture supported almost all the population in the most densely populated country in Africa. An average family had something between six and eight children; an average family farm was between one and two hectares (about three to four acres). Coffee, tea, and some tin ore were the only sources of foreign exchange. Rwanda was a very poor country, landlocked, densely populated and lacking much necessary social infrastructure, like schools and clinics, to care for its rapidly increasing population.

During the time I was there, Rwanda was a favorite of donor countries. Government officials said all the right things to development agencies, and they appeared to be taking careful steps toward managing the country's resources well. On the surface it seemed that corruption was minimal. With all these factors in its favor, there was, in fact, competition among donor countries to give money to Rwanda. In 1985, at a time when I was acting as *chargé*, I went to the Foreign Ministry to sign a multimillion-dollar assistance agreement to fund some agricultural projects. In the parking lot I ran into both the Japanese and German ambassadors, who were there for the same purpose. "How much are you giving?" one of them asked me. It was like kids comparing Christmas presents. The Foreign Minister was loving it.

At another time, a project under development by USAID ran into mysterious delays getting final approval from the Rwandans. It was to be a multi-faceted agricultural project, located in an area in which there was a settlement of Tutsi refugees who had fled into Rwanda to escape the civil war raging in Uganda to the north. We slowly became aware that the land on which it was proposed to establish the American-funded project was also being requested for a totally different project, funded, I think, by the World Bank. Each project had its supporters within the Rwandan government, and the competition was holding up final approval for either one. Economic assistance was a recipient's market at that time in Rwanda, and government officials had become adept at playing the game to their advantage.

What made Rwanda a physically beautiful country was also a factor that made it a poor one—most of the land was vertical rather than horizontal. Rwanda is called *"Pays des Mille Collines,"* meaning the country of a thousand hills. There are a lot more than a thousand, believe me. Much of the subsistence farming is carried out on painstakingly carved out terracing from bottom to top of hills. The bottom land is fertile for many crops, but much is owned communally. If I asked a Rwandan if he knew someone, his answer was likely to be something like, "He comes from the next hill to mine." People thought in terms of hills rather than villages to say where they came from. Finding suitable land for development projects, therefore, was not easy.

One of many beautiful sights I saw during my time in Kigali was, again, from the air. I can't quite remember what the occasion was—a visiting American was in a town to the north and had left something in Kigali he needed in a hurry. The Administrative Officer, Kathleen Austin, her pilot partner Tom Ferguson, and I decided to fly in a borrowed plane to Ruhengeri to deliver the necessary item. We took off in a tiny Piper Cub just after dawn and gained altitude as the rising sun hit the tops of all the hills at a glancing angle. In every direction you could see green hills, defined by a golden rim at the tops, stretching off to the northern horizon where the five volcanoes on the Rwanda/Uganda border rose high in the sky. It was breathtaking.

In Rwanda, a person was never alone. There were people literally everywhere: little children in bright blue school uniforms, aged grandfathers sucking on pipes, old ladies walking along the roads in bright wrappers and knitted wool tam o'shanters, the short, squat Twa people (the original forest dwellers of the region), lovely, graceful young women with the banana leaf band around their heads signifying readiness for marriage. A person who thought he was alone was likely to be disabused of the idea. One USAID employee told me he was on a field trip to a project when he urgently needed a toilet. As there was no conventional one anywhere around, he plunged down a hillside into what appeared a solitary piece of bush and took care of things. As he was reassembling his clothes, an old lady materialized from nowhere and remarked, "Ah, monsieur, tu étais pressé," meaning "Well, sir, you were in a hurry!"

The six weeks in summer 1984 when I was *chargé* are a blur in my memory. I was settling into the embassy and coming to know the personnel there; I was unpacking in my house and becoming acquainted with the staff there; and I was trying to take hold of the administration of the Peace Corps and military assistance programs. The embassy in Kigali had an entirely different focus from the two others I had served in, for our major interest was support for the United States assistance programs in Rwanda. There was a minimal amount of political and economic reporting. The consular section provided visa and United States citizen services, but in relatively low numbers. The USIS office was an active, although small, operation.

Administrative services were under heavy demand. We had personnel in many categories—commissioned members of Washington agencies, American-citizen contract personnel working for USAID projects, locally hired third-country nationals, locally hired Rwandans, and so on. Managing the various privileges (importing goods, diplomatic mail, car registration) and pay plans of all these people was a challenge. Finding suitable housing, renovating and maintaining it, and providing security for all the personnel took care and resources.

As I look back, I think probably the greatest challenge of all was keeping our personnel healthy. It only gradually became apparent during my time in Rwanda that the central part of Africa was a "hot" center for HIV infection. Accurate information about AIDS prevention and the spread of the infection was hard to come by and continually under revision. Families with young children were understandably concerned about the safety of their children and the possibility of the spread of infection from household servants to members of the family.

Although HIV and AIDS were more dramatically dangerous, malaria was common and more immediately threatening to all of us. Malaria is everywhere in Africa, and people coming from a non-malarial area for just a few years' stay are well-advised to take precautions against the disease. The first line of defense is to avoid mosquito bites, for the parasite is transferred to human hosts only by the female anopheles mosquito; generally this mosquito bites only at dusk and night, so all American houses were fitted with window screens. I also purchased a little apparatus that plugged into the socket in my bedroom and released a repellent all night long. During evening parties, we all tried to wear long clothing and use repellents.

In addition to all this, however, we were all urged to take a medication that would prevent the parasites from developing through their life cycle and bringing on the disease, in case we did get bitten. There is no such thing as a vaccine against malaria, badly as one is needed, nor is it easy to cure malaria if it develops in certain parts of the body, such as the liver or brain. Malaria is not an infectious disease, but a parasitical one. And the parasites are very crafty, learning over the years how to resist agents that prevent their development in human hosts. The malaria parasite resistant to chloroquine, a long-standing prophylaxis, had recently spread to Rwanda. Combating it in 1984-85 was a process of trial and error, and a number of personnel at the embassy did not wish to take the steps advised by the Department of State medical division.

Many cases of malaria in our staff were treated in Kigali. We were lucky to have a competent nurse on our staff, locally hired, as well as some Belgian doctors who were very good. But some cases could not be managed with the resources in Kigali or at the minimally equipped hospital, and we had to evacuate those people at least to Nairobi, if not to Europe. Keeping our people, including Peace Corps volunteers who lived out in the countryside, healthy was a continuing concern.

At the time I arrived in Rwanda, the country was undergoing a drought that threatened famine in the country. One season of rain had failed, and it was not certain if the expected "short rains" due to start in September would create favorable planting conditions. In a period of normal rains, Rwanda was just able at that time to achieve self-sufficiency in food, particularly the production of the staple crop of beans, but disruption in the rainfall tipped the food supply to insufficiency. During the summer of my arrival, the Rwandan government put out increasingly stark requests for emergency food assistance. USAID was our lead agency on this problem, and the director in Rwanda and I attended a number of donor meetings at which pledges of help were made and delivery schedules worked over. Happily, the assistance provided by the United States and other donors was sufficient to bridge the gap and the following rainy seasons were normal. Dating from this time, however, I have always regarded rain as a blessing, even if it disrupts my plans. I have seen too much suffering from the lack of it.

Once Ambassador Blane returned from his leave, I was freer to travel about the country and become better acquainted with it. The previous administrative capital of the Belgian protectors, Butare, was in the south, site of the major university campus. Two of our Peace Corps volunteers were stationed there as English instructors, and I drove down occasionally to check up on their well-being and the adequacy of the housing and other support the university was supposed to provide. Butare was a pleasant small town and the university campus was fairly attractive as well. One major feature of an outing to Butare was lunch on the veranda of one of the two hotels in town, Hotel Ibis or Hotel Faucon. The menu at both was pretty much the same—brochettes (skewers) of recently slaughtered goat and french fries served European style with mayonnaise. Sitting on the veranda you were likely to see about half the people you knew in Rwanda passing by, shopping at the good local bakery, stopping in for a soft drink or beer, or returning from a trip to Bujumbura, the capital of Burundi to the south.

To the north/northwest of Kigali were the towns of Ruhengeri and, right on the border with (then) Zaire, Gisenyi. In this direction ran a road, completed during my tour in Kigali, called by all residents "The Chinese Road." This appellation infuriated the German ambassador, since Germany had financed the road that was, however, being constructed by Chinese engineers and laborers. Since the Chinese were a far more visible component of the deal, they got the credit. As the road got closer to completion, the trip to Gisenyi took only about three hours at most; driving to Butare in the far south was about two hours, so most trips out of town did not have to involve an overnight stay.

Halfway to Gisenyi from Ruhengeri, turning north off the main road and crashing along a secondary road, we came to Mugongo, where an American citizen, Roz Carr, had a beautiful flower farm. Roz had first come to Central Africa immediately after World War II and had lived in Rwanda since 1956. Once she settled in Rwanda, she established a plantation for pyrethrum, a natural insect repellant produced from small daisy-like flowers, which for a time was one of Rwanda's major exports and foreign currency earners. Synthetic forms of the active ingredient and unsuccessful efforts on the part of the Rwandan government to establish factories to process the flowers to the next stage of production had caused a crash in the market for the flowers. Roz then turned to horticulture, producing flowers that could be sold to local flower stores in Kigali or Goma, Zaire, or else shipped to Europe by air from the airport in Goma.

Roz is a unique person. Her modest house, located at the foot of the volcanoes that rise up to 14,000 feet, stands 7,000 feet above sea level. It is surrounded by a lovely garden, with the commercial flower fields located at that time behind the garden. The entire Rwandan population surrounding her home, many of whose members worked on the plantation, knew Roz and called on her to meet many of their needs. She acted as a first-line dispensary, doling out aspirins and band-aids. She also ran a kind of informal scholarship program for children in the area who had done well enough in elementary school and lacked the funds to continue to secondary school, for which fees were required. Many current and former members of the foreign community in Rwanda provided money to Roz who gave each contribution to a particular student, whose results she checked periodically. She also sent to the donors photographs of "their" students and insisted the children write the donors, thus cementing the relationship to continue through the entire three or four years of school.

In addition to these activities, Roz's house was a center for visiting Europeans on Sunday afternoons when the local population gathered in her garden for a session of drumming and dancing. Rwandan drumming, on a variety of drums ranging up to about three or four feet tall, carved from tree trunks, is a well-known part of the cultural tradition; at a professional level it is a fascinating musical form. The dancing is also beautiful, although I was told it had become more touristic and less authentically ritual. At Roz's house you could enjoy good, albeit nonprofessional performances by the local people, beginning with young girls and boys and ending with the older dancers. As a result of their contacts with these performances, many visitors became donors to the scholarship program or contributors of other items such as used clothing. Roz once told me laughingly that the people living in her neighborhood generally had better clothing than they wore to her house on Sunday. They knew that seeing the children in their rather raggedy clothes could well stimulate more sympathy for their situation, which was all the same minimal by our standards.

I frequently stayed for a weekend with Roz. She was a gracious hostess, and her home was a wonderful place to relieve the tensions of work in Kigali. She had no electricity. She had a primitive system of running water, even hot running water that was warmed in a large boiler outside the back door. Baths were timed to coincide with the wood-fire heated water. In the early morning, one of the watchmen would knock on the back door of the bedroom and come in, as I snuggled under the animal skin blankets, to light a fire in the fireplace and take the chill off the room before I got up. During one visit, in the company of Kathleen Austin, we stepped outside at an exact time Kathleen had been told by her partner Tom to look up in the sky. Right on schedule, the Rwanda Airways 707 of which Tom was pilot, flew over Roz's house with all the lights on, briefly disturbing the utter quiet of the African night.

Fairly shortly after Ambassador Blane returned in August 1984, I had my first chance to visit the mountain gorillas that lived on the flanks of the volcanoes on the northern border. Six of us (the maximum-sized group) traveled to Ruhengeri and, in the early morning, continued on to the headquarters of the national park. From there we picked up guides who led us to the spot at the foot of the volcanoes where we had to leave the cars and start climbing, first through the farm fields that spread up the side of the mountain to the entry point of the forest. The guides knew where the gorilla group we were to visit had been the day before. The general procedure was to start from that area and track them to where they might have migrated. We were lucky that day, for only ten minutes into our uphill struggle, the guides hacking at the undergrowth with their machetes, we could hear the unmistakable sounds of gorillas—chest pounding and crashing in the thick vegetation. Not too long after we found the gorilla family.

Nothing at all prepared me for seeing these beautiful beasts in the wild where they belong, but where they face extinction. We had been told how to behave—to make no loud noise or sudden movement, not to rustle the vegetation, not to look the animals directly in the eye but to look down in submission. We were allowed to remain an hour, and it was an hour of enchantment. These gorillas were "habituated" meaning they were accustomed to seeing humans. Some of the bolder ones came right up to us and mugged for our cameras. The young played with each other and with the half-grown older brothers and sisters. They all ate pretty steadily and groomed each other constantly. The adult silverback male, a magnificent animal, maintained his dignity once he ascertained we were not going to harm his family.

I had been prepared to find the gorillas interesting, but not to find them beautiful. The sun was shining and their hair shone in the sunlight. As I looked into their faces, which of course resemble human faces more than those of most animals, I really did feel kinship, a sense of recognition. That is probably sentimental and "wrong" from the perspective of professional animal preservationists, but I was captivated by the animals, and particularly by seeing them in their natural habitat and family grouping. I have never since been able to visit a zoo.

Most of my work in Kigali was administrative or managerial; I did little reporting, and it felt peculiar. I had to learn the ways of two Washington agencies—the Peace Corps and the Department of Defense—that varied quite a bit from the Department of State. I believe Rwanda may have been the only country with Peace Corps volunteers already assigned there that did not have the normal Peace Corps administrative structure in the country. This state of affairs had come about by an accident of history. I was told that a director had been assigned to the country about six years earlier. When he arrived in the country, he met some resistance from government officials to his efforts to expand the number and work assignments of volunteers. According to the story I heard, he abandoned the post, leaving it to the DCM to care for the volunteers until their assignments were up, at which point natural attrition would end the program.

What had happened instead was a continuing request for volunteers from those places where they were already stationed, as well as an additional request for a volunteer at a reforestation program under USAID auspices. When I arrived in Rwanda, there were five volunteers assigned, two each to the university campuses as English instructors, and a forestry specialist who had broken his ankle and was undergoing medical treatment in the United States. Shortly after my arrival, I was asked for a second forestry volunteer for another USAID project and a physical therapist to work at a Catholic center for children suffering the after effects of polio and other physical disabilities. In fact, the number of volunteers appeared to be growing rather than shrinking to none.

I had never before been in a country with a Peace Corps presence. The culture of this agency is quite different from most, particularly in the requirement that after a total of five years' work for the Peace Corps in any capacity, as a volunteer or administrator overseas or in Washington, a person must take two-year break. This means constantly renewing the blood of the personnel, but it also means there is little institutional memory. I gradually found the mandated rate of change does not guarantee an absence of bureaucratic red tape. I became exasperated by the cables demanding monthly or quarterly reports on all kinds of budget items we did not have—staff housing, official vehicles, and the rest. I was also surprised during a subsequent assignment to Nigeria in which there was a Peace Corps program to learn that a fairly large percentage of volunteers ended their assignments before two years were up. In Rwanda I had to fight so hard to have volunteers assigned that I did not even consider the possibility that volunteers might leave before they were due.

Being a Peace Corps volunteer is not easy, and Rwanda was particularly difficult. Like the people in many mountainous lands, Rwandans were difficult to know and very slow to accept outsiders. The volunteers lived away from Kigali and the small American community there and could come to feel very isolated and lonely. Far more than for us in the town, it was hard for them to maintain their health. Fairly often, then, the volunteers came to Kigali, either to consult with the embassy nurse or just to have a little R&R. Several of them had friends among members of the embassy staff, some of whom had themselves been volunteers. I also told them they could find a haven at my house whenever they wanted, and they frequently did. It was not at all unusual to hear a knock on Friday night or Saturday morning and see one of the volunteers at the door. I had a video player, at that time a rather unusual toy, and one volunteer in particular used to sit up all night, watching one movie after another. I might get up in the middle of the night and find him sprawled on the living room floor, watching *The Big Chill* or *The Colditz Story*.

During my time in Kigali, we also had a visit from Loret Miller Ruppe, then the Director of the Peace Corps and a most enthusiastic and energizing woman. She stopped in Kigali for about twelve hours between a stay in Nairobi, where the UN Conference on Women had just closed, and a visit to the huge Peace Corps operation in Zaire. She met with most of the volunteers who traveled in from their workplaces, and with the deputy foreign minister. This was the sole time I was asked to serve as an interpreter. All went well during their meeting that lasted perhaps a half hour, until the wrap up. The deputy minister expressed his thanks to Mrs. Ruppe for visiting Rwanda and the appreciation of his government for the work the Peace Corps was doing. I listened to his words, then turned to Mrs. Ruppe and relayed what the deputy minister had said. She smiled beautifully and remarked, "Helen, your French is lovely, but if you could tell me in English what he has said, I could answer!" I had become so tired after a half-hour of interpreting that I was no longer aware what language I was speaking to whom. We all had a big laugh over it. I was happy to return to my office job.

After nearly a year in Rwanda, I became convinced that direction of the Peace Corps should be in the hands of staff from that agency. There were programming possibilities that were not being followed up because I did not have enough time with all my other

91

duties. Eventually the office in Washington sent a temporary contract specialist, a former Peace Corps volunteer, to run the program and spend a few months evaluating the potential for the program to grow. She recommended that a country director be assigned, and one eventually was. I regarded this as a positive outcome of my assignment to Rwanda.

The Defense Department is another institution that operates quite differently from the Department of State. We had a very small program of military assistance to Rwanda, centered largely on technical engineering training for personnel to operate heavy construction machinery we had provided Rwanda under a military grant program. Two to four people a year, half junior officers and half enlisted personnel, went to United States military facilities to learn the operation and maintenance of the machines. Inevitably they had to be scheduled as well for a preliminary intensive English course, for none of them could speak English. Getting one of these trainees into the pipeline took a great deal of effort. The kind of lead time required by the Pentagon to enroll people in the right courses in the right sequence was not the kind of lead time the Rwandan Army hierarchy was used to working with. I had to focus all my diplomatic skills on nagging in the most pleasant way possible so as not to lose the fiscal year funding altogether. The Rwandans did not understand the "use it or lose it" principle of hanging on to a piece of the foreign military assistance pie. If a fiscal year went by and the account set aside for the Rwandan program were not used, the chances of getting the same amount or more the following year were greatly reduced.

One particular trainee was memorable. When he arrived at the embassy to get his visa and the final briefing before his departure, he asked me shyly if I would be willing to use official channels to send a cable to the base where his course would be held. His wife was expecting a baby, he said, and the due date was a day or two after his departure. He would be anxious to know as soon as possible after the birth that everyone was all right. Of course I promised to do as he asked, and he gave me the name of the colleague who would deliver the news to the embassy.

The day came for his departure. I went out to the airport to see him off, only to find the Sabena flight was canceled for that day. The next scheduled flight was not for two days, so we all went home to wait. Two days later, the strike in Brussels led to a second Sabena cancellation. At the airport, I told the soldier we would do our best to get him on the Air France flight scheduled for that evening. I asked him how his wife was doing, and he said she was fine, but the baby had not yet been born. That evening, having succeeded in getting the soldier booked on the Air France flight, I went a third time to the airport. Third time lucky, for sure. The baby, a girl, had been born just a few hours earlier and my prospective trainee was in the airport bar, treating all his mates to a beer in honor of his new daughter whom he had been able to name (the father's responsibility in many African cultures) before his departure. I can't remember the name in Kinyarwanda (the language of Rwanda), but in English it meant something like "she whose father is traveling," reflecting as it was supposed to the circumstances of the birth.

The Kigali airport was on the top of one of the country's thousand plus hills that had been shaved flat to accommodate the runway and airport building. Very few flights a week landed at the airport—two Air France flights, three Sabena flights, two Ethiopian Air flights, and a couple from Kenya, the ones that brought in the all-important diplomatic pouches with our mail. The schedule was well known to all of us, and whenever we heard a large jet overhead we could be fairly certain which flight it was. Tom Ferguson, partner of our administrative officer, flew the irregularly scheduled Rwanda Air 707 flights, generally round-trip cargo flights to Mombasa on the Kenyan coast to deliver coffee, the most important Rwandan export. Occasionally, if Tom were arriving after a servicing trip to Europe, he would fly over the embassy or Kathleen's house in the next street to mine, buzzing her to let her know he was home. Once, during the embassy Christmas party, he buzzed the ambassador's house to let the children know Santa had arrived in his green and white 707.

Since flights were so few and there was fairly frequent travel among members of the foreign community, it was a common excursion to go out to the airport on the nights the flights to Europe were leaving. You were certain to run into a large percentage of your friends out there, so the evenings were almost like a reception at someone's home. Whenever a member of our embassy staff was leaving for good, or even for a long home leave, it was customary for all the staff to go to the airport to wish him or her well. Or we might know someone was traveling who could carry mail to be sent from Europe or the United States. During my time in Kigali the road to the airport was being widened into a four-lane divided highway (with the construction equipment we had provided to the army), so the last stretch was unpleasantly dusty. Except during the rainy season. At that time the red clay dirt turned into a slippery mud as treacherous as ice. It was during this period one year that one of our communicators was leaving post; he was an efficient and pleasant person, so everyone planned to go see him off. I never made it. The long hill just before the airport access road was greasy with mud churned up by all those who had traveled out ahead of me. The hill was littered with cars that had spun helplessly out of control, trying to climb the hill. Even if I got traction and a good head of steam, it wasn't possible to get all the way up, while dodging those who were failing. Ultimately I drove my car across the median, slid down to the bottom of the construction, and crawled home.

Our military assistance program in Rwanda was supported by the officer in charge of military training in Zaire, and two times a year, that officer and often someone from the military attaché office traveled to Rwanda in the attaché's airplane, a small King Air jet prop aircraft that seated about twenty at a pinch. On these occasions, I went out to the airport to welcome the visitors and also make certain all the arrangements for parking and fueling the plane were in place. It is an extraordinary sensation to stand on the tarmac at a virtually empty airport and see a small speck in the sky grow into an airplane with "The United States of America" painted on its side.

During one attaché visit, when a few of the wives had been able to come as well, we took a trip to Akagera National Park in the eastern part of the country. Although not as well stocked with animals as the parks in Kenya, Akagera was a pleasant place to spend a weekend. I usually stayed at a lodge at Gabiro that had a good dining room and spartan but comfortable rooms in low bungalow style buildings. The senior member of the entourage, the colonel who directed the attaché office in Kinshasa, was determined to see lions. We drove about for a brief time on our first evening in the van we rented in Kigali complete with a competent and friendly driver. We found no lions. The second day we were off and looking. We went down to a stretch of water where we saw wallowing hippos, some fairly bold monkeys and other wildlife. We ate our picnic lunch at a spot down near the river and got back in the van. Our colonel was sleepy from the food and heat, and we were all a bit dozy. All of a sudden from the back seat there erupted a yell: "Lions! Lions! Lots of them! Stop!" We all looked frantically around and then realized the lions were nearly at the roadside, lying still under a tree. There were, in fact, not lots, but rather two, male and female, obviously well fed themselves. We circled off the road and drove practically right up to them, cameras snapping away. Ultimately the male tired of our presence and got to his feet, making it clear we should go away.

Emboldened by the lion triumph, however, our colonel and his traveling companions were fired up. A short way down the road, and by now some distance from the river, we spotted a muddy pond in the center of which wallowed a hippopotamus. Although hippos look kind of funny, bulky and lazy when they are in the water, they are actually quite dangerous animals. One unbreakable rule is not to swim in water where hippos are present. Another is not to get close to a hippo on land, particularly between the hippo and the water. The driver stopped to let our group photograph the animal in the mud pond; our visitors were leaning out windows, standing up through the sunroof, shooting off one photo after another. The hippo rolled over to his feet and left the pond. The driver said, "Now we will move on." "No, no," shouted the photographers, "just a few more." The hippo was obviously irritated by our presence and began to move toward the van. I am certain the animal could have overturned us if really motivated. "Now we go," said the driver. "No, no," came the reply. The hippo picked up speed into a clumsy but determined trot. "Go ahead," I shouted. "Get back in the car and close the windows!" The driver did not hesitate but gunned us well ahead of our now quite riled up hippo.

There was in Kigali a group of Hash House Harriers, an informal organization that exists in a number of places around the world. The origin of this activity was, I believe, in Malaysia, where a group formed for a cross-country chase along a marked trail, always ending at a pub called the Hash House where they proceeded to get drunk. In Kigali there were some modifications to the program, due largely to the vertical terrain of the country. Women were also welcome to participate as, I believe, they had not been in the group's original incarnation. Every other Sunday or so, anyone who wanted to take a country walk gathered at the place where that day's trail started. Prior to the time the hike began, two or three people had played "hares," laying a trail across the countryside using little clumps of paper shred from the Belgian embassy. Off we went. A few determined types would actually try to jog, while the rest of us were content to hike, enjoying the countryside and what conversation was possible while walking almost straight uphill. One of the challenges was to stay on the trail, in spite of some false side trails left by the hares. Fairly often, at the intersection of the paths, we would come across an elderly Rwandan farmer smoking a pipe and bemusedly watching a crowd of Westerners making fools of themselves. We women were dressed in shorts, something I never did on other occasions, and that must have given the farmer some food for thought as well. Over time, I had learned some phrases in Kinyarwanda, and most of us greeted the farmer in his language. I would then peg on the question, "Which way is it?" Obligingly he would point out the real, as opposed to false, trail, saving us fruitless uphill struggle.

One special time, the group traveled all the way to Akagera Park where we spent the night. The park administration had given permission for us to hike through the hunting section, so that we could be on foot and not confined to cars. This was the section in which people with permits were allowed to shoot some of the wild animals. We were warned to stay together and told that three park guards had been assigned to accompany us with weapons, in case any animal threatened us. Off we went. Very shortly our group of thirty or forty was spread out over a half-mile distance, for some of the men did not wish to abandon their jogging and others were merely ambling along. The guards were armed with what appeared to be breech-loaded one-shot rifles. What possible use these might be against a charging buffalo I am glad we did not have to learn. The day was pure enchantment. At one point, we crested a gentle rise, to look down a long slope to a river bottom in which there was a herd of a hundred zebra or more. As if on cue, halfway down the slope and not far from where we stood, trotted from left to right a whole family of warthogs, father, mother, and children down to a little one perhaps a foot tall, all with their tail brushes thrust straight in the air. It was a fantastic sight. One member of the cluster in which I was walking kept muttering, somewhat like our colonel, that he wanted to see lions, but I was happy that the most dangerous beast we spotted (dangerous enough actually) was Cape buffalo. These animals are quite menacing up close and, particularly if separated from the herd and alone, can be unpredictable and aggressive. Fortunately the ones we saw were all in a large herd, crowded up under a grove of acacia trees to escape the heat. We walked past them very, very quietly and carefully. Being able to view large wild animals in their natural habitat without the framework and noise of a vehicle, is a treat fewer and fewer of us can enjoy.

Not all excursions into the countryside were play. Under the authoritarian nation-building program of President Juvenal Habyarimana, all Rwandan citizens were expected to perform communal manual labor, known as *umuganda*, every Saturday morning. Shops were closed for the three hours when teams, organized mostly by place of employment, went to their sites to ditch roads or cultivate communal lands, or something similar. The President made a show of performing this duty himself. Once, shortly after the shops opened, I ran into the number two ranked official in the country, his corduroy trousers tucked into Wellington boots, shopping for bread.

As diplomats we were exempt from *umuganda* except for one Saturday in the year. In October, the entire diplomatic corps was summoned by diplomatic note to report at 7:00 am at the Foreign Ministry with our hoes and shovels. This was the day we all traveled to that year's selected site to plant trees, a necessary job in this disastrously deforested country. The year before I arrived, it seemed, not many diplomats had turned out, irritating the President who announced they would be summoned a second time; this time there would be no excuses. Thus, in my first year, Ambassador Blane told the embassy staff we were all to report for duty and get it over with. It was kind of a lark. The Rwandans supplied the saplings, so all we had to do was dig spaced holes and stick them in, down the side of a hill not far out of Kigali. As with many projects of this kind, however, there was little follow-up, and almost all the saplings died within the year.

Most Rwandans were cynical about *umuganda*. One doctor responded to my question about where she had performed her service that morning by laughing and saying it was a waste of time to ask non-agriculturalists like her to hoe fields. Most of the time, she said, her unit just had a good gossip until it was time to go home. *Animation* was another politically decreed activity we did not have to conduct at the embassy. At most businesses, however, work ended at noon on Wednesday, and the personnel were then expected to listen to party training talks, hear other motivational harangues, and form singing and dancing groups that would compete with those of other businesses. In theory this was meant to build national consciousness and unity; in practice it probably did nothing.

My first year in Kigali passed pleasantly. Life there was safer and easier than in Lagos. Hotels and restaurants were better equipped to cater to visitors, the roads were safe to drive on alone, most necessities of life were obtainable through a few good stores oriented to the Western shopper. I was busy at work that absorbed me. I left for my R&R travel feeling I had put in a good effort. During my trip I spent one of the best vacations I have ever had, traveling through Normandy and Brittany, occasionally alone and occasionally with friends.

Shortly after my return to Kigali we were due for a Foreign Service inspection. Immediately thereafter, the ambassador was due to leave on transfer to another post. Preparing for an inspection is hard work, but useful in providing an occasion to check out procedures and make sure regulations are being followed. Both the ambassador and I were fairly confident we were in good shape when the team arrived. It was unfortunately headed by a former ambassador who, for reasons known to himself, was determined to find fault. Among other things he decided to insert himself into a local personnel decision in which I disagreed with one of the more junior officers about the qualifications of a Rwandan employee to take over a job that had opened up. I did not believe the person was competent for the sensitive and difficult job; the inspector decided to take the side of the junior officer, something he had absolutely no business doing. And so it went for over a week. We were also hampered by the unavoidable absence of the administrative officer in the United States with a medical emergency.

The quality of the inspection was revealed by one incident. I had a call from the junior administrative officer downstairs who asked me if we had used the ambassador's representational allowance to purchase large quantities of wine just before the previous fiscal year had expired. I said we had not done this to my knowledge; it was illegal to claim representational funds (for entertainment) prior to the actual event they were spent on. Apparently there were vouchers in the files that suggested we had done this, and the accounting inspector was all over us. What were these vouchers claiming expenditures on "red" and "white" items. As it turned out, when someone who could actually read French looked at them, the bills in question were for bathroom fixtures that had been purchased for renovating some of our housing. Inspections can be useful, and they are certainly necessary; that one was conducted like a witch hunt.

Immediately after the inspection, Ambassador Blane and Deedee left. The farewell party I gave in their honor was a happy one. All the guests, including the staff from our embassy and a number of other ambassadors, had been asked to come with a song, poem, or other contribution to perform. They all rose beautifully to the occasion, the Kenyan ambassador singing two wonderful songs in Swahili. Our staff put on a skit called, "The Ambassador Receives His Call," a spoof, based on truth, of the call he received from President Reagan asking him to accept an assignment to Chad. Among others, the Zairean Ambassador was in tears of laughter, unable to believe Reagan had spent almost the entire telephone call asking what time it was in Rwanda.

That evening was the last good time in Rwanda.

When John and Deedee boarded the plane for home, I became *chargé*, a state that continued for the next seven months. Inordinate delays held up the nomination of the next American ambassador to Rwanda, and even when confirmed for the post, he took forever to set an arrival date. Two other officers were transferred during the summer of 1985, and their replacements arrived only several months later. For some time, then, we had to operate with a skeleton staff. We would meet in the morning, all two of us officers, and decide who would do which jobs that day. Visas and passports could only be issued by a commissioned officer, and one of us had to do them.

Early in August, I had a visit from Dian Fossey, the well-known gorilla specialist and director of the Karisoke Center she had established to study the mountain gorillas in Rwanda. Dian was having problems renewing her residence visa, due to the obstinacy of the Director of National Parks, under whose authority her work was conducted. The immediate problem was sorted out, although the longer-range issue was not. Dian was a passionate defender of the gorilla with little sympathy for those who wanted to develop them as a tourist "resource." She was unpredictable in her likes and dislikes and highly emotional in her reactions to people and events. She had been a friend of the Blanes. Certainly her work had done a great deal to publicize the danger of extinction of the mountain gorilla. She was not a favorite of the National Parks Director, and she had opponents among other Rwandan officials as well as other Westerners working on gorilla-related programs.

Friday of the week when Dian visited from her volcano eyrie, I went home thankful the weekend had come. About eight in the evening, I had a call from Kathleen to tell me one of the embassy drivers, Valentin, had been in an automobile accident and had been rushed to the hospital where he was pronounced dead. I was devastated, as was Dian when I told her; she had been a good friend of Valentin. He had been at the embassy a long time and, when I was *chargé*, was the driver assigned to me. I liked his quiet sense of humor and cheerful behavior.

As the story became clearer in the next few days, it was an ugly one. Another driver who worked for USIS had been fired for stealing gasoline from the embassy pump, an activity to which we had been tipped off by Valentin. Of course, the fired driver was not told who had spilled the beans, but he suspected Valentin and, as he left the embassy, publicly threatened him in front of some other employees, told him he knew he was responsible, and that he would get even. Now, a few months later, this former employee had a new job as a driver for the publicly owned electric company, and, with a truck of his new employer, followed Valentin when he left the embassy on a motorbike. When Valentin slowed down at a corner, the man drove the truck into him and killed him.

Kathleen, Dian, and I attended the funeral mass and burial the next day. Valentin was Zairois, and the tradition in his group (as opposed to that in Rwanda) was for the widow and family to wear poor clothes and cover themselves with ashes from the dead fire in their compound. One of the daughters was carried into the church, wailing loudly. At the gravesite, his widow tried to hurl herself into the grave behind the coffin. It was a pretty terrible and emotional scene.

After we reported the death to Washington, we were given permission by the Department of State to inform the Minister of Justice that we would favorably consider waiving immunity for anyone they would like to have testify at the trial of the killer. We also offered to have our employees interviewed by the police about the circumstances of the threat. None of these offers was ever taken up. Some six months later, the trial was held and the murderer was found guilty only of some trifling crime like reckless driving; he was sentenced to time already served and fined a minimal amount even in Rwandan terms. He walked free. We understood he had powerful connections in the police. I was disgusted.

Very shortly after Valentin's death, I was speaking on the telephone with my counterpart at the French embassy, Isabelle du Tilleul. As another female deputy, she and I had a lot in common and had hung out a bit. At this point, Isabelle was also *chargé*, since her ambassador was in Tanzania on safari. She told me she had been ill for a week or so. I urged her to get to the bottom of it, and even call back her ambassador if she had to return to France for treatment. She decided to tough it out, and by the time her ambassador returned a week or so later, Isabelle was seriously ill. I never had a definite answer to what was wrong, but I believe it was a case of malaria that got established in her liver, causing acute hepatitis. A day or two later, it was decided Isabelle should be evacuated. I was at the airport the evening she flew out to France and was appalled. She was so jaundiced, she was almost orange, and she was clearly very sick. Almost as she got off the plane in Paris, she went into a coma and she died some days later, the only child of elderly parents. She was about my age, mid-forties, and had survived the terrifying month-long siege of Caen in 1944 during the liberation of Normandy.

With two such events, I began to wonder what more could happen. I soon found out. At the end of August or early September, a good Rwandan friend who worked in the Ministry of Justice was driving on the "Chinese" road when his car skidded on gravel and flipped over. He suffered terrible head and spinal injuries and was evacuated to Brussels where, after about a week, he died. I had recently attended the baptism of his sixth child who was not yet a year old. The evening I learned the news, I went with Helen Picard, USIS Director and also a good friend of the family, to call on Mrs. Biyibeshyo and condole with her. It was heart-rending. I am constitutionally unable to keep my composure during such times, although Rwandans are expected to be stoic at such loss. The widow sat in her bedroom receiving the women callers, while the males condoled in the outer room with the men in the family. At the burial I was weeping. In the car back to town for the reception, a Rwandan woman to whom I had offered a ride remarked, "She was very strong." This was said in admiring tones, reflecting the fact that the widow had gotten through the ceremonies without shedding a tear.

At this same time, a beloved aunt of mine died. It took three weeks for the news to reach me. I believed that my own general lassitude and uneasy feeling of bad health were due to all these tragic events, as well as overwork from our staff shortages. Gradually by late September, the gaps in our personnel were filled in, happily with competent and jolly types so that getting them up to speed was not difficult.

The process of naming a new ambassador can be time-consuming. A short list is developed, usually including both career diplomats and perhaps a political appointee; this list is then sent to the President for his final choice. Until the Carter presidency, political appointments were generally made only to high profile capitals where a senior career diplomat served as the deputy while the ambassador performed the "representational" functions of entertaining and showing the flag at trade events or cultural affairs. Jimmy Carter had changed this tradition with the appointment of quite a number of academics and other professionals, often women or African-Americans. Ronald Reagan continued the trend, appointing campaign contributors from business and the non-profit sectors to ambassadorial positions. In Rwanda, it turned out, we were to receive a political appointee.

I didn't believe this kind of appointment made any sense at a tiny embassy in a country in which American interests were minimal. For one thing, in Rwanda an ambassador should be a working, reporting member of the staff, and not a figurehead. For another, a small embassy like the one in Kigali is a perfect post for a Foreign Service officer to serve a first ambassadorial tour. However, sometime early in the fall I received a cable from Washington instructing me to request "*agrément*" (or approval) from the Rwandan government for the assignment of John Upston as United States ambassador. Upston had a career of moving in and out of the Department of State, receiving civil service jobs during Republican administrations and moving into non-profit foundation jobs during Democratic periods. He had worked most of his life on Caribbean affairs.

In November 1985, President Reagan met for the first time with Mikhail Gorbachev and Cold War rhetoric began to cool down. Shortly after the summit, the Soviet ambassador in Rwanda had a dinner party to which I was invited as the temporary head of our mission. I remember the party for three reasons. First, the host, who was a jovial, roly-poly man, appeared to believe that he and I could substantially advance the cause of peace in our little corner of the world. During the evening, he repeatedly invited me to agree with him that the summit now removed all barriers to an intense friendship, although I was a little more skeptical. Second, all the staff at the party—the bartender, the cook, the waiters—were Russians, whereas we depended entirely upon Rwandan staff. I wondered what the Congress would say if the State Department requested funding for posting an American cook and bartender at the Kigali embassy. Third, I had a heated argument with the papal nuncio (equivalent to an ambassador from the Vatican and, ex officio, the dean of the diplomatic corps in Rwanda). The nuncio was a pleasant man, but I did not judge him a great intellectual. We were seated near each other and I somehow raised the question of ordination of married and female priests, remarking that the Catholic Church over the centuries had always adapted itself in order to survive and I thought it would in this case as well. The nuncio became agitated, insisting it would never happen. Diplomats sitting near us joined the fray, and the discussion became somewhat noisy. Only about a week later, I had a dinner at my house to which the nuncio was invited; the seating was at small tables, and one of the nuncio's table partners was another unmarried female from our embassy who went at him on the subject of the Catholic Church's stand on birth control. I suspect that ever after the nuncio checked to see if single American women diplomats were on the guest list of any party before he accepted the invitation.

The Rwandan government agreed fairly quickly to receive Upston, and then the Washington mill took over, investigating his background, upgrading his security clearance, and preparing for Senate hearings. All these steps took time, and meanwhile I was not feeling much better than I had since the beginning of September. Finally, a week or two before Christmas, I decided to fly to Washington for some quick medical checks. The process turned out to take over six weeks. Ultimately I was permitted to return to Kigali at the end of January for only three weeks, enough time to pack up my house and get the new ambassador credentialed to the government.

While I was in Washington, I was shocked to find in the *Washington Post* one morning the report of the murder of Dian Fossey at her research station in the Rwandan mountains. Anyone who has seen the film *Gorillas in the Mist* will know the murder was a bloody and shocking one; although much of the movie is untrue or grossly exaggerated, it is true that Dian was killed in her bed by an intruder. During the next days, I followed the events in Rwanda from the State Department desk, frustrated at not being at my post.

By the time I returned to Kigali, very little progress had been made in the murder investigation. A number of people had been questioned by the police in Ruhengeri. Shortly after I got back, the American researcher who had been at Karisoke Research Station with Dian was asked to speak with the police. He had had a difficult month, continuing to live at the station as the only Westerner, a hike of some hours away from the nearest habitation. Understandably he was nervous. Our consular officer traveled to Ruhengeri, not to participate in the questioning but to be on hand in case the American needed assistance with legal problems. The uncertainty continued for some time, until after I left the country for good, but then it became clear the Rwandan government was very likely to charge the American with the crime. He left the country before he was apprehended and was convicted, *in absentia*, of murder. Given the lack of investigative diligence in the case of Valentin's death, it is difficult to believe the trial to find Dian's killer was a rigorous search for the truth.

The problems of Dian's death, as well as the necessity to tie up a lot of other details in Kigali, filled my days for the three weeks I was in Rwanda. I was still *chargé* as well and was called on to fulfill the duties of that job. One was to respond to the government's summons to all the chiefs of mission (ambassadors or *chargés*) to turn out early one morning for the arrival of the President of Zaire, Mobutu Sese Seko. I remember the morning well, for at the crack of dawn I had a call from our communicator to tell me a message had come in relaying the news of the explosion of the Challenger space shuttle. Many of the other diplomats at the Kigali airport that morning had heard the news and condoled with me about the tragedy. I also remember, of course, shaking hands with Mobutu as he went down the receiving line drawn up to greet him (in protocol rank, longest-serving ambassadors first, then *chargés*). He was by this time a legendary African strongman, and I was interested to note he was taller and more powerfully built than I had thought from photographs. Even shaking hands with him, as the representative of a power that was still friendly to him, was a mite intimidating, especially since his presidential guards, with distinctive green ascots tucked into the necks of their uniforms and the reflective sunglasses so beloved by thug types, followed his every move. By contrast President Habyarimana was a teddy bear.

During these three weeks, I also had to pack up my house. Generally we were permitted a day or two off work to take care of this, but I had so much to do at the office I could not take the time. Fortunately the packers were members of our own staff, and so could work for short periods every day. I worked until the office closed, and then went home to sort my belongings out from those that belonged to the embassy. I placed in the center of the living room the items to be packed the next day—kitchen equipment, household linens, books, whatever—and found a bigger stack of cartons when I returned home the next afternoon.

The biggest emergency came when I received a call one day from the cook while I was at work. "Madame," he exclaimed, "we cannot find the cat." All the household help I had while I was in the Foreign Service knew that one essential task was not to let the cat escape from the house. In Kigali, where the front door opened directly into the main part of the house, this could be difficult. Ruth, the cat, had never been outside and if she had really disappeared there was no telling where she might be. I rushed home and began to search frantically, asking the gate guard, the gardener, the maid, the cook, where they had last seen her. I looked under beds, in closets, and grew increasingly upset. Finally, in the living room, I opened the door of one section of a sideboard and there was Ruth, hiding where I stored vases, until they had been packed up that morning. She never apologized for creating such uproars.

I was sorry to leave the house in Kigali. The layout of bedrooms and bathrooms was not entirely comfortable, as one bathroom served three bedrooms on the main floor, while there was an entirely separate guest suite with bath on the floor below, accessible only by a door from the garden. But the living room was large and airy, and there was a porch and long verandah on the upper floor which was raised enough to give a view down the side of the hill. It was a breezy and comfortable place to eat lunch and to sit and read. One curious defect was that the powder room was tucked into a space off the dining room. During dinner parties, when I invited the guests to come in from the verandah to the dining room, one or two always asked for the powder room. The rest of us were then treated to all the sound effects as we took our seats around the table.

The garden was also pleasant. It was furnished with a few banana groves, which produced a stem of bananas once or twice a year, and two avocado trees, whose fruit I ate and shared with everyone I knew when they came in season. I tried to grow some vegetables when I first arrived. The cook told me the birds would eat the broccoli and cauliflower, but I persisted, and was happy to see them pushing up healthy and strong. I weeded and crooned over them. Once it was clear they would survive, I had to travel to Germany for some training in military assistance. I was gone about two weeks. Upon my return I went out to the garden to survey the scene. It was appalling—the only thing left of my strong healthy plants were the veins of the leaves, like green skeletons. I yelled out, "What happened to my garden," and the cook replied, "I told you, the birds ate it." That was the end of my vegetable garden.

A large tree stood at the corner of my property, covered with bougainvillea, a good deal of which grew in from the neighbor's garden. Bougainvillea is lovely from afar; the colors are brilliant and the whole effect is immediately tropical and lively. But what appears to be the flowers are, in fact, colored leaf bracts (like poinsettia, another plant that grew in the garden), and they turn brown and fall to the ground without stopping. My gardener, a listless chap named Ildephonse, whose claim to fame was a family of twelve children, more or less, spent almost his entire working day raking up these brown leaves. Over and over he raked, and the supply never stopped coming.

Also prior to leaving I had to reimburse the embassy for items destroyed by the cat. This was a ritual at most of my posts. At the end of a tour, an inspection of housing takes place, checking the inventory against the one completed when moving in. In Kigali Ruth had broken two pottery lamps which she knocked one after the other off a table. Behind the table was a large, screened window which I usually had open in the evening. One or two large moths flapped against the screen, and Ruth would try to grab them, becoming so agitated that twice she shoved the lamp right off the table. I also had to reimburse the State Department for reupholstering her favorite chair for claw care. It had come with such a tempting, nubby fabric that there was no way to keep her off it.

About a week before my departure, Ambassador Upston and his wife arrived in Kigali. My last major job was to get him through the formal credential ceremony prior to my departure, so there would be an orderly changeover from *chargé d'affaires* to ambassador. My successor would not arrive for quite a number of months, so there would be no deputy. The foreign ministry was quite accommodating, scheduling his call on the foreign minister within days and setting the date for his call on the President the day before I was due to leave. Among other things, Upston spoke no French, so an interpreter was required for all his meetings. In these two cases, the foreign ministry obliged. I was interested to see that the foreign minister, who always spoke French, carried on for several minutes at least while the interpreter frantically took notes. When time came to repeat the remarks in English, nevertheless, the minister carefully corrected the interpreter if he left out an item in a list of several.

Each country sets the exact protocol for the accreditation ceremony for a new ambassador; it is always a highly formal affair. I received the instructions from the protocol office and had our secretary type out the statement Upston was to make as he handed over each envelope to the President. We got into the car sent to take us to the reception hall. Immediately upon arrival, I was separated from the ambassador by several ranking Rwandans and the interpreter as Upston was introduced to the President who came out of the building to greet him. Habyarimana was dressed in a blue suit, rather than the military uniform shown in his official photograph, plastered in every government office and private place of business.

We went into the reception room, in which there were two rows of the massive plush armchairs that are standard furnishing for every African high-ranking office I have been in. I was seated two large chairs away from the ambassador. The President was opposite.

The President opened the conversation, asking if the Upstons had a good trip to Rwanda. Upston launched into a fairly long description of the travails of packing up and taking the long plane journey. At this point, he was supposed to rise and address the President, handing over the letters of recall of his predecessor and of accreditation, but instead he talked on. I was unable to prompt him to stand up. Finally the President said, "Do you have something for me?" Upston then jumped to his feet and got through the formal part of the ceremony. In the car on the way back, he told me that until that nudge from the President he had not realized the man opposite him was the President. "He doesn't look at all like his photographs," he remarked, true enough since the military cap changes the shape of the face and the hairline.

The next evening I boarded the Air France flight, leaving behind the land of a thousand hills.

Bad Times

My early departure from Kigali had thoroughly upset the normal assignment rhythm. I scrambled around and learned there was an opening in the office handling United Nations affairs. This seemed an interesting job, and I was officially assigned to that office. The person I was to replace could not decide on a departure date, however, so for several months I was a loose end without any clear responsibilities. I didn't find that situation very comfortable.

Much worse was ahead. Numerous personnel changes occurred up the entire chain of command, including our office director, the deputy assistant secretary who supervised our office, and the assistant secretary. The new assistant secretary was Alan Keyes. Keyes had joined the Foreign Service some eight years or so before in the normal way, beginning as a junior officer. While serving in the office of Southern African affairs, he caught the eye of Jeane Kirkpatrick, newly appointed ambassador to the United Nations, who insisted she wanted Keyes to be one of the deputies (who also carry ambassadorial rank) at the UN Mission. The Department of State refused to appoint such a junior officer to an ambassadorial job, so Keyes resigned his commission and immediately received a political appointment to the post. With Kirkpatrick's departure from her job in 1985 and the appointment of Vernon Walters as ambassador to the UN, Keyes was reassigned to the department as Assistant Secretary of State for International Organizations. He was an outspoken and fervent conservative, eager to make his mark.

While I disagreed, and still do, with many of Keyes's policies and implementation procedures, I was not high ranking enough to engage in any genuine policy debate. Narcissistically, I was more interested in his effect on my daily working life. One of my colleagues in the office told me Keyes had openly stated his management style

107

was to govern by terror, a practice I have always believed is counter-productive. Generally, I stayed out of the way of our assistant secretary. One day, however, all of us in the office were summoned to a brown-bag-lunch session with Keyes, billed as an opportunity to exchange opinions with him about UN policy and approaches to foreign policy in general. We all filed into the conference room with our apples and yogurts, ready to have a friendly give-and-take. Keyes opened the meeting by expressing himself genuinely interested in our opinions. After a short introduction, someone asked a first question. Keyes then launched into a response that took up the rest of the hour. There is no question he was smart; certainly he could speak forcefully. But when he said, at the end of his speech, that he was grateful to us for coming and that he had found the session useful, I had to work hard not to laugh out loud. So much for getting to know the troops.

The new deputy assistant secretary (DAS) under Keyes was a career Foreign Service officer. He assessed his situation and realized that, although he answered directly to Keyes, the higher reaches of the department intensely disliked the assistant secretary, who had been forced on them. I believe the DAS decided to insure his own career by keeping the work of the bureau going smoothly and bypassing Keyes as much as possible. At one point, he actually convened a meeting of all the officers in our unit and told us he knew it was difficult to work with Keyes. He was there, he said, to run interference for us. I was astonished, for under unspoken State Department manners, a DAS should not in any way criticize his superior and invite the subordinates to conspire to bypass him.

The DAS had other drawbacks so far as I was concerned. He was a screamer, one of those managers who believe that yelling at people who fail to do what they want gets results. He was also inefficient in moving paper, an infuriating habit when he failed to make a decision within the working day. He frequently insisted that I or others stay after hours to make revisions or take care of jobs that could have been accomplished in the allotted time. Worst of all, he was a micromanager when he believed he could gain visibility helpful to his own career. In my position, for example, I was responsible for planning the President's attendance at the United Nations General Assembly in September. I found myself accompanied to every meeting at the White House by the DAS as babysitter. He made commitments to the staff of high-ranking officers and forgot to tell me, so I would suddenly have a complaining special assistant on the line wondering, for example, where a luncheon guest list was.

Our new office director, third down the chain of command, was simply a nebbish. He had been appointed as assistant office director, the position that accorded with his personal rank. Keyes wanted to have him officially assigned to the full director's job, which was open and which Keyes had promised when he recruited him. The Department personnel office refused to do this. As acting director, he was afraid to make any decision or give any direction until he had checked with his bosses.

All through the summer of 1986, once I had fully assumed the job, I worked with this group of careerists and ideologues. It was the first time I ever worked with an entire group of superiors for whom I had contempt, and it was amazingly uncomfortable.

In early October, things came to a head. One task for which I was responsible was the approval of travel out of New York of UN diplomats from unfriendly countries. I worked with an officer, junior to me, who did the actual calling around and checking before recommending action on a request. He had briefed me on an application from the head of the PLO Representative office to travel to Washington to attend a funeral. There were many precedents for this kind of travel, and offices in the Near-East Bureau and the Office of Foreign Missions had approved the trip. We, therefore, approved the travel for the purpose and time requested.

The first I knew there was a problem was when the office director called me in. Keyes and the DAS were both there. Keyes was furious, demanding to know who had approved the trip. He had actually been informed of it by a pro-Israeli employee in the Office of Foreign Missions whose duties had nothing to do with approving this kind of request. I explained that there were many precedents and that the relevant people on the Near-East desks had approved. Keyes was not placated and demanded to know how it was such a decision could have been made without alerting him. He was shouting by this time, and I shouted back that we never referred these kinds of requests to him, that unless there were some unprecedented problem, they were treated as routine. The DAS stepped in between us. Keyes said he had to go to a reception, but he wanted a full investigation of who had approved the travel.

It was well after hours. My assistant was not at his home, so I began phoning around the department to check on how the clearances had been procured. I was all the way at one end of the office suite speaking to the Near-East office director, when I suddenly became aware that my office director, at the other end, was listening in on my call, checking up on me. After all the upset and the difficulty of finding people still at work in the early evening, everyone up the line agreed the decision had been the right one. I assume Keyes also agreed, although no one, including the office director, had the courtesy to tell me that. The decision to grant the travel permission was allowed to stand.

The next day I requested reassignment. It was impossible to work in a situation in which I was not trusted to do my job properly. I felt my superiors questioned both my competence and my loyalty.

It is not easy to break an assignment, unless the Department itself sees a compelling reason for it—perhaps because there is an urgent need for precisely your skills or experience in a crisis. It was particularly difficult for me to do it in the fall of the year, since almost all the open positions had been filled during the summer changeover period. After some scurrying around, I did manage to find a job into which I could move, permitting my personnel counselor (who himself had experience with the DAS and the acting office director) to apply for my transfer.

As part of the process, I was told to go speak with one of the deputies in the Director General's office to explain my reasons for requesting a transfer. I had already written a lengthy memorandum explaining why I found it impossible to work under the management of the bureau. During my talk with the Assistant DG, it became obvious to me that his office wanted to use me as a lever against the acting office director, while my major complaints were against the DAS. All the questions the Assistant DG asked me were about the office director; my attempt to explain why the DAS was unable to manage the work fell on deaf ears. My usefulness as a pawn in the ongoing guerilla war against Alan Keyes was limited.

I have never been able to conceal emotional distress very well, and during this interview it was obvious I was upset and angry at the conditions of my job. The Assistant DG thus informed me that he wanted me to go have a consultation with a psychiatrist on the staff of the medical division. He assured me unequivocally that this consultation would be completely off the record and that it would be kept confidential from my current bosses. With these assurances, I agreed to set up the appointment, although I found it humiliating to be treated this way. I spoke with the psychiatrist. I came to two conclusions. One was that he assumed my emotional reaction to my job situation stemmed from my recent illness in Kigali. The second was that he would not recommend any intervention with the DAS. The psychiatrist asked me, among other things, what I really wanted. I replied that I wanted the DAS to be counseled on his bad management. The psychiatrist simply laughed at the mere idea; I'm sure he noted "delusional" on his little notepad. He did inform me, nevertheless, that he would recommend that I be permitted to leave my job.

A short time later, I discovered how firm the assurances of confidentiality were. The DAS, informed by this time that the personnel office was going to permit my transfer, took me to the cafeteria for coffee. He brought all his charm to bear asking me if I

110

wouldn't consider staying on and what changes might make this possible. He prefaced all this by saying he had been unaware of my "medical problems" and was so sorry to learn of them. I was furious—at the man in the DG's office, who had obviously given him at least the bare outlines of something that should have remained confidential, at the psychiatrist, and at the DAS.

I was successful in leaving the job, but I learned a number of things. One was that no effort would be made to work with the DAS to improve his style of management. He would never be urged to organize his work to avoid last minute crises, including ones that got a black eye for the State Department in the press. He would not be counseled to curb his temper and stop yelling at people. Another was that the higher reaches of the personnel system were interested in my situation as a way to get at the office director, who they judged was unqualified for the job. If they could find some way to shift him out of his place, they would have scored a point against Keyes. I did not have much against the office director, except for listening in to my phone calls; it was possible to ignore him and work around him.

During the next year, three more people at my level left the office prematurely for some of the same reasons that had driven me out. Alan Keyes also did not finish out his term. I am not certain of the details; I heard he had an argument with the deputy secretary of the Department and, having lost it within the walls of the State Department, attempted to carry it on through the pages of the conservative newspaper, *The Washington Times*, in which he accused the deputy secretary of racism. Very shortly, Keyes left the State Department altogether. His departure also removed the protection for the office director.

I won my personal battle, but I lost the war. The job into which I was moved failed to develop into anything useful or interesting, making it impossible to get the kind of evaluation that would get me promoted. The fact that I had left an assignment also counted against me. I had failed to get a promotion I might have received at the end of my Kigali assignment, and my career was in limbo for the next few years. I suspect, although I could never prove it, that corridor gossip began to circulate that I was not good material for more senior jobs.

I began at this point to consider leaving the Foreign Service in eight years as soon as I became eligible for a pension.

During the remainder of my years in Washington, I became increasingly aware of the politically charged atmosphere of the later Reagan years. I was assigned in turn to two different offices handling African issues, first to the Intelligence Bureau and then to the Zimbabwe desk in the Office of Southern African Affairs. These were Assistant Secretary Chester Crocker's final years in office. For his

111

entire tenure, he had worked to broker an agreement to settle the civil war in Angola and grant independence to Namibia in a way the South African government would accept. Part of the problem in Angola was the military support the Cubans provided, with financial assistance from the Soviet Union, to the MPLA government in Luanda. This meant, almost by default, that the United States was supporting Jonas Savimbi, who was challenging that government. American conservatives praised Savimbi as a fighter for freedom and democracy, and a trip to his bush headquarters became a regular stop on congressional travel.

An ugly civil war was also ravaging the countryside in Mozambique on the other flank of southern Africa. The official government in Maputo, with which we had relations, was fighting against an insurgent group formed by the Rhodesian intelligence service during the independence struggle in Southern Rhodesia, now Zimbabwe. Renamo, as the Mozambique group was known, first had the job of harassing the Zimbabwe independence fighters who took refuge across the border in Mozambique. Now that Zimbabwe was free, the South Africans had taken over the financing of the group, which controlled large areas of Mozambique.

Many conservatives in the United States had a symmetrically rigorous attitude to these two struggles: in Angola, the MPLA/Cuban/Soviet constellation was communist, hostile to democracy and market forces, automatically meaning that Savimbi, supported by South Africa and Zaire, was democratic, capitalist, and good. They believed the same formula could be applied in Mozambique: the government in Maputo was socialist and bad, while Renamo was democratic and good. Quite apart from an ignorance of the origins of these groups and their activities in their respective countries, people who adopt simplistic formulas like these quickly become hardened in their positions. Jesse Helms, *The Washington Times*, and a number of White House advisers put constant pressure on the State Department and the intelligence community to throw their weight on the side of Renamo.

Forces outside the control of the United States ultimately resolved these issues. The end of the Cold War, the difficulties of the Soviet Union and the end of its subsidies for Cuba, and the end of *apartheid* in South Africa shifted the intense focus on these regional struggles away from southern Africa. The MPLA government made a kind of peace with Savimbi who ended his days as an abandoned warlord; he continued to make terrible trouble until his death. The same happened in Mozambique—a negotiated truce with Renamo that gave them some concessions but not much power in the central government.

Although these particular struggles between the State Department and the conservatives in Congress have faded away, the 1980s was a decade in which congressional micromanagement of foreign affairs markedly increased. One challenge facing me on the Zimbabwe desk resulted from the Pressler Amendment, attached to the foreign assistance appropriation bill. USAID funded a number of regional projects supported by the nine-nation Southern African Development Coordination Conference (SADCC). The Pressler Amendment stated that no assistance could be given to any of the nine countries until each specifically affirmed that its government did not practice, or support anyone who did practice, "necklacing." Necklacing was a horrific form of revenge practiced largely in South African townships by one group of black South Africans against another. A tire was placed over the head of the victim and shoved down to hold his arms against his side, filled with gasoline, and set afire. It was not practiced by black South Africans against whites, nor was it anything the nine governments of SADCC had anything to do with. The Pressler amendment was a pointless irrelevancy, and the SADCC governments were outraged. The State Department and USAID had argued strenuously against its inclusion in the bill, but it became law. It was my job to instruct our ambassadors in the nine countries involved to approach the governments and get their official statements that they did not practice or support necklacing.

Ultimately, Zimbabwe was the only holdout. President Robert Mugabe was a proud man, and had fought long years from the bush to win independence for his country. The United States had given him no help in that struggle. Now he was asked to provide an assurance to satisfy the Pressler Amendment's requirements, and he wanted no part of it. Unlike the other leaders, he was unwilling to wink at the whole process and just get it over with. In the end, as I recall, there was a contorted process in which a few separate, verbal statements were pieced together which satisfied the requirements set out by Senator Pressler. The cost in my view was too high—the United States looked ridiculous asking sovereign governments to swear off a practice that did not occur in their countries and to go through a *pro forma* renunciation just to satisfy a United States senator who had a bee in his bonnet.

After fighting several battles of this kind, either against members of Congress or against public opinion aroused by leaks from political appointees within the government, I decided life in Washington was too contentious.

I certainly believe members of Congress have a constitutional obligation to involve themselves in foreign policy formulation and implementation. I do not for a minute fail to support that role, and I believe it plays a crucial part in gaining popular support for much of our action in the world. Some members of both the Senate and the House of Representatives (although a diminishing number) are knowledgeable about foreign affairs and provide crucial advice and consultation. Richard Lugar and Lee Hamilton were two of a number of such legislators. What I do think is harmful is the attempt of Congress to involve itself in detailed policy instruction; the legislative process is not designed for the kind of nuance and give and take that pushes along our foreign policy. Much of the time congressional micro-management is like performing surgery with a machete; one has only to consider the increasing dependence on unilateral sanctions (say, the ones against Cuba) in recent years to judge that they do not succeed in gaining our objectives.

I was due for reassignment in summer 1989. I thought I would take an interesting job but not one directly in the center of attention. On July 21, 1989, I landed at Tegel Airport, Berlin.

The Wall Falls

Berlin was a strange city in 1989. The Berlin Wall was still standing in July. So far as anyone could judge at that point, it was likely to go on standing for a good long time. It was visually offensive. Additionally, it gave the city a lopsided feeling, particularly on the western side. All the traditional, old part of the central city was in the east—many of the surviving old churches, the State Opera, the City Hall, the museums, and the main streets, Unter den Linden and Friedrichstrasse. On the western side, jammed right up against the Wall was the Reichstag (parliament) building. The Wall, making a great, fortified semicircle around the Brandenburg Gate, meant that little life went on in its vicinity. Western Berlin, therefore, was found some distance away in little clumps. The hotel and commercial area was along the Kurfürstendamm, with what passed for a central train station and the bombed remains of the Kaiser-Wilhelm Gedächtniskirche at one end. The government center was in the former city hall of one of the twelve boroughs of western Berlin—Schöneberg—a good distance away from Ku'damm.

I was assigned to the United States mission in western Berlin, the office that still administered what was the vestige of the military occupation regime established at the end of World War II. Our headquarters were a long way from either the commercial center (which lay in the British sector) or the city government building (in the United States sector). The headquarters building for both the United States Army and the diplomatic entity that was under Army authority was the wartime office of the Berlin-area Luftwaffe. It had been relatively untouched by bombing, unlike about seventy percent of all the buildings in Berlin at the end of the war, and thus was commandeered by the Americans. When I was in Berlin, the United States maintained about five thousand troops in the city (the Berlin

115

Brigade), which had to operate entirely within the boundary of West Berlin. Outside that border lay the German Democratic Republic (East Germany); the Federal Republic (West Germany) was 100 kilometers away. All military housing, all training, including tank maneuvers, and all support operations were located within the confines of the "island city." The British and French had similar military establishments.

Western Berlin was divided into three sectors encompassing twelve of the twenty-four boroughs; the other twelve boroughs formed the Soviet sector in the east. The western sectors were administered by the three allies, the Americans, the British, and the French. Over time, the three missions developed structures that mirrored each other, so we participated in groups of three when we discussed issues requiring allied agreement. The three army commanders met jointly, the three ministers (the top diplomats), the political advisers, and so on.

My title in Berlin was most impressive in German: *Verbindungsoffizier beim Senat und Abgeordnetenhaus von Berlin.* Translated it means Liaison Officer to the Senate and House of Representatives of Berlin. My job, similar to that of my French and British counterparts, was to act as the working level go-between from our mission to the city government of Berlin. All three of us had offices in the Schöneberg City Hall in addition to our offices in our respective mission headquarters. In the nearly fifty years since the end of the war, many of the functions of a sovereign city had been restored to Berlin, but legally and technically the city was still subject to the approval of the allies. This meant, for example, that laws passed in the Federal Republic of Germany (West Germany) did not automatically become law in Berlin; rather they had to be "carried over" by the House of Representatives, the legislative body, with allied acquiescence. In some cases, for example on questions involving the continuing stricture on any German military presence in the city, we insisted that some clauses in federal legislation be inoperative. Commercial and transportation issues also brought close scrutiny. We had a lawyer on our staff, as did the other missions, whose job it was to screen all legislation and put up flags when "status" questions appeared to be involved.

Shortly after my arrival, a German working for our USIS office asked if I would like a ride in an Army helicopter taking two film crews up for aerial shots for a TV series. Because of the demilitarized status of Berlin, no German aircraft were permitted to operate in Berlin airspace. Thus, even for commercial filming like this, United States Army aircraft had to be used. The rule served additional purposes, including asserting the rights of the western allies to operate their aircraft in Berlin airspace and training the crews to fly over the city. Our USIS employee told me the helicopter would fly over a large area, and I would be able to see the city as I never could from the ground. I jumped at the chance. The day before the flight he warned me to wear warm clothing, because the doors of the helicopter would be open. I reported in my jeans and sweater to Tempelhof Airport, one of the largest buildings in the world. It was built by the Nazis to overwhelm, and it does.

Only as I walked out on the tarmac with the other passengers did I realize what I was going up in. The helicopter was the standard Huey of the Vietnam War. Immediately behind the pilot and co-pilot, there were two forward facing seats; all the other places were on two benches along the sides, facing outwards. The sliding doors that formed the two sides of the copter were open. With most of the others, I was to sit on one of these benches, with only a lap belt fastened around me, my toes about three inches from the completely open side of the helicopter. There was nothing to hang on to—no grip or rail. I took one look and informed the pilot I suffered from acrophobia. He surveyed me with pity and asked if I wanted to bail out. I simply could not—the experience was going to be too interesting.

We lifted straight up off the tarmac, tipped forward and headed for the first filming site—a housing complex in the southwestern part of the city. I was wedged at the end of the bench, my eyes tightly shut. I found I could open them for very brief moments and control my panic this way, opening them for longer and longer periods until I amazed myself by being able to keep my eyes open almost all the time. Once over the housing complex, the film crew spoke into the little microphones we all wore and asked the pilot to circle the building in a tight, tilted-over circle while they shot their footage. That was the ultimate test, for my side of the helicopter was tipped over at about a forty-five degree angle.

From there, we headed for the southwestern edge of the city, to the border between West Berlin and East Germany. From fifteen hundred feet in the air, it was possible to see the scar that ran around the city—the wall, a wide sand track, watchtowers: the lot. We then turned north and overflew the beautiful chain of lakes and rivers that border Berlin on the west, separating it from Potsdam in East Germany. More filming was scheduled over Charlottenburg, site of a lovely palace. That was where one of the film-crew members of the party lost his breakfast. The pilot then asked over the intercom, "How is that lady in the back doing?" and I muttered "Fine" into the mike, forgetting to cover it with the hand that was tightly braced against the top of the cabin. The pilot got an earful of wind noise. At the end of our trip, which lasted over an hour, we snaked along the actual Wall that ran through the center of the city. From the air, it

117

was possible to see the stark contrast between the prosperous and well-maintained buildings on the western side and the grimy, ill-kempt buildings in the east. It was an unforgettable introduction to the city where I would live for almost two years.

During my first few months in Berlin, I was kept busy learning the job, unique in the Foreign Service, and covering various additional positions that awaited replacements or returns from vacations. I did not get into the center of town for some weeks. Our mission headquarters were plopped down in a residential area where there was not even an adequate lunch-time restaurant. My office at the City Hall was off the beaten track as well, and I spent a great deal of time moving back and forth between the two. I became acquainted with my French and British counterparts and German national assistants and introduced myself to members of the *Senat*, the administrative body of the Berlin government, headed by the Governing Mayor.

The Berlin government with which I dealt was in theory the government of the entire city, but in practice only governed the twelve districts in the sectors of the three western allies. Immediately after the end of World War II, the twelve eastern districts had formed the Soviet sector. When the Soviet Union had acquiesced in the creation of the German Democratic Republic, it had also allowed the GDR to reclaim its sector as the capital of the country. The western allies had never recognized these arrangements as legal, nor had they permitted the Federal Republic to assert sovereign control over the western part of the city. We refused to deal with any GDR authority so far as managing the city was concerned, although by this time we had an embassy in East Berlin that dealt country-to-country with the GDR government. So far as the western allies were concerned, the Soviets continued to be the operative power in their sector as we were in ours.

Every Tuesday, I met with my British colleague, John Freeman, and our French counterpart, André Destoup. We got along quite well, generally speaking English among ourselves. André had some difficulty with the language, while John and I ribbed each other mercilessly about words and phrases the other used. I kept complaining that John thought he spoke "standard" English, while I came from a country with roughly four times as many people; that gave me the right, I asserted, to decide what was standard pronunciation and usage. When we got wound up over, for example, my use of the term "grandfathered" about some piece of legislation, we would hurl mock insults back and forth across the table. André became very anxious at such times, for he seemed not to understand this form of friendly ribbing. He could not quite figure out if John and I were really angry or not.

Tuesdays had a regular routine. Before I left for City Hall, the senior political assistant working under my direction, Erika Nassiri, would have digested a huge stack of papers sent to each of the allied missions by the Berlin government. They included all the administrative decisions ready for approval by the *Senat*, proposed legislation, and other matters that affected relations between the Berlin government and the allied occupation personnel. Erika screened these papers, and she briefed me on their contents and any particular problems that might affect status or our operations. Our legal advisor also informed me of any potential problems.

At the City Hall, my two colleagues and I met with Gerhard Kunze, a senior civil servant of the Berlin government, who went over a list of concerns with us, ranging from some of the issues raised by the stack of papers to complaints from the citizens of Berlin about noise and environmental problems caused by our troops. One case that came up for a number of weeks involved an escape attempt by two East Germans prior to my arrival. One of the escapees managed to swim across the canal that runs just past the Reichstag building and get up the bricked side of the canal. The other was not so lucky; he was attempting to scale the slippery canal wall when he was intercepted and shot by an eastern Berlin police patrol boat. He was the last east Berliner to die during an escape attempt; he was nineteen years old.

The Berlin government proposed to deal with one of the problems this escape caused by installing some kind of mechanism that could be used by anyone trying again to scale the canal wall. But whether this mechanism should be a rope that could be pulled up out of the water when not needed, or a fixed ladder extending down below the surface of the water, was not clear. The ladder would obviously be easier for escapees to use. The actual border at that location, however, came right up to the wall itself, so there was a question whether the East Germans would see the ladders as provocation, whether they would try to cut them off, what the British (in whose sector this part of the border was) would do if the East Germans did cut the ladders off, and so on. Ultimately, we approved the installation of the ladders. These kinds of choices were by no means clear or easy to make.

In addition to our regular meetings with Herr Kunze and Herr Schroeder, the political director in the administrative offices, we three liaison officers also attended meetings of the Berlin House of Representatives when it was in session. We met during the legislative season with the senior civil servant of the House, again to review what might come up during debate that would affect the allies. If there were something on the legislative docket that affected us, we took special note since political maneuvering would play a role. During my time in Berlin, the Social Democrats were the major government party, in coalition with the Alternative Liste/Green Party, and not all members of these parties were as staunch supporters of the allied role and presence in Berlin as the opposition Christian Democrats. When I attended the legislative sessions, I was as interested in party behavior and politics as in the fate of particular pieces of legislation. We three liaison officers had reserved seats just behind the rows of legislators, at desks raised slightly above the well of the House. It was a good spot for observation. As representatives moved in and out of the chamber, they frequently stopped to greet one or the other of us and exchange a little political gossip.

Each month, one of the three western allies was the "chair" mission, meaning that the members of that mission became the lead persons in each of the functional triads, as well as the person called by contacts in the Berlin city government when some immediate issue came up for decision. The United States became chair mission in August, ten days after my arrival. One day during the month, I had a call from Herr Kunze at City Hall. He informed me that shots had been heard in the night at an area along the western border of the city with East Germany. This suggested there had been an escape attempt, although no one was known to have arrived in West Berlin. He asked what we planned to do. Herr Kunze and his administration were not, of course, permitted to deal directly with the East German authorities. I had to ask around a bit. It turned out we first checked with our army, since that part of the border was in our sector. We also had to get approval from the other two missions both for a press release deploring the shooting and for a *démarche* (an official statement of our interest and disapproval), by our mission as chair, to the Soviets. We considered the Soviets responsible for finding out what had happened.

Our refusal to speak directly to the German Democratic Republic about Berlin matters reflected what was true about so much of our work in Berlin—what existed in reality on the ground was not reality in how we managed our solutions of problems and issues. We insisted in cases like this that the Russians speak to the East Germans. Our embassy in eastern Berlin was not permitted to discuss Berlin administrative issues with that government. It is possible to ask what the point of all this was, forty-five years after the end of World War II. Even if no formal treaty ending the war had been signed, what was the sense of all this intricate behavior based on conditions that no longer existed. In Washington, in fact, it was called the "Berlin theology," suggesting an intellectual construct concerning things that could not be seen.

I strongly believe the rules by which we lived and worked were essential to maintaining the freedom of western Berlin over all the years until the collapse of the German Democratic Republic. Berlin was more than fifty miles inside the GDR, which completely surrounded it. Had we not continued to insist on the uninterrupted existence of the occupation and on the daily exercise of the western allies' rights of access and supervision of their sectors of the city, the Soviets and East Germans would have eroded those rights to non-existence. The Soviets had tried once, in establishing the blockade of the access routes in 1948, to end the occupation and had failed. We were determined not to let it end by default.

The Berliners knew this too. Some younger Berliners, particularly those in the Alternative or Green Party or on the left of the Social Democratic Party, chafed at the allied presence and found it ridiculous. At one time, quite a large number of people had moved into Berlin for the tax benefits and other advantages it gave them. Berlin's demilitarized status meant young men who lived there were exempt from the West German draft. Many of these people enjoyed the sense of being free of complete control under the Federal Republic of Germany; they often pursued intellectual or artistic professions, living in areas where the rents were very cheap for a time. They developed an island mentality, savoring the free float of the city.

But older Berliners, particularly those who lived there uninterruptedly from the end of the war, knew they maintained their freedom because of the commitment of the western allies. Although they might wish for more authority for their elected government, and although they might get annoyed at the noise of military maneuvers in the middle of the night, they supported our presence as a guarantee that the division of Germany and Berlin could not be considered a final arrangement. The division of Berlin meant that nothing could be settled finally until that division was settled. And our presence meant the division still existed and would only be ended with western agreement.

I bent my effort to mastering the Berlin theology. I became more sensitive to those issues likely to create problems for us. I learned how all of us, particularly the political section, had to interact to carry out our occupation functions. I dealt with the city government, while another member of the section served as the assistant to the monthly meeting of the three commandants and ministers, a third was the legal advisor, a fourth was the person designated to liaise with the Soviets when necessary, and a fifth was the link between the diplomats and the army (who transmitted the city government's concerns to the army and gave me answers to relay back). It was all a delicate minuet.

When I was assigned to Berlin in spring 1989, the Hungarians had just reduced their physical border with Austria. Fences, guard posts, and border control booths were either torn down completely or reduced to token importance. In Washington, friends began to joke about sending me to Berlin to rip down the wall there. "Oh, no," I replied with the received wisdom of the State Department at that point, "no time soon. Whatever is going on in Hungary, Germany is an entirely different situation. Berlin is even tougher." So much for received wisdom.

All summer long, larger and larger numbers of East Germans traveled to Czechoslovakia, also still behind the Iron Curtain, which they were freely permitted to visit. Once in Prague, many of them simply walked up the street to the West German embassy and either plunged through the gate or jumped over the fence that ran at the back of the property. Very quickly the West German compound became overcrowded with people, including a large number of families with small children, for whom the Germans had to provide some kind of shelter, sanitary facilities, food, and other amenities. Intense negotiations began between the Federal Republic and the Democratic Republic, as well as the Czechoslovaks, about what to do with the crowd, which had grown to over five thousand people. The West Germans would not permit them to be removed and sent back to the GDR; the Czechoslovaks would not permit them to travel directly to the Federal Republic. In the end a solution was found by providing a train that would carry the crowd through the GDR and on, without stopping, to the FRG. This was obviously only a short-term solution since there was nothing to stop the same thing happening, over and over, causing a never-ending hemorrhage of eastern Germans.

The sclerotic East German government at this point only wanted a short-term end to the embarrassment to get them past their fortieth anniversary as a nation. Gorbachev was due in town in early October for the celebrations, and the East Germans hoped to pull off the anniversary with no serious trouble. The major dissident demonstrations were taking place in Leipzig, well away from Berlin and Gorbachev's view. What happened during Gorbachev's visit, in spite of all the panoply and parades, was that the Soviet leader told his East German clients they could no longer count on the Soviet army to help them out in repressing their own people. Any use of force against the Leipzig demonstrators and the groups developing in Berlin and elsewhere was going to have to be German. And that was something GDR head Erich Honnecker was unwilling to order. A week or two after the fortieth anniversary, Honnecker resigned and a younger, more reformist, though still communist government took over.

One of the major complaints of East Germans, and indeed all citizens of Warsaw Pact states, was the strict control of their travel, with regulations that made it nearly impossible to visit West Berlin or West Germany to see relatives or just look around. Pressure on this point built up rapidly, especially in the wake of the merely temporary solution of the Czechoslovak escape route. Why should people have to go to Prague and jump over the wall of the West German embassy there when the regime in East Berlin could simply let them get on a train or bus and head west? By early November, it was clear the issue of free travel was a flash point. The East Germans issued new regulations that still seemed too restrictive, and the demonstrations continued to grow in numbers and impact.

The Central Committee met to try to find a solution.

On November 9, the Thursday before the three-day Veterans' Day weekend, I finished work and went home to enjoy a quiet evening. I changed into my bathrobe and flopped down to watch the evening news on TV. The broadcast led off with the introduction of the spokesperson for the Central Committee addressing a press conference, announcing the decision to liberalize the travel regulations more or less along the lines demanded by the demonstrators—East Germans would be able to travel freely to the West. Someone in the ranks of the reporters asked a follow-up question, a practice to which communist officials were not accustomed. "When do these regulations go into effect?" asked the newsman.

The spokesperson had no briefing book to cover this question. He looked down at his prepared statement, looked back up, and said, "Well, I guess from right now."

I was flabbergasted, not completely sure I had understood what I had heard. But the news broadcast cut back to the studio and an interview with the Governing Mayor of Berlin, Walter Momper. Momper was a cheerful, self-possessed politician, but on this evening he was white with excitement, almost incoherent as he tried to answer the news anchor's questions. I was now certain what I had heard. It was also certain that anyone who wanted to could walk through the Wall into West Berlin. I went to the phone to call the duty officer, a colleague in the political section.

"John," I asked, "are you aware of what is going on?"

"You mean that Soviet plane that strayed into the allied corridors?" he answered. This was a common duty-officer crisis in Berlin.

I then told him I had just watched the evening news, that the Wall was open, and that I suspected a flood of humanity would soon be pouring through Checkpoint Charlie in our sector. He was off and running.

Although the next day was an American holiday, we all reported to work. My major task on November 10 was to be at the City Hall where the Berlin government was struggling to deal with events. Safety was, of course, a big concern, since east Berliners were surging around and through the Wall, while west Berliners were celebrating on top of it, particularly at the Brandenburg Gate where it was about six or eight feet wide and flat on top. In the middle of all these celebratory types, many of them fortified with beer or champagne, were the Volkspolizei (Vopo), East German policemen. Less than twenty-four hours before, they were supposed to shoot anybody trying to get near the wall. No one was clear what orders the Vopos now had. Luckily they realized they were outnumbered and permitted the celebration to proceed without intervening. Any injuries that did occur were the result of high spirits, booze, and partying in a large crowd.

Another concern was to create more openings in the Wall, so more people could cross in orderly fashion. The Berlin government urgently needed to discuss these issues with the east Berlin authorities, although in the past allied occupation regulations had tried to keep such contacts at a minimum. A great number of ad hoc decisions and contacts were made in the next three or four days, some of which created a certain level of tension between the various authorities, who wanted to keep matters within channels and established procedures. The Governing Mayor met with a number of officials in the East, and there were meetings between public safety people of various ranks as well. These meetings took place in some cases without notification to the western allies and the kind of careful discussion of agendas that had been the rule in the past. The orthodoxy of the Berlin theology was difficult to maintain in the force of events over the weekend of November 10-12.

In the afternoon of November 10, I attended the hastily called session of the Berlin House of Representatives to listen to the speeches and reactions to events of the past day by the leaders of all the political parties. This assembly was followed by a large, public rally outside, in front of the Schöneberg City Hall, the location of President John Kennedy's "Ich bin ein Berliner" speech. The crowd was huge. John Freeman, his German wife, and I stood nearly at the back of the mass that almost filled the square and listened as Governing Mayor Momper, President of the House of Representatives Jürgen Wohlrabe, Former Berlin Mayor and Chancellor Willy Brandt, Foreign Minister Genscher, and others addressed the crowd. The replica of the Liberty Bell that hung in the tower of City Hall was rung. It was an unforgettable moment of pure euphoria.

I had to report everything by phone from my City Hall office back to the mission where "SitReps" (situation reports as the State

124

Department calls them) were being assembled every few hours. Whenever a fast-breaking story like this happens anywhere overseas, the post on the spot is required to keep Washington fully briefed by regularly scheduled, consecutively numbered cables. Such cables receive very wide distribution in Washington—all foreign affairs agencies, the White House, the Pentagon, and on and on.

It was not until Sunday that I had enough time to go myself to the center of the city, to see one of the new openings in the Wall (cut just that morning), to stroll past the Brandenburg Gate, and to see some of the small holes that had already been made in the concrete monstrosity by the group of chisel-wielders who came to be known as the "Wallpeckers." All over the city you could hear the put-put of the East German Trabants or "Trabis," the horrible, smoke-belching two-stroke car that was all many easterners could afford. In an endless stream they were pouring through the new hole at Potsdammer Platz, the central traffic circle of pre-war Berlin but now a deserted part of no-man's-land. Solid walls of pedestrians also pushed through, in both directions, those returning home carrying shopping bags filled with, among other things, bananas, a rare fruit in eastern Europe because the imports had to be paid for with hard currency. Flanking the two streams of humanity were west Berliners greeting their eastern cousins, handing them flowers if they had any. The British Army, in whose sector this new crossing was, had set up a mobile field kitchen to provide hot drinks on the chilly November day; there was also a little trailer from Burger King handing out free Whoppers. My companion, the legal advisor from our mission, and I just stood and gawked at everything, taking pictures, and drinking in the moment. As we walked back to the underground, we were stopped by a couple in a Trabi asking directions. Maps of west Berlin were unavailable to easterners, and they had no idea where they were or how to get back to a crossing point.

It is difficult to remember now that the reunification of Berlin and of Germany were not foregone conclusions by any means on November 15, 1989. The German Democratic Republic was still a sovereign nation, the capital of which was legally still under four-power occupation (according to the western allies); no treaty ending the war and occupation had ever been signed, nor was one under negotiation. The Federal Republic of Germany was divided about how to deal with the newly opened up neighbor to the east.

In Berlin, nevertheless, the pressure almost from the beginning was for a more normal relationship between the city government in the west and the administration in the east. The western allies might wish to put brakes on contacts and joint operations, but to continue the separate administration of transportation, communications, and all kinds of municipal services

125

made less and less sense to the two Berlin governments. The position of the western allies was that the city government in the east was illegitimate, having been installed after the mayor and his supporters had been so intimidated in 1948 by communist inspired mobs that they had moved "temporarily" to the west. Governing Mayor Walter Momper was by western reckoning the successor to Governing Mayor Ernst Reuter who had administered the entire city in 1948. It was difficult to stand firm on this point when urgent daily issues such as coordination of security forces or the provision of health services kept coming up for resolution.

During all this time of reassessment and procedural revision, the Wall kept coming down. When I walked in the center of the city in the cold, clear evening air, I heard the metallic ring of chisels in every direction. We at the mission were forbidden to approach the wall or to try to chip out our own souvenir pieces. Yet we kept seeing the United States Commandant, General Ray Haddock, on TV, constantly visiting new wall openings. He secured three large panels of wall and had them erected in the lobby of the headquarters building.

One day a close friend in the political section told me she and her family had gone up to town and the Wall the previous night. Both she and her husband began to pound away with the hammers and chisels they brought with them. She managed to dislodge a large piece of concrete, but it started to fall through the hole to the other side. She grabbed and caught it, but her fist was now sticking through the Wall; if she opened it she would lose the souvenir. Just at this point, she realized a Vopo, an East German policeman, was standing on the other side, contemplating her fist. He asked her what she was doing and suggested she remove her hand. She said if she did, she would lose the piece of wall she had just chopped out. Ultimately they negotiated a deal; he would take the piece of Wall, she would remove her hand, and then he would hand the concrete through to hole back to her. East-West cooperation at its finest.

Not long after that, I was at the same friend's house for supper. After we ate, I said, "Well, it's time to do a little Christmas shopping for our friends and family." We boarded the S-bahn and rode to the end of the line, near the Wall and Checkpoint Charlie. (Almost all Berlin city transport lines ended at the Wall, where most of the pre-Wall tunnels were blocked.) We snuck through the darkness to an obscure corner; I felt like a kid breaking the rules, since we were still officially forbidden to touch the Wall. Out came the hammers and chisels. This was the first time I had actually tried to break off pieces of the Wall, and it was incredibly difficult. The concrete was reinforced with rebar all through, and it was extremely hard. I found you had to start at a seam, where the cement was softer, and then work outwards. I did finally manage to collect enough so that at Christmas I gave each family member a little box with a certified crumb of the Berlin Wall.

During one weekend visit to the Wall, I saw a man renting hammers and chisels by the hour to anyone who wanted to take a turn collecting his or her own piece. I asked him if he were from east or west Berlin. He was from the east, and I then remarked that he was making money from something that had caused a lot of trouble over the years. He admitted that was true, but added, "I had to pay to put it up, so I should be able to make something out of taking it down!" True enough.

Meanwhile, the opening of the Wall meant that Berlin suddenly moved front and center in the minds and travel plans of Washington politicos. By the end of November, we had such a list of congressional delegations and other visitors that we needed a large wall chart to keep straight who was coming when, who was to take care of their schedules, and what they wanted to do. The first visitor I was responsible for was Ron Brown, at that time the chairperson of the Democratic Party. Ostensibly he came to participate in a program at the Aspen Institute, a think tank in western Berlin headed by retired United States Ambassador David Anderson. Another part of Brown's interest was, I think, to explore the idea of a visit by Ted Kennedy.

My major memory of Brown's visit is that, as I rushed out the door of the headquarters building on the way to meet him at the airport, I slipped on ice on the top step, sailed off into the air, and landed on the cobblestoned courtyard with my foot twisted below me. The driver standing at the door of the van watched my flight with dropped jaw. From that dramatic exit, I acquired a sprained ankle that hobbled me for the next few weeks.

Shortly after, we received word that Secretary of State James Baker was coming to Berlin with a substantial party. Secretarial visits had become steadily more elaborate since the Kissinger visits to Zurich; every new Secretary added to the requirements and acquired staff members who were more demanding and less flexible. In early December, about ten days before the visit, the first members of the advance team arrived and began working on the schedule. A basic outline of the various events was established. A mission officer was assigned as the "site officer" for each event, responsible for developing the detailed scenario, beginning with the exact minute the motorcade arrived, proceeding minute by minute, walking up the stairs, shaking hands (names of all persons and biographic information on each attached here), signing guest book, sitting in holding room, taking place on podium for remarks, list of all persons sharing podium (and biographic information), and so on all the way back to getting in the car. Press arrangements were handled by USIS. I was site officer for Baker's appearance at City Hall and the remarks that would be made to a gathering of the city government.

Over and over we were required to work on revising and refining these scenarios. As the security officers on the Secretary's detail arrived, we had to walk each of them through the site, indicating which stairs or elevators the Secretary and the others would use, where he would stand to do what, where the press would be, and on and on. Hobbling around on crutches with a sprained ankle, I found it pretty uncomfortable to participate in all these visits. The State Department officer coordinating the advance work was not at all sympathetic when I told her late on Friday before the visit that I was in pain and had to go home to elevate my foot. Otherwise, I would be useless when the visit began Monday. There was one little change, I told her: the Secretary would be going up the stairs on the left rather than on the right. She began to insist I go back with the security guys to walk through it again; I declined. "Helen," she said, "when the Secretary of State visits, we all have to make sacrifices." I refused and went home. The name of the advance lady, forever etched on my memory, was Lisa *Tender.*

The Secretary and his entire party arrived on Monday evening. We had been told to stand ready to go, along with his Washington-based staff, on a final run-through of all the sites for the next day. At about 9:30 pm, we boarded a school bus and headed off to run through the schedule one last time. Those of us from Berlin had complete confidence the visit would go without a hitch; most of us had been through numerous VIP visits and thought much of the advance work was monumentally silly. In the bus we began to joke and fool around, telling disaster stories of other visits. The State Department staff pulled in their skirts, sniffing that they found us very unprofessional.

The visit, of course, was a complete success.

In addition to my duties as *Senat* Liaison Officer, I had more recognizable duties as a political officer. I reported on the parties and personalities that were active in Berlin. One job that came up irregularly was attending the various party conferences. A few times there were national conferences held in Berlin that I was expected to cover, but more commonly they were meetings of just the Berlin organizations. The two major parties, SDP and CDU, generally produced well-managed events at which there were few surprises. The same was true of the FDP, the center party dominated by liberal business interests. The two parties on the right and left edges of the alignment were, however, less predictable.

The Republikaner, a right-wing organization that appealed to disenchanted working-class people who resented immigrants among other things, held one convention I attended. Members of this party were more suspicious of American diplomats than any other politicians I ran into, and I had few contacts among the leadership. Covering this party was further complicated by its tendency to expel its parliamentary representatives at regular intervals; party chairmen were also regularly deposed. When I attended their convention, a good deal of time was consumed by complaints over the chair's decree that there would be no smoking within the conference hall proper. Ultimately, the chairperson tired of all the grumbling and broke into the deliberations to announce that smoking would be permitted. A member of the no-smoke brigade then pointed out to the chair that there were large "no smoking" signs posted all through the hall, and he had to reverse his ruling once again. It was that kind of party.

The Green/Alternative Liste party on the left prided itself specifically on its relaxed methods of running a party conference. Their conferences tended to be held in places like technical school cafeterias and to proceed without much of an agenda or effort to impose structure on the meeting. I attended one such conference, in a cafeteria, at which some question of policy was to come up. The leader of the AL party in the House of Representatives, a partner in the coalition after all, suddenly announced she could no longer continue in the leadership because of the party's position over some issue. The meeting then broke down into wrangling over that issue, with members proposing motions, and then amendments to motions. Unlike all the other parties, members of the press and diplomatic corps were not seated apart from the delegates in their own sections. We were sprinkled throughout the cafeteria at tables with all the voting members of the group. Things became more and more complicated and confusing. A series of votes was finally called, and the delegate across the table from Erika and me voted a few times. Then she asked us what the votes had been about. Such conventions could be amusing at times, but since they were always on Saturdays, it was occasionally irritating to have to sit there until six or seven in the evening before major decisions were taken.

By December 1989, talk of German reunification began to buzz in the air. By this time, Federal Republic Chancellor Helmut Kohl started floating long-term conditions that might bring the two Germanies together over a period of perhaps five to ten years. The United States embassy in East Berlin was not convinced reunification would ever happen, envisioning instead some kind of new, democratic political arrangement that would permit continued sovereignty for the German Democratic Republic. In our mission in west Berlin, we began to wonder how such a halfway measure could work out. The city was moving steadily toward some kind of reunification. In a strictly legal sense, however, the city could not be unified and maintain its ties to the western German state unless and until the occupation regime in both Berlin and Germany ended with agreement between the four wartime allies, including the Soviet Union. We could not see how the current arrangements could be maintained for the five to ten years Kohl was talking about. In some ways, the logic of the Berlin situation drove German reunification. The city was entirely inside East Germany, and the eastern half was the capital of that state. Half of it was western however. The anomalies of this circumstance could not be resolved within a divided Germany. Of the three United States diplomatic establishments, the Bonn embassy, the Berlin embassy and the Berlin mission, we at the mission were the first to get the story right—unification was coming fast.

The first six months of 1990 at work were consumed with discussions of the legal, political, and logical questions among our staff, among the allies, between the two Germanies, and between NATO powers and the Soviet Union. Simultaneously the rest of the Warsaw Pact countries were breaking out: Czechoslovakia in the "Velvet Revolution" of November-December 1989, Rumania in a bloody coup against the Ceaucescu dictatorship, Hungary gradually expanding its freedoms, and Poland on Germany's eastern border moving to replace the Communist Jaruzelski government.

I was busier than ever, carrying on the still-routine business of *Senat* Liaison Officer with the weekly meetings at City Hall and consultations with my two counterparts, while putting out an increasing amount of reporting on the *de facto* reunification of the city all around us and trying, with all the others in the mission, to work out what might lie ahead.

Meanwhile my house became one of the most desirable bed and breakfast spots on the continent. I have never been so popular as I was then; everyone I knew wanted to come to Berlin and see the end of the Cold War. It was for me a wonderful time, and instructive as well. Since there was a certain obligatory route every visitor wanted to trace, if I were free to go with them, I was able to see week by week the changes in Berlin, at the center of the city near the Wall and at the border along the outer boundary.

The Brandenburg Gate area had opened to foot traffic at New Year's, but much of the Wall in front of the Gate itself still stood. Gradually it became more and more fragmented by the wallpeckers, and we were able to see why it had not been opened immediately. At that spot, the Wall had been six or eight feet wide, because behind the western facade (all that could be seen from that side) was a tight row of x-shaped steel tank traps sunk in the street pavement; behind that, on the eastern side was another concrete facade. For a while, we mission folk were not supposed to cross from west to east at the Gate or slightly to the north behind the Reichstag building. At some point, imperceptibly, that rule changed.

More and more crossing points opened, some to car traffic and others to foot traffic. The rule for those of us assigned to the western missions was always, even in the days of Checkpoint Charlie and the Wall, that we could not treat the Wall as any kind of international boundary. We were not permitted, therefore, to present passports to the Vopos in the east or even speak to them; all we could do was hold our military ID cards up to the car window and we would be waved through. These rules persisted, even as the travel restrictions on west Berliners became more relaxed (much later than the relaxation on east Berliners traveling west), and they could transit the old wall boundary with their ID cards. For a period, however, they could not travel in our military-plate cars. In late February, I was traveling to a concert in east Berlin with Erika Nassiri, my German assistant. We decided to cross at a point most convenient to get to Gethsemene Church where a combined Berlin youth orchestra was to perform a Bruckner symphony. The crossing point was recently approved for my use, but Erika could not drive through with me. I had to stop twenty-five yards from the crossing, let Erika out, and drive through while she walked and presented her ID. As Erika approached my car, in the foggy February night, her high heels tapping on the uneven paving stones, I felt I was living a Le Carré novel.

Only a month later, an American friend was visiting from England and the two of us with Erika drove through the same point, all together, each of us presenting a different form of identification. No problem!

The concert Erika and I went to was one of a growing number of events that took place across the previous divide in the city. One of the most moving and memorable was at Easter 1990, when I attended the Easter Vigil service at the Catholic cathedral. The cathedral stood in east Berlin. Interestingly, the division of the city never divided the diocese, and the bishop continued through all the Wall years to serve both halves of his diocese, even if the people could not meet together. This service was the first post-Wall Easter. For those who have never attended an Easter Vigil, the service takes place on the Saturday evening before Easter. It begins in total darkness, which was kind of alarming when we entered the cathedral. I knew from previous visits that there was a wide staircase in the center of the round sanctuary descending to the crypt. I was slightly disoriented in the darkness and was afraid I would pitch down the stairs. We finally found the base of a pillar to sit on, all the seats being filled. The bishop and the procession entered in the darkness, carrying the large Paschal candle and gradually the light was passed through the congregation so we could all light the candles we had purchased. It was a moving service, proceeding through the readings and the proclamation of Christ's resurrection when all the lights blazed on and we greeted one another, East and West. The domed, circular space rang with the Easter alleluias.

The 1990 spate of house guests also meant I was able, when I could get away from work, to explore the city ever more intensively. Depending on my friends' particular interests, I could rustle up a variety of things to do. One French couple included an architect who wanted to see many buildings all over the city. We went to the Le Corbusier apartment house, and we explored all over the parts of postwar Berlin reconstructed in the center of the city, looking for housing units and office buildings. Most of them failed to stir me to any admiration; my architect friend remarked, "Even great architects seem to do their worst work here in Berlin!"

The American from England was a church musician who visited just a few weeks before Easter. The Berlin musical calendar was filled with wonderful choral music, and we were able to attend a full-blown St. Mathew Passion in the Philharmonic Hall, a more intimate performance of the St. John Passion in a large church, a wonderful concert by a boy's choir in a small local church, and so on. The impetus to check schedules, go out and get tickets, and attend such events was provided by my guests. I was very grateful to them all.

It may sound terrible to those to whom hospitality comes more easily than to me, but I also enjoyed my friends' cooking! Quite a number of them, realizing it was hard for me to cater meals while remaining late at the office, would purchase food during their day's explorations and cook a meal for me to enjoy when I got home. As Berlin food shops were not open at any times convenient to a working person this was a great boon.

Since many guests stayed a while once they got to me, I made up what I called the guest kit. I provided an excellent street atlas of Berlin, guides to all the museums and architectural sites, a pass to the underground system, a key to the house, and a few other aids to effective sightseeing. It worked pretty well. I had only one guest who, not speaking German, appeared terrified to venture out without me at her side. That was a kind of drag but lasted only for a weekend.

The photographs of my guests trace the rapid disappearance of the Wall. While the early ones, in January and February, show them standing next to chipped out sections of the Wall, by May and June they are photographed in the former no-man's land, next to heaps of completely dismantled wall sections with demolished watchtowers, rolls of barbed wire, and other paraphernalia nearby. By July it was getting more and more difficult to find very much standing Wall at all. We were now taking bike rides along the excellent tracks built through the former no-man's land between the inner and outer wall.

The first time I visited Potsdam, I needed to get an East German visa and stop at the East German border point just beyond Checkpoint Bravo (on the western edge of the city) to get visas for my friends. We were supposed to return by the same route, but found ourselves instead driving over the newly opened Glienecke Bridge (the famous bridge for East-West spy exchanges) before we knew it, back into Berlin and the American sector. Not more than a week or two later, I headed for Potsdam with a visitor and found the post where I had gotten the visas locked up and deserted. On we went to a lovely day in Potsdam, returning by the much shorter route over the Glienecke Bridge.

Since the entire city of Berlin was within the Soviet occupation zone, i.e., the German Democratic Republic, access for people, freight, military personnel and equipment was a crucial question that, over the years, had been a major concern and frequent flashpoint. Berlin occupation rules stated that all allies could travel to all parts of the city, even though it was divided into sectors. Our military made the constant exercise of this right, by car and by airplane, a means to insure the city would stay open. The definition of air corridors into the city for use by the western allies and their commercial aircraft (the only air companies allowed to operate to Berlin were American, French, and British) was of overriding importance. The existence of these corridors was the only factor that kept West Berlin alive during the Berlin Blockade of 1948—49. In fact, the only remnant of four-power occupation that lasted beyond the Soviet walkout from the Kommandatura in 1947 was the air traffic control center which, until the city was unified and air traffic control turned over to German civilians, remained in continuous operation—Soviet air controllers sitting beside American, French and German colleagues.

In addition to air traffic, the western allies also maintained access to Berlin by railroad. Each day, in each direction, all three allies ran a "duty train" between Berlin and the Federal Republic of Germany. Due to our assignment to the United States mission, we were permitted to ride any one of these trains free of charge, to Frankfort (American), to Bremerhaven (British), or Strasbourg (French). One time I took the train to Frankfort, partly to see what it was all about. First I had to request travel orders from the military travel office and get assignment to the train. Then, at about 6 pm, I reported to a small suburban station in our sector, at Lichterfelde-

West, where all the passengers collected and were briefed by the military. We had to hand in our passports and travel orders, and we were instructed not to lean out the windows or attempt in any way to speak with the Soviets who would be controlling the crossing points. We boarded the train. As I carried a rank that in military terms was somewhere between a lieutenant colonel and colonel, I had two-bunk compartment I shared with an instructor at the University of Maryland campus attached to the Army. The trip was pleasant, and I slept most of the way, except at those times when we were lurching across points at junctions. The formalities of border crossing were handled by the commander of the train, who was empowered to deal with the Soviets controlling our passage; the right of the East Germans to control these trains across their territory was not recognized.

I also decided to travel by car one time before the entire regime came to an end, and that, too, was a strange experience. I again needed military travel orders. I crossed into East Germany through Checkpoint Bravo, the only point we were permitted at that time to use. I had to check in with an American military policeman, who recorded the time of my transit and briefed me on proper behavior. "Return all salutes," said the MP. I protested that I was a civilian, in civilian clothes, and I didn't know how to salute. "Return all salutes," he repeated in that stern, expressionless way law enforcement officers have of dealing with recalcitrants.

We were required to avoid crossing through the East German control booths that ordinary westerners took. Instead, we followed the curving bypass route marked for military personnel and came to a Soviet control point. There was a young soldier there by the side of the road, who motioned me over. As I got out of the car, he saluted me in my blue jeans and windbreaker, and I solemnly saluted back. I then had to go into a shed to hand my orders and passport through one of those slots favored by Warsaw Pact border controllers; you can't see a thing on the other side of the wall and can only hear muted conversation, rustling of paper, and thumping rubber stamps. Eventually my passport was handed back, and, after saluting the young boy outside, I was on my way, following the map and photos of autobahn junctions provided at Checkpoint Bravo. We were permitted to use only the central route to the west, had to stay on the road at all times, and were not permitted to pull over. We were instructed to wait for one of the American MPs patrolling the autobahn to help us out if we had any kind of trouble en route. At the other end of the route, two hours later, I went through the procedure in reverse—salutes, check-in with MPs at Checkpoint Alpha and then I was in the west. Coming back, I was in a line at the Soviet control point behind a civilian Englishman who, instead of saluting, performed a kind of Japanese bow to the Soviet soldier, and a short, stout American serviceman in lycra shorts and t-shirt who snapped to attention and saluted so professionally that his buns quivered very temptingly to my view.

Although the train trip occurred before the opening of the Wall, all my other border crossings came later. The cumulative effect of living with the regulations, developed for a time when every tiny infringement of the rules risked setting precedents that could not be rolled back and were now changing and disappearing every day, created a never-never land. Even when I arrived, three months before the events of November 9, the regulations were based on non-reality; we understood the need for observing them, but it was strange. After November 9, they became increasingly bizarre. None of my visitors could understand the restraints on me; it is *not* normal, of course, to have a major European city divided with walls and crossing points, and it is *not* normal to be unable to drive from one street of a city into an outlying suburb without going past guard towers and barbed wire. Normality slowly returned and seemed abnormal only to me.

In March 1990, elections were held in the German Democratic Republic, ousting the remade communists and bringing the eastern version of the Christian Democratic Party, the same as Chancellor Kohl's, to head the new government. At this point, both Germanies agreed that on the first of July, the old GDR currency would be converted to a unified German mark used in both East and West. Momentum was building by now for political unity. Within NATO, the British and even more the French, resisted the reunification of a country that would almost certainly dominate the European Union. The United States was in favor of such a move, and ultimately won support for the three western allies to approach the Soviet Union to go along with the deal as well. The biggest concern of the Soviet Union was the prospect of NATO forces stationed in their former Warsaw Pact client state. The negotiations that led, by the end of June, to an agreement among the four wartime allies to conclude a treaty ending the occupation, were full of roadblocks that had to be patiently dismantled.

Within the city, steps to permit easier movement of traffic and people continued. Checkpoint Charlie, symbol of the Cold War and one phrase that immediately meant Berlin to the world, ceased its work controlling traffic on the west side of that crossing point. One day, my British counterpart confronted me, asking if it were true that the United States Commandant, General Haddock, was planning some kind of huge ceremony for the removal of the modular building at the crossing. I found out, in fact, it was true; Haddock had the idea for some kind of celebratory event, in which he would be the leading figure, to remove the building and donate it to a local museum as an artifact of the Cold War period. It was a bit embarrassing to contemplate what the American commandant was going to do with the event, and the three allied ministers were trying to roll him back from his more spectacular ideas.

In the end, Haddock was upstaged. By June, the details of the agreements that would end the occupation and permit reunification of Berlin and Germany were ready for initialing. The Foreign Ministers of the four wartime allies and the two Germanies agreed to meet in Berlin to approve the agreement. One of the events planned for this historic step was a ceremony at Checkpoint Charlie, concluded by the dismantling of the border shed. Haddock was no match for James Baker, Edward Schevardnadze, Genscher, and the rest. I sat in my chair, facing the checkpoint shed, as each of the six foreign ministers, the two mayors of still-divided Berlin, and the three commandants spoke their thoughts on that day, recalling those who had died at the Wall while seeking freedom and looking ahead to a reunited city and country. At the end of the speechifying, as the military band played "Up, Up, and Away," a large construction crane lifted the shed from its foundation and swung it away from the Friedrichstrasse crossing point. (This maneuver had been rehearsed at 4 am that morning, to be certain the chains would hold and the shed would not be dumped on the heads of the assembled notables.)

The actual date for reunification was October 3. Until then, the occupation legally continued in force. Through the summer, planning for the new arrangements for the army units and the merging of the embassy in east Berlin and our mission in west Berlin picked up speed. For us who were assigned to the mission, it was an uncomfortable time, as it was for the embassy. Somehow, a large number of personnel had to be reduced, either by normal transfers for the Americans or by reductions in force for the Germans. In the west, we had 277 German national employees who had to be whittled down to 77 defined positions. A few decided to retire on their comfortable pensions, but not that many employees were close to retirement age. Many of the rest applied for the published list of positions for the final configuration of the Berlin office. The day on which the decisions were announced was a grim one indeed. I was pleased that all three of the assistants who worked under my supervision were offered jobs in the new office, but it was a tense time for them as well as for those who had been let go. Any sympathy they offered was rejected by the unfortunate contenders for the jobs they had gotten. The woman who ran my City Hall office was kept on as the Protocol Assistant, while two employees in the Protocol Office were let go, with great bitterness on their part.

For us Americans, the arrangements also caused a lot of hard feeling. I was not due for transfer in the summer of 1990, and the earliest I could be put into the normal transfer pipeline was the following summer. We were told that the main center of operations would be moved to the embassy building in east Berlin, although there was not enough room for the overstaffed political section that would exist until the next summer. We lived in the west, close to the offices in the headquarters building where we had both computer workstations in our offices and functioning telephones, neither of which existed in the east. We also had our own offices, while in the east we would have to share with others. I was not only removed from my position as the number two ranking person in the section in favor of someone lower ranking (because he would remain at post longer, I was told) but I also learned I would have to share an office with the college intern in the east. I stayed in the west, even though this caused bad feelings between me and my boss. For the most part, my colleagues in the political and economic sections also continued to work where we were.

Even though the center of action switched over time to the former embassy, there was resentment from the Americans there. They continued to live in the fairly uncomfortable housing made available by the former East German government, while they saw us inhabiting the very large and comfortable houses that, under occupation law, had been paid for and provided to us by the West German government. It is amazing how snarly we can get under stressful working conditions. Many of the decisions about who would stay on and what positions they would get had been made in great secrecy in our embassy in Bonn, with little consultation with any of us. There was much backbiting over the nine months following reunification.

In the week prior to reunification, we three allied liaison officers were entertained by the staff of the *Senat* with whom we had worked so closely, as well as by the President of the House of Representatives. We were taken to lunch, with speeches, gifts, and good food. It was clear, however, that we were being seen off with a sigh of relief. Whatever problems lay ahead, no one was going to have to check any longer with the allies. Our administrative section moved my office furniture and that of my assistant out of City Hall. The American flag in the office was folded up and removed, and we unscrewed the plate on the door that read "United States Liaison-Offizier." I still have that plate, as well as the small one from the desk in the front row of public seats in the House of Representatives.

The formal proceedings took place in the House of Representatives as the French Commandant (chairman commandant for that month) and the Berlin dignitaries spoke of the long relationship between the allies and the city, keeping the city open and free over all the troubled years of the Cold War. The whole process was strange. Most Berliners were aware of the sustained commitment the western allies had made, and they were profoundly grateful for it. Much more than in West Germany itself, pro-American feeling was high in Berlin. Yet there was no mistaking the eager anticipation and enthusiasm for a united Germany and their wish to have us gone. For some months, people in City Hall had been asking me when I was moving out; a number had their eye on my office, which was a large and airy one. Ambivalence lay all over the farewell.

Once the speeches were done, my flag folded, and the occupation a thing of the past, I became a political reporting officer pure and simple. The political section was grossly overstaffed, now operating out of two locations. It was difficult to speak with each other, as there were insufficient and inadequate phone lines between the east and west halves of the now-united city. There was no e-mail; courier service was sporadic and shrank constantly. The underground rail line that ran right in front of our western mission headquarters had originally run to the center of eastern Berlin; a train ride between the two offices should have been a simple twenty-minute trip. However, when the city was split down the center, three miles of track on that line were torn up and the tunnels sealed; journey by public transport now took almost an hour with two changes between lines. The route by car ran through the center of the increasingly congested city with parking problems at the eastern end. Those of us in the former mission were pretty much on our own.

The first two and a half months were busy. I had responsibility for reporting on the reunited Berlin. National and city elections were scheduled for early December, so I had to make contacts with party organizations in the former eastern part of the city and with the leading politicians there. I also attended sessions of both Berlin Houses of Representatives, still meeting separately until the elections that would create one unified legislature. For the first time, I traveled extensively around eastern Berlin. Many of the party headquarters in the outlying districts ("Bezirke") were in the ugly, badly built apartment complexes of the communist period. I was shocked by their shoddy condition—uneven stairs that were crumbling, holes in the cheesy sheetrock walls that appeared to have no structure behind them, and walls in apartments that were not true.

In and out, up and down I trudged, encouraged for the most part by the enthusiasm with which the easterners were facing the elections that would unify the political structures. The former

Communist Party had already renamed itself the "Party of Social Democracy" and, alone of the political parties, possessed real party headquarters, whole buildings centrally located in the boroughs.

In addition to meeting the leaders of the various parties and talking with them about their platforms and candidates, I attended as many rallies as I could. These were taking place constantly, all over the city, in any place—shopping areas, parks, open spaces—where a large crowd could get together. I went to about a dozen for all parties, listening to the speeches, judging the enthusiasm of the crowds, and seeing which western political leaders turned up at eastern rallies and vice versa. This kind of legwork political reporting is enormous fun, and I enjoyed every bit of it.

The elections were a triumph for Chancellor Kohl's Christian Democrats at both the national and city level. Easterners saw his party, much more than the Social Democrats or Green/Alternative, as the one that had embraced reunification. The result for Berlin was that Governing Mayor Walter Momper and his "red-green" *Senat* (Social Democrats and Green/Alternative) were turned out, and the Christian Democrats and Free Democrats formed the new *Senat*. There was a new constellation at City Hall.

From the time of the election until my departure the following May, I had less and less work to do. Quite naturally, Berlin and its politics were less interesting after reunification; fewer Washington policy makers were absorbed in what was now, after all, merely a city government. More interest focused on what was going on in the five states of the former East Germany, and I did not have much direct responsibility for reporting on that. After about a month or so of sitting around twiddling my thumbs, I talked the economic officer of our former mission into doing a big project on the unification of the church organizations in eastern and western Germany. Such a project would give us an excuse for doing some traveling in the provinces and permit us to report on something no one else was interested in.

There were actually some substantial issues involved in this project. One was the east-west resentment that occurred in all other institutions of the former Germanies. Many easterners felt, even before reunification but increasingly after, that western Germans looked down on them as lazy, inept at the skills that got them ahead in business or politics, and in need of instruction and direction from the big brother in the west. Westerners held, and often expressed, their conviction that easterners couldn't do anything efficiently; they also began to realize the financial sacrifice that was going to be demanded from them to turn around the state enterprises and clean up the ecological disasters in the east. Eastern church organizations, too, began to feel the condescension of the western churches. They resented it, particularly as churches had served as centers for dissidence under the communist regime.

Eastern churches, both Catholic and reformed, almost because of their role in the dissident movement, now had a major task ahead. If the possibility for limited opposition to the communist regime attracted people to join churches prior to reunification, that attraction had now disappeared. Churches had to shift rapidly to finding other messages and other purposes that would bind their members to them.

The churches in western Germany were traditionally financed by a surtax, collected by the state, levied on all workers who did not opt out of the system; seven percent of a person's income tax was deducted from the paycheck and made over to the specified denomination. Each denomination then paid its ministers and provided for the upkeep and work of the parishes. Eastern churches, under communism, had provided for themselves and were proud of the fact that they lived off free contributions from members. They saw no reason simply to sign on to the western religious tax system without even a discussion. Westerners could not understand why easterners saw the church tax as a problem.

The eastern churches needed a lot of money at this point. The fabric of their buildings in many cases was deteriorating badly. Furthermore, they had to obtain materials and provide for services they had not been able to perform during the communist period—proper church schools and youth groups, hospital and prison visiting, and the like.

Traveling around eastern Germany and talking with bishops, parish priests, and lay people was an interesting window into the painful process of reunification. Once we finished collecting our data, my colleague and I decided to let it rip and write a report that would start at the beginning, go on to the end, and then stop. We produced a seventeen-page cable. I doubt that anybody in Washington read it, with the possible exception of one or two green eye shade analysts at the CIA. But it sure was fun doing it. I was able to escape all the office politics and resentments and just beaver away.

Meanwhile, I received my new assignment and, like my fellow *Senat* liaison officers who left Berlin during the winter, was getting ready to move on. I had asked for and been assigned to be the United States Consul General in Kaduna, Nigeria. When I told one colleague visiting from the embassy in Bonn where I was headed, he made a face of disdain. That was a typical reaction from a member of the "German club" as a certain group of officers in the State Department is known. These are people who spend almost their entire careers moving from one German-speaking post to the next, from Bonn to Vienna to Dusseldorf, and back again. During my time in Berlin, I gained my own disdain for them as fairly unimaginative people who were quite dependent on instruction from above or from Washington. In Berlin, for example, when I was unable to get in touch with people in the eastern part of the city by phone, I simply got in a car and went there. If they were in, fine; if they were out, I would leave a note saying when I planned to return and whom I would like to see. Meantime, my "German club" colleagues would sit in their offices complaining that the phones did not work and they couldn't get through. After a tour in Lagos, I had learned how to function without modern technology. In Kaduna, as in Kigali, I would be in a place where I could be my own boss, where Washington would find it difficult or unimportant to deliver detailed instructions, and where I could make my own decisions about what to report and how to do it.

I was not sorry to be leaving my house in Berlin either. I lived in a place that was the envy of all, but it had never felt like a home to me. It was actually a duplex, although that term hardly applied to the postmodern, palladian-style edifice, one of three buildings in a large compound. The original idea for the construction project was to build housing for mission staff personnel—communicators and secretaries—who might feel more comfortable living in a compound in which everyone spoke English. The architect chosen to design these town houses, however, was determined to win a prize for his work, and what could have been relatively cozy little townhouses turned out to be mock-mansions, each unit of which cost about a half million dollars. The bill was footed by the Germans, under occupation rules, and the German government demurred at the idea of support staff personnel inhabiting such expensive houses. Thus I was moved into 36B Im Dol.

Approaching by car, I opened the electronically controlled gates that gave on to a short driveway into the underground garage, big enough for eight cars. All the basements for the three buildings opened off the garage, and each basement had several huge, unfurnished rooms. The house itself rose three stories above ground, and was, to my thinking, laid out in the most inconvenient way possible. The kitchen was enormous; I used to say I had to walk several miles to bake a batch of brownies, since refrigerator, sink, and stove were all a good hike away from each other. The best working space was close to none of them.

The laundry room was at the top of the house, close to neither the main bedroom nor the kitchen. There was no plumbing in the basement. There was a bedroom on the top floor but no bathroom; the guest bathroom was one floor down. My bathroom was enormous, as big as my bedroom; the toilet was ten or fifteen feet from the double sink. The entire room—tiles and fixtures—was in gray-blue, the most depressing color I could think of during the gray Berlin winter.

When I moved in, the living room was not completely furnished so I had some control over choice. But, along the only solid wall in the room already stood the central feature of the German living room—the "*Schrank.*" This word refers to a large cabinet, some parts with solid doors, others with glass doors or open shelves; mine also had a pull-down desk. This *Schrank* was about fifteen feet long and made in dark, rosewood veneer. In what was actually a fairly sunny room, it loomed on one side, completely dominating the place and taking up the one wall where large pictures could be hung. I told the woman who controlled furnishings that I wanted it taken out and put in someone else's room. She fought me, kept "forgetting," told me it was the most expensive piece of furniture they had put in the house. Finally, I said, "Frau Schwandt, by Friday the *Schrank* has to be gone or I will commit suicide." She sent the carpenters over, and they disassembled it and stuck it in one of the empty rooms in the basement.

I spent almost two years in the house but just never felt I really lived in it. The other four people in the compound seemed happy in their homes, but for me the atmosphere was always hostile.

Aside from my housing, however, Berlin was a wonderful place. Before living there, I had not realized how large it was and what possibilities existed, even within the borders of the divided city, for recreation. There were beautiful lakes, and the United States Commandant had a motor launch we were allowed to use for our own entertainment or for representation; I once took my two allied colleagues out for lunch on a trip on the canals. There were several large parks with walking trails where we could spend a full day. Another feature of Berlin was the "Gartenkolonie," various spaces set aside for small garden plots assigned to the lucky applicant. Many holders of these small gardens constructed little cottages on the site where they could entertain friends or spend a night "in the country." As a group, these gardeners were a powerful political lobby.

Another great advantage of Berlin is that it is nearly flat and has an extensive network of biking lanes. I purchased a good bike that I often used on weekends to explore the city, either alone or with friends. I even used it occasionally to commute between my two offices, putting on walking shoes while I pedaled to City Hall, wearing my tomato-soup colored bike helmet. I gained the admiration of one of the Green members of the House of Representatives, when he found me locking my bike into the bike rack next to his.

I was trained as a historian and was interested in tracing the growth of the city, tracking down where various buildings and streets had been in the pre-World War II era, prior to the bombing that pulverized the center of the city. Equally interesting was tracing the growth of the city outward by the process of annexing settlements that had been self-contained villages until the early twentieth century. In the American sector, for example, there were numerous old village centers with parish churches that could easily be four or five hundred years old. They often stood on a village green, surrounded by old houses. Connecting these various village centers were wide, modern roads with modern housing and commercial establishments. I lived in the area known as Dahlem, one of the former villages. The church in Dahlem, St. Anne, dated from the fourteenth century and had the distinction of being the church where Martin Niemoeller served as pastor in the 1930s and 1940s. Niemoeller was close to Dietrich Bonhoeffer and resisted much of the Nazi effort to take over the Christian churches.

Lubars was another small village incorporated into Greater Berlin; it was in the French sector, in the very northeast corner of West Berlin where The Wall and The Border met. I first went there for a Sunday outing in August 1989, when both Wall and Border were still standing. My visitor and I strolled out after lunch at a village cafe to look at the inner city boundary. Here, on the western side, there was only a chain link fence, with a no-man's land about 100 yards across to a wall and watchtower. Following the fence north, we came to a pretty meadow with a stream at the bottom; warning signs well before the stream announced the border and the danger of approaching any further.

In March, seven months later, another friend and I drove to Lubars for a similar outing. The chain link fence had been torn open at places, and we could look across the no-man's land to the still existing watchtower. French tourists were climbing all over the watchtower. My friend suddenly decided to walk across the hundred yards where, presumably, there had recently been mines or automatic firing devices. In spite of my protestations (I was still not allowed as a member of the mission to cross from west to east except at the recognized crossing points), my friend strolled across the space, clambering down and up the sides of a sandy ditch in the middle. At the tower, he disappeared from view. Just then an East German jeep, driving along the track in the no-man's land, pulled up at the tower. I stood there, wondering what was going to happen— particularly if they were going to take my friend away from the tower toward the east. I didn't know if he had his passport, nor could I think where I would start first to find out where he was. How could I call the embassy in East Berlin and tell them that I had mislaid a house guest? Naturally my panic was premature and excessive, as it often is, and my friend reappeared some minutes later having savored his experience.

The cultural life of Berlin was also rich. One of the most wonderful perks of being a *Senat* Liaison Officer was that I received two tickets to every premiere of a new production at the opera or theatre. I also was able to subscribe to season tickets at the Berlin Philharmonic. Since I knew that such treats are rare in life, I took advantage of as many of these opportunities as possible.

Shopping in Berlin was another matter. Unlike the United States, where salespersons are frequently of indifferent quality, German sales personnel are well trained and unionized. When I first arrived in Berlin there was a great and ultimately unsuccessful struggle going on to extend the open hours of department and food stores by some small increment. Before the final decision, I met with the member of the *Senat* responsible for labor, and, almost as a joke, I remarked I hoped he would support the longer opening hours. He had a long history as a leading unionist and said he would certainly not support longer hours. "Salespeople need time with their families, you know," he said.

I countered that working people needed to have shops open at convenient times as well. I found it almost impossible to shop in Berlin stores, I said, since they were just not open most of the time I was not working. He suggested I could save my money in that case. Except for food, I followed his advice. Food, however, I could not do without. The Army had a commissary in which I was permitted to shop, but I didn't like a lot of the food there—processed cheese, squishy bread, aisles filled with easy-to-fix foods.

Every Saturday morning, therefore, I arranged to be at the door of the closest supermarket at 8 am. If I waited until 9, there was total cart gridlock inside the store. Even though the store was a supermarket, I still had to line up for many things—meat, deli, cheese, bakery, and so on. After 9 am, each of these lines was about fifteen minutes long. At 8 am, however, the coast was relatively clear, particularly after I knew the layout of the store and had mapped my route. I found I could do a week's shopping in about a half hour, including the self-bagging at the cashier.

Generally I also included my recycling chore in my Saturday outing. There was a complete recycling setup on one of the corners I had to pass—three colors of glass, cardboard, newspaper, and batteries. The collection containers for glass were shaped like what I called personal bomb shelters, six-foot high mound shapes with several holes to throw the bottles in, painted the color of the glass each one was for. When they were full, a truck came to grab them by the handles welded on top. One of my friends told me she saved up glass at her house until some point when tensions began to get high or the kids started fighting with each other. A trip to the glass recycling corner was then in order, and all the aggression could be worked off by throwing bottles and jars in the mound as hard as possible and listening for the satisfying crash.

As time wore on and the date of my departure came closer, I had less and less to do. I still didn't feel like working in the eastern part of the city much. I also began to realize that my boss and others were arranging luncheons and meetings with "my" contacts without telling me. Such behavior was not entirely courteous, according to Foreign Service protocol, although I realized I would soon be leaving. The Army presence was also being reduced; the Commandant and his staff had already left at the time of reunification. The headquarters building had more empty offices in it. One morning, about a month before I was scheduled to leave, I walked down the hall to the ladies room I usually used, only to find it locked. This was an unmistakable message that I was not a functioning part of the mission any longer.

In mid-May, I was happy to get in a taxi and drive to Tegel Airport. My cat Ruth, in her carrying case, was less happy. I was not pleased to find at the airport that TWA had contracted out its check-in services to a firm that appeared to hire only gorgeous young men and women, dressed in the latest styles and completely unaware how to check in passengers. The plane was two hours late leaving Berlin because the check-in took so long. My particular gorgeous man had to refer every question to his supervisor. He was unaware how to permit pets in the cabin and get payment for it. Ruth ended up traveling free because he could not think how to charge me. At the next hurdle, the x-ray machine, I had another argument with the security man who wanted Ruth to go through the x-ray. Finally, when all the luggage was loaded and Ruth (un-x-rayed) and I staggered on to the plane for the first leg of the journey, we lifted off from Tegel and the runway that had first been constructed during the Berlin Blockade with bomb rubble. Now the city was open and reunited, and I had seen the process from ground level.

My Own African Place

Home leave between Berlin and Kaduna was as enjoyable as could be imagined. I spent the six weeks largely in Maine, where I had already purchased a retirement home. I celebrated my fiftieth birthday and then traveled to Michigan for the wedding of my oldest nephew. I was rested and ready for the challenges of running my own post in a country I already knew and liked well.

The departure was total chaos. Hurricane Bob passed through the day before I was to leave, and not one commuter-sized plane on the eastern seaboard was where it was supposed to be. My mother took me to the tiny airport in White Plains, New York, only to find a morass of canceled flights and hundreds of angry and desperate passengers whose ranks I joined. I was to take a commuter flight to Boston where I would catch the trans-Atlantic Northwest flight. My flight was canceled, although I had been assured all morning on the phone it would fly. I changed to an airline that would not permit Ruth to travel in the cabin. In the midst of the uproar I had to change her to a different traveling case and then, with minutes to spare, run through a pounding rain to the aircraft, Ruth in one hand, and my carry-on luggage in the other. I was dripping wet when I took my seat, and my hair and clothes slowly dried on my body during the flight to Boston. Thirty hours later, Ruth and I unloaded ourselves, somewhat disheveled, at Murtala Muhammed Airport in Lagos, Nigeria.

It was strange to be back in Lagos. It seemed the same and not the same. Buildings that had been brand new when I was there in 1981 were now weather-stained; a couple of them had burned down. I had forgotten how lush the vegetation was at the end of the rains. Most of all, Victoria Island was now heavily built up. In 1981, most of the buildings there were residential and had no landscaping around them at all. The land was so sandy that the impression was of a suburb in the desert. There were now multi-story office buildings on the major roads, and all the residential compounds had high walls around them. Huge green trees and plants hung over all the walls.

After several days of consultations and meetings at the embassy, I went to the airport, this time to the domestic side, for my flight to Kaduna. Traveling by plane within Nigeria is an experience no one can believe until it happens. I sat in the embassy car while the driver took my money and booked the seat. He returned with my ticket and a baggage handler who took my suitcases and threw them into an open wagon being pulled across the access road to the airplanes. The driver asked around and discovered which aircraft was headed to Kaduna, and I went and lined up at the plane's rear entrance. Even if the flight had not been called, I knew better than to wait in the lounge. The flights get oversold, and there are many touts out on the tarmac who bribe the boarding agents for boarding passes; passengers at the end of the line pay this unofficial middleman for a boarding pass in order to board ahead of the others. I knew that if the plane was full, I could be out of luck, even with a boarding pass. Thus, I got in line, carrying Ruth who was going crazy with the noise of aircraft taxiing around. I guarded my rear flank from the touts and their customers and, after standing there about a half hour, managed to take my seat.

An hour later I landed at Kaduna. Here I met Adamu Asuku who was to be my driver for the next two and a half years. I probably spent more time during my years in Kaduna with Adamu than with any other person. I soon came to value his driving skill, but even more his loyalty and good sense. In Nigeria, a driver needs to find places within cities strange to him for which there are no maps. He has to perform simple repairs to the car, which is likely to break down far from home. He must assess the quality and negotiate the price of gasoline at bush stations, often the only places at which gasoline was available at all—illegal, roadside tanks with primitive pumps or jerry cans to fill the car. He has to be a well-spoken, problem-solving sort of person who can run errands, make appointments, and provide advice. Adamu was the second person I met when I stepped off the plane in Kaduna. The first was Alex Martschenko, the political officer during my first year.

I had been to Kaduna a few times before, but I could not remember all that much of the city as we drove in from the airport. It is a much more attractive place than Lagos, and, of course, much smaller. There is a great deal more space around buildings and along the major roads. It is in the north of the country, but not in the sub-Saharan region of the far north. It is a lot drier than Lagos, however, and vegetation is less lush. The general impression is less tropical, sparer, more bleached out.

At the time when British administration of Nigeria established three regions in Nigeria, Kaduna became the capital of the northern region, by far the largest with well over half the land area of the entire country. Kaduna was not by any means the largest town in the north, but it had the advantage of not being the residence of any of the northern emirs or other traditional rulers. More in the north than anywhere else, the British practiced indirect rule, through the traditional rulers, and wanted their capital to be apart from them. After independence, Kaduna continued in this role during the first six years, when the regional governments were power centers and the national government was relatively weak. The premier of the Northern Region in 1960 was Sir Ahmadu Bello. He came from the royal house of Sokoto and held the highest title, "Sardauna," under the Sultan himself. He was slaughtered in the first military coup of 1966, and his residence was maintained as a museum in 1991.

By the time I arrived in Kaduna, the former northern region had been divided into eleven or twelve states and Kaduna was the capital of just one, within a now highly centralized nation. Nevertheless, Kaduna was still recognized in many ways as a capital—partly because manufacturing and commercial development were strong there, partly because it was settled by people from all over Nigeria, of many ethnic groups and religions, and partly just as habit. Many of the wealthier and more prominent people in northern Nigeria maintained a home in Kaduna, even if their real origins and homes were elsewhere in the north. There were several important military establishments in and around Kaduna, and the town was a popular place for officers to retire. The establishment of the United States consulate dated from independence, although its continued existence was under question.

In the next couple of weeks, I settled into my house and office. The office itself was a pleasant building, constructed as a traditional northern house, with public entry areas in the front, and the living quarters (where traditionally the women and children would be found) in the rear. The offices in the back of the building all opened onto a covered walkway, with a pretty garden courtyard in the middle. Access to the compound was controlled at the gate, opened only for cars belonging to the consulate, and at a small, pedestrian entry controlled by our contract guard force. We had no Marine guards in Kaduna and depended entirely on the Nigerians who were trained by the Regional Security Officer in Lagos. They were stationed at all our houses, as well as at our offices and the warehouse compound.

The consulate covered many of the normal functions of American posts overseas. In the front of the building, we had the consular section, presided over by a Foreign Service officer and staffed with two others. This was where a good number of our visitors were headed, to get passports or assistance (if American) or visas (if Nigerian). Many other visitors used the library maintained by our USIS branch (headed by Michael Pelletier with about eight Nigerians) or called at the small outpost of the Foreign Commercial Service (staffed by a locally hired American and a Nigerian). In the back of the building, our fairly large administrative section worked at all their challenging tasks under the direction of Larry André. The Communications Section was tucked all the way in the back in a vault area that was closed and locked at night. The rest of the building was inhabited by me, the Consul General; my secretary, who was an American Foreign Service employee; and Alex Martschenko, who did most of our reporting.

In addition to this staff, there were two additional offices in different buildings—the newly established Peace Corps office gearing up for the arrival of the first group of volunteers and another that served as headquarters for a public health project funded by USAID and headed by an employee of the Centers for Disease Control in Atlanta.

One of my first jobs was to get to know all the people who worked for me or for the other agencies at my post. Although some of them, like the recently hired Peace Corps people, were new to the consulate family, a number of others had worked for the United States government for twenty years or so. Taken as a group, they were a good crowd. Individually there were a few bad apples, with whom we gradually had to deal. One of the worst was the Nigerian who supervised quite a number of the employees in our administrative section. He was abrasive with the people under him and unctuous in a way I hated to me and the other Americans. I believe a source of tension between him and the other Nigerian employees was his intensely evangelical Christianity. After more than a year, we fired him for having contributed comments to a virulently anti-Moslem paper in the aftermath of serious ethnic riots; he identified himself as a member of the consulate in a way that made it appear he was the consulate spokesperson. He also gave the consulate telephone number as a contact phone for a meeting of some new, evangelical Christian organization he was sponsoring. Although many of the consulate employees were devout Christians, others were equally devout Moslems, and it was essential for the peace of the workplace to leave the evangelizing at the door. We were quite relieved to have good reason to get rid of this employee.

149

Many employees were Moslem; one of the drivers was actually an Alhaji, meaning he had made the pilgrimage to Mecca during the annual Hajj. On one side of the building there was a small room where employees could perform the mid-day prayers, and we broke up at noon on Friday to permit anyone who wished to attend mosque. A number of the Christians on the staff were members of the active evangelical churches found all over Kaduna State. One tradition was changed under my leadership—the annual "Christmas" party. This change came partly by accident, since my first year we found that most of the Americans were going somewhere else at the holidays and it would be better to schedule the party for early in the new year. After that, we called it the New Year party, disassociating it from any religious connotation. There was some grumbling among the Christians on the staff, so at a full staff gathering, we talked it out.

As I became more familiar with the office and the staff, I began to see where the strong and weak links among the Americans lay as well. Alex, the political-economic officer, had been in Kaduna a year and had a good feel for the Nigerian north. He had a quirky sense of humor and was a resourceful and interesting travel companion. Larry, the Administrative Officer, was a Rock of Gibraltar in a sea of difficulties. Michael ran the USIS operation very effectively. He, too, had been in Kaduna for a year and had an excellent network of contacts on the press and cultural side.

My secretary had arrived only a few weeks before me. She was experienced, but seemed timid. She was also distracted by the presence of her daughter, a troubled and manipulative young woman who was about to travel back to the United States to finish high school. A tougher nut was the communicator. He was a man with wide-ranging skills, a retired Air Force sergeant, who single-handedly ran all the communications functions and also would rush out to fix generators or take care of other maintenance problems in "off-duty" hours. He had an unpredictably violent temper as well, which caused tension between him and the secretary whom he was supposed to be training to act as his backup in case he became ill or had to be pulled out for some reason. The secretary was not making rapid progress in learning the communications trade, and frequently came out of the vault in tears, unable to tell me what the actual problem was. In the end, I had to declare the training over.

A somewhat different problem was the consular officer who was in her first tour with the Department of State but was several years older than I was. Since white Americans look alike to Nigerians, and since she and I had, I suppose, several similar characteristics—we were tall and a little heavy, had short, graying hair, and seemed about the same age—she was often mistaken for me. I had the distinct impression she did not disabuse people of this notion with much force. She also enjoyed playing hostess at my dinners and receptions, which annoyed me no end; I had to impress on her several times that I was the hostess and she was there to help.

I knew from my experiences in Kigali that dealing with such conflicts on the staff went with the territory. I also knew from experience that when I was boss, I could not vent my frustration about anyone to some other member of the staff or, indeed, to anyone in the community at large. For me, this was one of the most difficult things about being head of a post and also being single—I had no one at home in the evening to bitch to and I didn't feel like kicking the cat.

Well before we had all settled in and shaken down with each other, I was summoned along with Alex to Abuja, the new national capital under construction about two hours' drive south of Kaduna. Vice President Dan Quayle was coming for a visit, and the embassy was collecting every spare body it could. Alex and I were completely superfluous to the operation, but it made the embassy people feel better to have us there, installed in the Abuja Hilton Hotel and milling about at all the meetings. We did go out one day to a village, where Quayle was to visit a development project, and speak to some of the people there about the visit. A major concern of the Vice Presidential advance party was "no funny clothes;" one of the most popular gifts for northern Nigerians to give visitors is a suit of traditional clothing, with a hat. Quayle was to visit another village with some crafts industries where they wanted to invest him as chief, with clothes, sword, horse, the whole bit. One American site control officer had the delicate task of explaining that the Vice President would be happy to accept the gifts but he would not put them on, nor would he get on the horse. There was great fear he would be made to look foolish in front of the press.

What drove the advance party the craziest, however, was the laid-back approach of the Nigerians. What drove the Nigerians crazy was that the Americans would not just let them get on with arranging the visit the way they wanted; rather the Americans kept insisting on changing the program, approving everything, inspecting every site, including the Presidential villa which was off limits, and in general taking over. The biggest job for us based in Nigeria was running interference between the two groups and interpreting the reactions of one to the other.

Things fell apart at the very start. The Secret Service had rehearsed the motorcade with the Nigerians, and the line of twenty or thirty vehicles left the Hilton for the first event of the day: the official greeting and meeting with the Head of State. Unfortunately, the motorcade thought the meeting was in one place on the presidential compound while the mounted horse guard that met the motorcade at the compound gate thought it was somewhere else. Horses and cars got completely entangled, and it took quite a while to get everyone lined up again and headed in the right direction. The meeting started twenty minutes late and, as such things are apt to do, went a lot longer than the scenarios said it should. From then on, the entire schedule was out of kilter.

My job, after whatever it was I was supposed to be doing at the presidential villa, was to be site control person for an afternoon meeting scheduled for Mrs. Quayle with a group of leading women professionals. This was to take place over tea at a lovely, thatched gazebo at the side of a lake. I arrived well ahead of the professional ladies, but they gradually collected under the leadership of the wife of the administrator of the Federal Capital Territory. They were all interesting women—lawyers, engineers, teachers, social workers—about twenty in all. Mrs. Quayle was very late, so I enjoyed immensely my opportunity to chat with them all. As I discovered during my time in northern Nigeria, if you could meet alone with women, they were lively, opinionated, strong people; only in the company of their husbands did they become quiet and deferential. When Mrs. Quayle finally arrived, I dropped to the background, and she began, quite stiffly, to converse with her hostesses. The Secret Service man accompanying her looked with some concern at the sky where an imposing late-afternoon storm was assembling. He wanted to bail out; I said maybe it would blow by. The thunder got closer and closer, a few drops of rain began to fall. Then the heavens opened, and we had a tropical downpour on our hands. We fled to the cars; umbrellas were useless. The party was over only twenty minutes after it started, and I collapsed in my car, soaked to the skin, laughing about the whole business with Adamu.

Back in Kaduna, I gradually settled in. Together with Alex and the political/protocol assistant, Mukhtari Shittu, we drew up a list of people in Kaduna I should call on. Bit by bit, I met the northern elders, some of the religious leaders, and the heads of commercial organizations and local businesses. Several Nigerian military training establishments were located in or near Kaduna, and I called on the commanders of those organizations. It took a lot longer to get an appointment with the military governor of Kaduna State, who appeared to be not very friendly to Americans.

In the fall of 1991, Nigeria was in the process of a transition to civilian rule. Elections to local government councils, the smallest political entity in Nigeria, about the size of an American county, had already taken place. Elections for state governments—governors and state legislatures—were a short time ahead. In addition to meeting the current leaders, therefore, I called on political party chairmen and candidates for office. The military government in 1991, in power since a coup in 1985, had constantly promised the return to civilian rule, but just as constantly canceled the process and changed the rules. At first, politicians were permitted to form their own parties, but then the Head of State, Ibrahim Babangida, stepped in and declared the process not representative of the nation as a whole. He banned a large number of politicians who had been active in the 1979-83 civilian government (the group I had known during my tour in Lagos). Then Babangida and his supporters simply created two political parties and began to control the entire process through influence, banning, and even occasionally detaining people. The group running for office in 1991 had been sifted through this sieve and consisted of largely untested, inexperienced politicians. Some of the more practiced politicians, having now been unbanned but not allowed to run themselves, stood behind these figures. It was a complicated situation, but we in the American diplomatic posts hoped it would go well and did what we could to encourage it.

In addition to these calls, I also met a number of the local media heads, under the auspices of our USIS director. Some of these meetings were pro forma—for example, with the editorial board of the oldest newspaper in the north, the *New Nigerian*. Others were highly interesting, off-the-record chats with some of the newer, more dynamic editors, such as the group that ran a weekly magazine called *The Citizen*. One was purely awful. There was a newspaper in Kaduna, *The Democrat*, owned by a wealthy businessman who was close to the military rulers. He was also the owner of the consulate office building. The editors at the paper were the worst kind of ignorant fools, full of themselves, jokily hostile to the United States, ill-educated and narrow-minded. We agreed before my visit they could tape the session for use in the paper, but I had the right to request the tape recorder to be turned off if I wished to speak off the record. After the normal greetings, I remarked I would be glad to hear their questions. The first one out of the mouth of the editor was, "Why does the United States hate all Moslems?" I knew I didn't want to be quoted responding to that question, as whatever I said would be twisted, so I had the recorder turned off before giving a careful, nuanced answer that most likely landed on deaf ears. As the interview began, so it went to the end, the editorial board enjoying what they thought was their proper put-down of an American diplomat.

I tried to travel as much as I could out of town—to Jos, in Plateau State; to Kano, the largest city in the north; to Zaria, the other large town in Kaduna State, home to the premier northern university and seat of the Emir. In November, I had a trip planned to

Sokoto, in the northwest corner of the country, seat of the Sultan of Sokoto, the nominal head of all Nigerian Moslems. We planned as well to visit Kebbi, a brand-new state that had been formed by splitting Sokoto. As it turned out, our trip to Sokoto coincided with a grand ceremony planned to "turban" a new Sardauna, the first one who would be named since the previous Sardauna had been murdered in the 1966 coup. The ambassador and his wife planned to come to the ceremony, so our trip also became one to support the ambassador's visit.

The Sultan had only been on his throne a year or two. His predecessor held the title for over fifty years. Generally a new traditional ruler is chosen by a council of "kingmakers" and comes from the royal family; the new ruler need not be the eldest son or a direct descendant, but rather is the most suitable person from among the extended family. The selection in Sokoto had fallen upon a retiring, scholarly member of the family but had been set aside by Head of State Babangida in favor of Ibrahim Dasuki, an enormously wealthy businessman. Before Babangida placed him on the throne, Dasuki had been head of the Nigerian branch of the BCCI, the scandal-ridden, Pakistan-based bank that had recently been reorganized. When it was announced that Dasuki would take the Sultan's throne, there had been bad riots in Sokoto and there continued to be great discontent under the surface. The Sardauna to be installed was a well-known figure, Alhaji Abubakar Alhaji (known as "Triple-A"), who served at different times as Minister of Finance and Ambassador to London.

During my call on the Sultan, a few days before the turbaning ceremony, I was amazed and appalled at the renovations he had made to the royal palace in Sokoto. I had visited there during the reign of the previous Sultan, when it was a simple, whitewashed building, quietly furnished, and, so far as a palace can be said to be, modest. It had now been turned into an opulent pad, with marble facings on the walls, ornate, gilded and imported light fixtures, and thrones in several of the public rooms with gilded work and fancy upholstery. Although Nigerians take the outward symbols of authority and power seriously, believing a man is as important as the car he drives, the house he lives in, and the jewelry he wears, this kind of ostentation was excessive. Traditional rulers were expected to live somewhat more simply than millionaire businessmen.

I remember the two or three days before the turbaning itself as ones of total frustration. Although we were out of phone range of the embassy, we did have a high frequency radio in our car. If we drove a short way out of town, we could radio the embassy and speak to the ambassador to tell him what arrangements we had made for his hotel room and onward travel. The ambassador at this time (one of three I served under while in Kaduna) was demanding when it came to his wishes on these matters, to the point of unreason. It turned out there was another event he wished to attend after the turbaning, and he wanted to fly directly to that town from Sokoto. There was simply no such flight, although he insisted there was. In Lagos, he kept being told there was this or that flight, but on the ground in Sokoto we were told there was not. He insisted on having a hotel room in the hotel he wanted, even though the protocol people wanted to place him somewhere else. We spent a lot of time looking for people who would know about the flight, or be able to put pressure on about the hotel; in the end, he flew on to the next place in a private plane of some businessman and didn't even stay in the hotel room.

The day of the ceremony itself came, along with one of the first days that year of *Harmattan*. *Harmattan* is a winter weather pattern, when the wind blows in from the Sahara carrying an abundance of fine sand; the air actually looks like fog, and, because the sun is covered, it can get quite chilly. November was early for *Harmattan*, but when we got to the airport, we could hardly see a hundred yards. The state protocol officer who was there to greet all the visitors coming for the ceremony told us there were up to twenty or twenty-five planes expected, from a large Airbus to small, private planes. We could not imagine how they could land, particularly as the air control radar was not functioning. There we stood, looking upwards, every once in a while hearing a plane pass overhead. Occasionally over the three hours we waited one would land. We thought the ambassador was coming in the Airbus, but could not be all that certain it had even left Lagos, so we had to watch each plane unload. After about an hour, we knew that the Airbus was overhead, since we could hear it and once or twice even saw its belly as it passed over the airport, crossing the runway at right angles. I began to be somewhat alarmed; the protocol officer was moaning, "Please, please don't land here. Go back. Go to Kano." I felt the same way. It was getting close to the time for the ceremony.

Finally the Airbus swooped down, this time on track with the runway, and managed to land. The ambassador and his wife disembarked. As annoyed as I had become in the past days at his unreasonable demands, I greeted them by saying with more than pro forma force, "I am very glad to see you." He answered, "Not as glad as I am." They had had a truly harrowing trip and had been overhead for almost two hours before landing.

We then went to the palace, where chaos reigned. We were shown into a kind of holding room, while the ambassador and his wife were invited to meet with the Sultan in a private reception room.

155

It was clear the ceremony, extremely late at this point because of all the holdup at the airport, was not going to be in the room where we were, but no one seemed to know where it would be or how we could get in to see it. Finally, the proprietor of *The Democrat* spotted Alex and me (the ambassador and his wife having disappeared) and led us to the place where the turbaning would be, shoehorning us in to sit on the floor in front of the throne, immediately behind the ambassador. More and more people packed into the room, which became dangerously overcrowded. The press corps was immediately behind me, shoving forward to get a better view. Finally the Sultan entered, and then Triple-A. A turbaning itself is just what the word implies—the honoree kneels before the ruler, while two members of the royal court wind a new turban on his head. In this case, there was a speech and some prayers and it was all over.

Getting out of the room was as difficult as getting in—a matter of shoving, trying not to lose sight of all the members of the party. The ambassador and I were waylaid by a TV crew and asked for comments. Then, we gathered up a traditional ruler from some place in southern Nigeria, whose royal regalia included an enormous collar and conical crown made entirely from coral beads; he also carried an elaborate staff. He had lost his car, and we offered him a ride back to the hotel. We had to shove through all the waiting vehicles, parked willy-nilly in front of the palace, where police in riot gear attempted to keep order. The coral-studded ruler was ahead of me as I indicated our Toyota Land Cruiser. He seized the back door handle to step up into the car, while poor Adamu tried to block him out, not knowing I was right behind. We ultimately got ourselves and our royal passenger sorted out, had lunch at the hotel, and then got the ambassador and his wife off in the plane in which he had found a seat. What relief.

Like the ambassador, I enjoyed some of the perks of office, but I did try to keep it in bounds. When I first arrived and began to pay my arrival calls on various people, they addressed me as "Your Excellency," a title we generally do not use in egalitarian America. For a bit, I tried to get people not to use the title but gradually realized I had to use some of the perks in order to have the necessary profile in the community to do my job. Within the consulate, the Nigerians referred to me as "CG" for Consul General, which I kind of liked. The American flag flew outside my house when I was in town, raised and lowered every morning by my steward. I also had the right to fly a fender flag, a small United States flag mounted on the right fender of the car, a perk I had always thought was reserved for Ambassadors and Heads of State. I only used it when I was on official calls, and even then, we only took off its cover a quarter mile down the road. One of my much earlier predecessors had been known in Kaduna as "Flags Walker" because he flew the flag every time he drove out the gate, even to go buy bananas down the street.

A perk I came to enjoy greatly was an invitation to the VIP area at the Kaduna Polo Club during tournaments. There were two big tournaments a year, and many of the prominent northerners attended. Either they played themselves, or their sons did, and I was often invited to sit next to them in the big, plush-upholstered chairs at the front of the grandstand. During the week of the tournament, all the horses were stabled or staked out in the shade underneath the unused grandstands that had been put up for a big African arts festival in the 1970s. Occasionally I was asked to flip coins at the start of a match or hand out cups to the winners. The second year I was in Kaduna, one of the leading Nigerian polo players (and also a member of one of the leading industrial families) invited an American team with which he had played in Palm Beach to come to Kaduna, so we had the fun of housing some of the members of the team and hosting a evening party for them.

The state government elections were finally held in fall 1991. The new governors were to be installed on January 2, 1992. I was asked by the ambassador to travel to Kano to represent him at the inauguration of that governor, who had called on him in Lagos. On that day, we had the very heavy *Harmattan* common that winter. I found myself in a cotton suit, sitting in an outdoor grandstand, facing directly into the sharp, cold wind. The dust was ceaseless, the din from the crowd down below was deafening, particularly after the new governor arrived. The ceremony was to take place on a covered stand constructed a short distance from where we were seated, but in the dust we could hardly see it. We could not hear a thing; we almost didn't hear the National Anthem when it was blared over the loudspeakers. I was freezing cold. I noticed that all the Nigerian men seated around me, wearing their traditional cotton baban riga (the flowing, embroidered gown), were also wearing heavy, padded jackets underneath. I wished for my long underwear. Another phenomenon of *Harmattan* is that the hair, eyebrows, and eyelashes of Nigerians catch all the dust, so that you have the impression of living in a land populated entirely by the elderly. When I finally got home that day and washed my own face and hair, I realized the skin on my face had been completely abraded by sitting in that dusty wind for two hours.

With elected state governments in place, it began to appear that the promised transition to civilian rule might actually occur. It was the second time I had witnessed the process in Nigeria. I was aware both that the first experiment of 1979-83 had failed and also that the current exercise had already been subject to capricious delay and manipulation. Many of the people I spoke with endorsed the idea of democratic, civilian rule for Nigeria, but as conversations with them continued it seemed to me the notion of how a citizen under such a system behaves was not internalized as it is in an American.

On our visit to Kebbi State in November 1991, I had met with the newly installed Secretary to the State Government, the highest ranking civil servant in the state. He told me he had been on a tour of the United States the previous spring, organized by USIS for officers in his position, to observe state governments in our country. One experience had stuck in his mind, and as we became more relaxed with each other, it burst out. "You Americans are so disrespectful to your President," he exclaimed. "While I was in the United States, I watched your news on TV, and I could not believe the things that were said about President Bush." This conversation was in late 1991. I tried to explain that even while he had been in the United States, the ranks were forming up for the presidential election the next year. I emphasized that in America we respect the office and its incumbent for the office he holds without unreservedly supporting the person. This distinction is not one most Africans are culturally prepared to understand. The elders in Nigeria, particularly in the North, are offered respect in their person as well as for their office. Far more than in the United States, incumbency carries an advantage since criticism of political leaders can be seen as disloyalty and lack of patriotism (to ethnic group as well as to country).

I had a conversation with the editorial board of the state-owned newspaper in Jos, capital of Plateau State in the center of Nigeria. The group was one of the most interesting of all the newspaper boards I met, and a number of the journalists were well informed about United States politics and policies. One of them asked me, apropos of our discussion of American and Nigerian elections, if money played an important role in American elections. I laughed and said it certainly did, for most campaigns depended heavily on TV advertisements that were expensive. I then explained that money in the United States was used in the opposite way from Nigeria—United States citizens paid money to political candidates to finance the campaign and exercise influence if the person got into office. The editors and reporters were astounded, for in Nigeria, the candidate pays the citizens to vote for him or her. It seems perfectly normal to the Nigerian voter to expect the candidate to pass out free soft drinks, t-shirts and money at rallies, paid for by the candidate and not by any election organization supported by citizen donations.

At this time and partly to support grassroots understanding of democracy, a program proposed by our Ambassador was finally approved. A little over a million dollars, provided from USAID funding and administered through USIS, would be used to establish linkages between various non-profit volunteer organizations in the United States and Nigeria. Thus the League of Women Voters connected to various women's organizations in Nigeria; an effort was made to bring the two bar associations together and so on. I generally felt the program looked good on paper but had the failing of many such ideas in practice—most of the money was spent on short-term visiting back and forth with relatively ephemeral enlightenment. In one case, in which the Nigerian organization, the University of Jos, was in our district, we became aware that the university official running the program used it to reward his supporters in campus politics with free trips to the United States. Many of those who took the all-expenses-paid (by United States taxpayers) tours were not directly connected to courses in political science or constitutional law.

In Kaduna State, the new civilian governor was a perfectly pleasant man, well connected to the military through his family, who clearly had no impulse to improve funding for the social infrastructure in the state. Payment for teachers and health workers was made irregularly at best. Hospital and clinic supplies and equipment continued to run out or deteriorate without replacement. As a prolonged strike by the public school teachers continued after his inauguration, I concluded I had to pay the private school tuition for the elementary school children who lived on my compound (six of them), who otherwise were running wild and forgetting what little they did know. I paid dental bills for one of them to see a private dentist after neglectful treatment at the public clinic. These were facts of life in all Nigeria.

During 1992, the civilian state governments were in office, but it became ever more apparent they had to take their direction from the military. One major cause for this was the way state governments were funded. Although they did collect a small amount of taxation and fees locally, by far the largest part of the available money came from the allocation to the states of their portion of the oil revenues collected by the national government from the oil producers. The governors and their cabinets had relatively little leeway. There was no nationally elected legislature or government to allocate the oil funds, but rather a commission appointed by the military rulers of the country. The cow providing the milk to the governors was milked by the military.

I found it interesting but discouraging by fall of 1992, when I was accompanying the new Ambassador on a trip through the north, to hear one of the elected governors echo a line the military was putting out about yet another delay and revision of the civilian turnover. The new message was that the transition would take place, "so long as the political class, the civilians, behave themselves." Here was a civilian, elected governor siding with the military against a free elective process. The attitude also revealed why, universally I believe, military government cannot succeed. Soldiers like a clear chain of command; they are trained to be precise and clear in giving orders; they do not look for discussion and negotiation, but for compliance. The messiness and compromise of democratic politics are not compatible with the discipline of military life.

In late 1992, General Colin Powell, then Chairman of the Joint Chiefs of Staff, paid a visit to Kaduna during a stop in Nigeria. He addressed the students of the Command and Staff College, and eloquently defended the American tradition of civilian control of the military. His remarks met with great enthusiasm from his audience, but it was a visit of one afternoon.

Against this background of political transition, the rest of the business of the consulate went forward. I had to do a fair amount of official entertaining, often on the occasion of visits of people from Washington or Lagos. Since the two hotels in Kaduna were deteriorating in quality, I housed most of the visitors as well. I was lucky to have two men working for me who were experienced, capable, and honest. Saleh, the steward, who did all the cleaning and laundry, had worked for my predecessors for eighteen years. Sebastian, the cook, had been with the consul general for only about two or three years before my arrival, but he was experienced in producing western-style food. This was the first and only time in my life I had a household staff to which I could announce that twenty-four people were coming for dinner in a week's time and find the entire party properly produced.

Sometimes visits took unexpected turns. At one point we had a visit from a group of three people conducting some kind of study of the Foreign Service personnel system. They came to Kaduna over the weekend, and on Sunday a number of us from the consulate went with them for lunch at a pleasant, outdoor restaurant some miles out of town. We enjoyed an excellent meal and chat with the visitors, who were to catch a flight back to Lagos scheduled for late afternoon. As we broke up from lunch, it was decided that Adamu would take the visitors directly to the airport on a bypass road, while I would drive through town to drop off two of the consulate people and continue on to say goodbye to the visitors. The traffic in to town was dreadful due to streets flooded in a sudden downpour. I was later getting to the airport access road than I planned, and as I sped along, I suddenly saw Adamu coming the other way, a half hour before the flight was to leave.

It turned out the flight had left forty-five minutes early, no reason being given. Adamu had arrived with the visitors, and when he purchased their tickets he learned the flight had boarded and was ready to taxi for takeoff. He dashed out on to the aircraft parking area, the visitors in faint pursuit, and waved down the pilot who was indeed turning the aircraft around to head for the runway. The plane stopped and the steps were let down for the visitors, one of whom was an elderly, somewhat stout, retired senior civil service employee who had never run to catch a plane in her life. Only in Nigeria did we flag down a jet plane the same way a New Yorker waves at a taxi.

Another Sunday afternoon, following something like the same program, I drove the DCM and his wife, who had spent the weekend with me, to the airport. The flight they hoped to catch appeared not to be there. The only aircraft in sight was a commuter-sized Tupelov plane purchased by a new airline that was offered a good deal from the collapsing former Soviet economy. This aircraft was flown by Bulgarian crews, and, while the flight was boarding, the two crew members stood off on the side, watching in disbelief. It appeared this flight would be the last of the day, and there was a shoving crowd trying to get on before the seats ran out. The plane entry was in the rear. People were crowding up the rather fragile set of steps and being squeezed over the sides. The boarding officials were literally stuffing people up through the entryway, heaving one woman so that her skirt was rucked up, showing quite a bit of underwear. Perhaps the ground crew had seen film of Japanese subway stuffers on TV. Although the DCM and his wife had legitimate boarding passes, they decided, after we watched the scrum with increasing dismay, to stay another night and take the first flight in the morning.

The airport was almost always a rich source of stories. One time I went there to meet a flight from Lagos, bringing with it the head of the counter-terrorism office at the State Department. He intended to spend only a brief time with us, and the embassy had decided to rent a small private plane for his trip. A major concern had been getting a promise of fuel for the return flight; we also had to get overflight and landing clearance for the flight, given by an office out at the airport. I arrived in good time and stood out on the arrival side of the airport, where I was joined by a Nigerian wearing the cheap black suit that was inevitably a uniform of the security services. This person asked me who I was, and I gave him my card, adding I was there to meet a flight from our embassy. He said I had not asked him for permission for the flight to land, and I countered with the information about our clearance. He insisted he had to be asked for clearance, so I asked him for his card "so I know where to find you the next time." He said he had no card and wanted to know why I wanted it. By this time I knew such a ridiculous conversation could only be carried on by someone from the State Security Service. It was of course no secret that our counter-terrorism man was in the country, but that title had produced this man at the airport.

The reason we were particularly anxious to have the head of the counter-terrorism office visit us in Kaduna was an outbreak of serious rioting in Kaduna State and town some months before. The trouble happened while I was on leave in Washington. A long-simmering dispute in a village about an hour's drive from Kaduna erupted on a day when an investigative report about the trouble was to be released. Both Moslems and Christians lived in the village, from which the trouble spread to Kaduna where there were settlements of people from the same area. Although the dispute initially was about land and the location of the village market, it became an ethnic and religious fight. In Kaduna the trouble went on for several days and caused many deaths and a lot of damage.

By the time I got back from Washington, the violence had been brought under control, but people were understandably very upset and frightened. On my first day back, I tried to see all our employees and make sure they were unharmed and that their families were okay. Many had been close to the trouble, but fortunately no one in their immediate families had been killed or injured. Our staff was concerned about what could be done for them if trouble broke out again. They were aware that we had contingency plans for Americans, and they wanted to know what protection might be extended to them. It was that concern that the counter-terrorism chief addressed during his short visit to Kaduna.

Much of our reporting in this first year, then, centered on the political activity in the northern states, the new state governments, and the aftermath of the trouble in Kaduna.

Another side of my duties involved attending various ceremonies or calling on families that had suffered bereavement. Under Moslem tradition, although the burial is held within the day of death, the family holds a wake at home for seven days after the death. The men and women sit in different rooms. Since I had an official standing and also was a woman, I was fortunate to be able to participate on both sides of the gender divide. Generally my condolence call was official, but once or twice the family were friends, making the visit more important and also more personal.

Weddings were obviously more enjoyable, but could be confusing as well. One time the bride was the daughter of an important local businessman and politician, whose wife I knew as the proprietor of a school on whose board I served. I received the invitation, which outlined about five days of events, all explained in Hausa, the *lingua franca* of northern Nigeria. The protocol assistant tried to tell me which ones were appropriate for me to attend. Invited guests do not, under Moslem tradition, actually attend the marriage itself, nor, interestingly, do the bride and groom. The tie is actually bound by representatives of the family who meet together with the imam and agree between themselves that the young couple should be married and discuss the terms of the union. The imam then blesses it. Around the edges of this transaction, various parties take place, usually sex-segregated in more traditional families. The bride's girlfriends and sisters help her move her things to the house the groom has prepared for her; the groom's male buddies get together with him. There is music and dancing in traditional forms. More modern families are now including one or two joint parties for all the friends, male and female, but this is by no means the rule. I went to one such wedding, when there was a luncheon in the afternoon for just female guests to congratulate the bride and then a large dinner-reception in the evening for both male and female friends. The groom's father remarked to me that the elders of the community were not there, as they found such an event too modern and untraditional.

Another time I was taken to a naming ceremony by a friend of mine, the wife of my polo-playing acquaintance. This took place in Kano, a far more thoroughly Moslem and traditional city than Kaduna. The baby had been born into the Dantata family, one of the wealthiest and yet most traditional of the Kano families. The scion of the family, on whom I called when I was in Kano, had four wives and twenty-seven children, and many of his children were also in polygamous marriages. The new baby was the son of one of the sons; the mother of my polo friend was a Dantata cousin. The Dantata compound was teeming with people when we arrived, both on the male side and on the female side. My friend led me in, and we greeted the baby's mother, inspected the cause of all the excitement, and congratulated everyone. We then went into a smaller room where the older women, including my friend's mother-in-law, were seated on floor-mats; they laughed as I tried to get down to floor level in my high-heeled shoes and tight skirt. After we paid our respects, we then moved through the crowd as my friend was whispering to me, "This is Amina, who is the second wife of Bello's son by his third wife," and other such confusing explanations of who was who. At the end of the afternoon, I asked her if she had to pass an exam on the family before her own marriage.

In addition to these family ceremonies, I also attended the traditional public ones that took place on Moslem holidays. At the end of the fasting month of Ramadan and again, seventy days later, during the period of the Hajj, there are big festivals, marked at the courts of the Emirs by elaborate ceremonies. I tried to attend these in different towns, although the general outline was the same. The

163

Emir rode on his horse to the public prayer ground (no mosque being large enough to hold the crowd), offered prayers and, on the second of the two feasts, slaughtered a ram to mark the remembrance of Abraham's sacrifice of the ram in place of Isaac. Then, with great celebration, the Emir rode back to his palace and, seated on a grandstand, received the greetings of his people. Each major member of his council led a group of mounted followers to salute the Emir; often they galloped up as fast as possible and reined in the horses just in the nick of time. They dressed in traditional clothes, many as warriors, carrying spears. Foot soldiers throughout the crowd carried "Dane guns," primitive one-shot rifles, which they shot off to great effect from time to time. There was great color, noise, and dust, and it was all a good deal of fun. For those who had been keeping a strict fast for thirty days, there was more than enough reason to let go. Modern, up-to-date citizens in the north don't pay all that much attention to these court ceremonies; they often find the emirs outdated and powerless. But I was an outsider and a visitor, and it provided a glimpse of cultural color from the old days.

One year, I spent a full day of Ramadan, the thirty-day Moslem fast, with my friend in Kano. I traveled up the evening before and then woke before daylight to have some breakfast. Once there was a faint daylight (enough light to distinguish the color of a red thread), the fasting started. From this point, until the evening and the breaking of the fast, no food or water could be consumed. The exact times of the fast are published in the newspapers and announced over the radio. In the evening, my friend told the kitchen staff the fast could be broken. Everyone at that point took a drink of milk and then performed the evening prayers. Following the prayers, the real breaking of the fast began. We sat on the living room floor and enjoyed a succession of tasty appetizers, fruit salads, and later on, delicious stews. This is a time when many Nigerians will drop in on friends to break the fast with them and nibble on the food. I only kept the fast for a day, but it was an interesting insight into an important part of the year for northern Nigerians.

A ceremony recognizable to Americans was the university convocation I attended at Ahmadu Bello University, in Zaria. ABU is the oldest university in the north; it has suffered like all the rest of Nigeria's universities from the deterioration of its physical plant, nonpayment of the staff (who then must look for other sources of income), and lack of funds for such basic items as library acquisitions and laboratory supplies. It is depressing to see institutions like this that started off with high standards and hopes now unable to maintain them.

In the fall of 1992 I was approached by a member of the ABU administration about the university's wish to confer an honorary degree on former President Jimmy Carter. Carter enjoys enormous popularity in Nigeria, as the first sitting American president to visit Africa and also as head of an organization that still does many valuable things for grassroots Africa. Carter's schedule did not permit him to come in person to receive the degree, and I was asked to receive it in his place. Our USIS library provided information to the professor who was writing the citation for the degree. In January 1993, therefore, I found myself processing in to the stands, with trumpet fanfare, academic robes all around me, and rows of students about to receive their own degrees.

About three hours in to the ceremony, the time came for the honorary degrees, and I stood up when President Carter's name was called. I stood at the edge of the stage, facing the University Pro-Chancellor (somewhat akin to the Chairman of the Board of Trustees). In this case, the Pro-Chancellor was a traditional ruler, the Lamido of Adamawa, an emirate in the far east of Nigeria. He was an ascetic looking, bespectacled man, dressed in his traditional robes with the white turban tied with two wings sticking out the top—I called these rabbit ears within the consulate walls. We snapped to our marks, and the citation began with the sentence, "Jimmy Carter was the first American president born in a hospital." I knew at that point, with a sinking heart and a full bladder, that I would be standing there quite a while, looking in the eyes of the Lamido, who was about two feet away. I tried to remember advice I had once received from a military attaché when we watched military students fainting at a parade—do not lock your knees. The TV cameras were also whirring away, so internally I kept saying to myself, "Don't lock the knees. Don't fold your hands together around the bottom of your stomach. Look interested and engaged!"

Finally the citation ended, the degree and robes of office were handed over, I shook the Lamido's hand and took my seat. A pleasant memento of that day, which I did enjoy, is a signed photo from President Carter and a warm letter of thanks from him. I believe a number of people in the audience thought I was Mrs. Carter, for several of them made it a point to come up and ask me to convey their greetings to "my husband."

The "launching" was another public event I often attended. What I enjoyed most was dedicating a project funded by the United States. In one case, we had used the Ambassador's Special Self-Help Fund that makes small grants of up to $5000 to communities with project proposals. A Peace Corps volunteer working in a local government area had organized the local villagers to apply for funds for a proper dug well to replace the surface wells they had been using. A deeper supply of water would help control the infestations of guinea worm. The head of the particular local government area struck me as an energetic leader who was trying hard to make a difference to his community.

The ceremony itself was terrific. There were, of course, speeches from all and sundry. But there was also a period when everyone got up to perform a kind of line dance around the area where the ceremony was held. A play staged by local villagers dramatized the need to use safe drinking water to control disease. The crowd was large and affable. We were offered lunch in one of the family compounds, and finally I got back in the car to return to Kaduna. Adamu informed me the villagers had insisted on presenting two chickens and a heap of yams as a gift to me. As we drove toward the divided highway, the chickens clucked for a while and then fell silent.

About thirty miles from Kaduna, we suddenly had two blowouts. This was a serious problem, since our Chevy Suburban had tubeless tires that were not easy to get fixed in Nigeria. Adamu replaced one of the tires with the spare, and then jacked up the other side and removed that tire. Rolling both tires in front of him, he set off in the direction we had come from where he had seen some roadside vulcanizing shops. There are no recognizable service stations along Nigerian roads outside towns, just huts where equipment is stored. All kinds of services are provided out of these minimal workshops, often of skilled quality. A late-model Mercedes stopped to offer Adamu a ride, and it proved to be the proprietor of *The Democrat*. He returned Adamu to our vehicle with the patched tires and stayed to be sure all would go well. When Adamu opened the back of the van to replace his tools, the publisher began laughing. It was now clear why the chickens had stopped squawking—they had been feasting on the yams, which had large bites out of them.

Meanwhile, the build-up to the elections for the national government came closer. The two-chamber National Assembly was elected in early 1993. At this election, as at the previous ones, embassy and consulate officers tried to observe as many of the polling places as possible. Polling was held openly. First, all the registered voters reported to their polling stations with registration cards, and their names were checked off on the registers. Once there, they were not allowed to leave, and the crowd became larger and larger. At the appointed time, perhaps two hours after the gates first opened, the election officers announced that the voting would start. Photos of the candidates were displayed, and everyone was invited to line up in front of the photo of his or her choice. In Moslem areas, men and women formed different lines to preserve modesty, for they all had to pack closely together. A voting officer then walked down the line, counting out loud as he or she tapped the shoulder of each person. The number at the end of the line was then entered on sheets, observed by representatives of each candidate. The purpose of this system was to eliminate the possibility of ballot stuffing and manipulating ballot boxes at the end of the day; transparency won out over the secret ballot.

With the National Assembly elected, there remained only the Presidential elections to complete the transition that had begun with the local government elections two years before.

The civilian governors had settled into office; many of them were proving to be fairly mediocre, including the one in Kaduna State. We became aware through the visa window of some strange shenanigans involved in a business deal in which an American was involved. Over the months in which this deal simmered along, I was convinced that someone was snookering someone else. The only question in my mind was whether the American was snookering the Nigerians, or the Nigerians him, or whether each thought he/they was snookering the other.

In the winter of 1993, when I was visiting the Kaduna Chamber of Commerce offices to firm up arrangements for our participation in the annual trade fair, one of the people in the room approached me about some visas refused to colleagues of his. I looked into the matter and learned that about ten people had applied for business travel visas to "inspect a bus factory." The person who refused the visas told me the applicants mentioned rather large sums (several million dollars) but seemed to have no knowledge of business practices at all. As time unfolded, it also became apparent many of the men involved, and particularly the chief Nigerian on the project, belonged to a trade organization in town theoretically established to promote Nigerian-American trade which the members believed gave them automatic rights to American visas. We had continual trouble with this organization.

The bus factory became a nightmare. After we granted several visas for the more reputable members in the group to travel to the United States, we then faced repeated requests for more visas for various "experts." One, claiming to be an electrical engineer, was asked by the consular officer precisely what his role in this venture was. He replied, "Oh, you know, I look at the wires and see where they go." Then the visa requests escalated into a gubernatorial progress, almost on the scale of Queen Elizabeth I. Kaduna State funds had apparently been committed to the project by the governor, and now he proposed to travel to the United States, accompanied by several members of his cabinet, his personal assistant, a security man or two, and two "secretaries."

167

Gradually the outline of the project came to light. An American businessman specialized in buying up disused factories and machinery, and then either selling the entire building and contents off or disposing of the machinery. He advertised in a journal published by the United States Department of Commerce. The head of the project in Nigeria was drawn to the idea of buying an entire abandoned factory in Oklahoma that had manufactured buses. All the machinery would apparently be disassembled and shipped to Nigeria and make its way from the port at Lagos, five hundred miles by two-lane road, to Kaduna. There it would be reassembled on land made available by the governor and produce buses. It seemed a transportation company in the east of Nigeria had been lined up as a major customer. The engines, I was told, would be shipped in from Romania; the sheet metal for the bodies would come from a steel factory the Soviets had been building for over fifteen years in Nigeria that had virtually no chance at all of being completed. All this was to take place at the same time as General Motors had a joint venture in Lagos to produce buses. I asked at some point in these conversations if the buses to be produced by the Kaduna factory could be manufactured at a unit price that would be competitive with the Lagos operation. I got blank stares.

Two things distressed me. One was that public money in Kaduna State had been invested in this feckless adventure. There must have been kickbacks all over town to have secured that commitment. The second was that, when the American businessman involved in the venture finally turned up in Kaduna, I had him come privately to my office where I tried to explain my uneasiness with the project. He had been properly wined and dined, introduced to folks he believed to be influential, and he was having a great time. The more I tried to point out the unreality of the plans, the more he assured me he knew what he was doing and if he did not get his payment by a date certain, he would back out. I told him the consulate was not going to issue visas to all kinds of seemingly unqualified people to keep traveling to Oklahoma to "inspect" the factory. What finally happened to this project I cannot say. For one thing the military coup in the fall of 1993 removed the governor from office and I have no idea whether the new military administrator was brought in to the deal or not. Whenever I am tempted to think protection of American interests abroad is an easy job, I remember this saga and the difficulty of determining exactly where American interests in the entire matter lay.

As the supervisor of the consular officer, I was required to review all her refusals at the end of the day. I frequently questioned them, particularly in cases in which the person had reapplied with additional documentation or some prominent person was interested.

We had a change in consular officers in the winter of 1993, and the new arrival had some interesting talents. Two officers before her, there had been an incumbent who attended religious seminary for a time, and word was out on the street since then that ministers of religion or Bible students would receive especially sympathetic treatment. This actually was not the case, but the flow of purported men of the cloth continued. As I read Monica's grounds for visa refusal in such cases, I kept finding remarks such as "Claims to be Bible student but can't name books of Pentateuch," or "Has no idea where Paul's first missionary journey went." Monica was the daughter of a Baptist pastor and knew her Bible backwards and forwards; I can't imagine what the people standing at the window in a clerical collar rented for the day thought when subjected to what I called "The Eppinger Bible Quiz."

By late winter 1993, the presidential election was in full gear. The military government had thought up a nomination process that was incredibly complicated. Anyone running for president had to jump through a series of conventions, beginning at the local government (roughly county) level. Delegates for each hopeful candidate would be elected at that level, and then move on to state, and finally national nomination conventions. This was the good, military, chain-of-command concept—squad, platoon, company and so on. Its underlying purpose was to insure that the final two candidates had organized and garnered support throughout the country. The specter of regional dissolution is a constant presence in Nigeria; it happened once in the Biafra secession, and fear of a repeat is not necessarily misplaced.

In practice, however, one thing that happened was that several prospective candidates realized they could knock off serious competition at the local level and thus not have to face genuine competition when they got to the national conventions. The two who ultimately won their parties' nominations set out to buy up delegates at the local level to vote for them, and a few well-respected politicians were eliminated in the first round. More fell at the second hurdle. The candidate for the NRC, supposedly the right-of-center party, a northern businessman named Tofa, engaged in this behavior to the anger of the Northern elders, who still thought they should have a major influence in choosing a candidate. The SDP, left-of-center, candidate was Mashood Abiola who also had millions to spend. Both men, interestingly, thought the military head-of-state General Babangida was behind them; Abiola in particular thought Babangida was a friend whose support would permit him in the end to win the election.

The campaign proceeded normally until just the week or so before the election, scheduled for Saturday, June 12, 1993. A challenge to Abiola arose in the courts, and a decision was announced on the Thursday before the election that the election should be delayed. Our embassy issued a press release the following morning regretting the decision and stating our belief that the election should go forward. By about noon on Friday, the government announced the election was on. I set off for Kano where I was to observe the election; another officer went to Jos, and two others were to observe in Kaduna. All inter-city movement was forbidden during election day, to prevent people from moving about to tamper with the process.

I was in the lobby of my hotel in Kano, speaking with one of the local political types at about 10:00 pm, when I had a call from Kaduna telling me the Nigerian government had reacted badly to the press release and withdrawn permission for United States diplomats to observe the elections. The next day, forbidden to travel until late afternoon, I had to putter about, visiting with a few people and otherwise cooling my heels. This was a pity, since Kano was a key area of support for Abiola, in spite of the fact that Tofa was a native son. Turnout was relatively light, but many northerners were irritated by Tofa's manipulation of the process. Abiola, a southerner and a Moslem, was seen by the less well-to-do as a man of the people, more energetic and more sympathetic than Tofa.

Once the travel ban was lifted, I returned to Kaduna and waited with everyone else for the results to be announced. Preliminary indications were that Abiola had carried the election easily and won support across the country. Suddenly, with about half the count finished, Babangida and the military council announced that the election was annulled, the counting would stop, and no results would be announced. It is still difficult to know exactly why Babangida took this step. My own belief is that he had assumed all along that neither of the two candidates would gain the necessary support in the different regions of the country, and he could then make a plausible case for stepping in to "save" the nation. When it became certain that Abiola would emerge a clear winner and would be accepted in the north in spite of his ethnicity, Babangida aborted the process.

Great trouble broke out in the Yoruba southwest of the country; there were riots and looting in Lagos and other cities in that area. There was some tension in the north, but no actual violence. Nevertheless, the State Department issued a travel warning for the entire country and, after a few weeks, decreed a drawdown of personnel. This meant that all dependents and non-essential personnel had to leave the country; people due for reassignment during the summer were asked to move up their departure dates; and anyone who was on leave or waiting to come to us on reassignment was not permitted to travel in to Nigeria. Such measures reduce the number of people who might have to be extracted in a hurry, but they understandably put pressure on the morale of the office.

At the same time, Abiola, the presumed winner of the election, took some unwise steps. He left the country in one of his own airline's planes and traveled to Washington where he enlisted the sympathy of the United States Congress. The Black Congressional Caucus, several of whose members knew Abiola in his business capacity, issued statements in support of his election. These statements were highlighted in the Nigerian press. In Kaduna, my least favorite paper, *The Democrat*, carried headlines claiming that Abiola had made a secret deal: in exchange for American military support to put him in office, he would grant the United States two military bases in Nigeria. Some people really thought this was true and refused to believe my argument that the United States was hardly interested in accumulating more bases at a time when, with great political and economic pain, it was closing a substantial number of bases everywhere else. I wondered out loud what use such bases would be and was told they could be used to attack Libya or Iraq; I pointed out that we had better places from which to do that.

One morning the ranking Nigerian employee at USIS told me the editor of *The Democrat* was in the lobby and wanted to interview me. I tried to evade the visitor but he told me he had just a few simple questions about our "evacuation." Once ensconced on the sofa in my office, he led off with a slam to the jaw. "Everyone in Kaduna thinks this United States evacuation is in preparation for a military attack on our country," he said, inviting me to deny we had such plans. It was hard to explain the difference between an actual evacuation and an ordered departure of dependents. It was tempting to say, "What possible interest would the United States have in invading Nigeria?" The ordinary citizen could not understand that since we had access to the crude oil in any case, there was no compelling interest. The editor sat there, his notebook open, ready to write down my denial. Finally, I said to him, "Write this down exactly. The United States has no interest in any violence or unrest in Nigeria. Our policy is to support peace and stability in this country.'" To his credit, he did quote me accurately the next morning in the paper, under a headline something like "UNITED STATES WANTS STABILITY, SAYS ENVOY."

The atmosphere of the two months following the annulled election was unsettled. The air was full of rumors about one plan or the next that Babangida might be contemplating. We had plenty of reporting to do, trying to sort out the more plausible possibilities from the cranky. The National Assembly that had been elected the previous winter was in session in Abuja, the new capital city. The big question was whether Babangida would go on the date in August he had announced or whether he would manipulate the process to get an endorsement from the Assembly to stay in power as the champion of order. Friends who were in the Abuja Hilton as the issue came to a head told me that the night before the Assembly vote, the halls were filled all night long with people caucusing and passing out money to secure votes. In the end, Babangida's efforts came to nothing, for by the narrowest of chances and procedural maneuvers, he failed to get the call from the nation he sought. He then announced the appointment of a civilian transitional cabinet that would govern until new presidential elections could be organized. At the ceremony when the handover took place, the face of Babangida's wife, Maryam, was carved in stone.

Babangida was gone, but the military establishment was still firmly in place. The civilian head of state was considered to be an honest man and good administrator, but he was no match for the army boys.

In November I was in Kano, accompanying our new Ambassador, the third during my time in Kaduna, on his first swing through the north. I had arranged a dinner for him at a local restaurant where he met a number of leading businessmen. We had a good evening, with lots of lively chat. We got in the car to return to our hotel and, some blocks away, were stopped by a policeman. I was in the front seat and thought Adamu answered the questions the policeman asked with less than his usual aplomb. I asked him if something were wrong. He answered that he had heard on the radio while waiting for us that there had been a coup and the military Chief of Staff, Sani Abacha, had taken over the government. We were not totally surprised, as just before leaving for the restaurant we had a call from the embassy to report rumors of such a move. In the car, the first word from the ambassador was, "Shit." He said it, but we all thought it.

Fairly rapidly the familiar forms of military government reappeared—the military council, military administrators in the states to replace the government, a cabinet of civilians who were relatively powerless, and so on. The United States announced a set of toothless sanctions on the Nigerian government. All persons in the government and all military officers who benefited in any way from the political arrangements were declared ineligible for a United States visa, and those visas they held were revoked. This ban extended to immediate family members, and that caused me some heartburn. One acquaintance was an adult daughter of a former politician who had agreed to be a member of Abacha's cabinet; there can be a number of reasons for such a decision, including a sense of patriotism and probably also a wish not to get on the wrong side of the top guy. The daughter had been accepted for an MA program in international law to supplement her first law degree, but we had to deny the visa because of her relationship to a member of the Abacha government. Although we appealed the decision to the highest reaches of the State Department, the answer remained no. This kind of guilt by association seems to me a major fault of a sanctions policy.

Even at the time I had accepted the assignment to Kaduna, there were plans to close the consulate. The new Nigerian capital in Abuja, planned for over fifteen years, was well along in construction, although much of the government continued to spend more time in Lagos than Abuja. Abuja was only about two hours by road from Kaduna, making the existence of two offices so close together redundant. For most of my time in Kaduna, a juggling act went on. The embassy did not wish to acquire a lot of real estate in Abuja if that was not to be where the business was conducted, but if the government really was going to move there with the transition to civilian government, we had to be ready with suitable office space modified for security and housing for our personnel. In an era of tight budgets, we could not pay rent for unused real estate. By the last year and a half I was in Kaduna, however, the decision was made to close Kaduna and move at least some of its operations to Abuja.

My biggest concern was the future of the Foreign Service Nationals in Kaduna. Just like Berlin where several offices had to be combined, rumors began to fly. If a Nigerian can imagine a conspiracy against him, it quickly assumes reality. I spent a good deal of time trying to find out from the administrative offices in Lagos what was planned and trying to assure the FSN's that nothing concrete had been decided. In favor of the Kaduna crowd were two factors: a large consulate would be maintained in Lagos even after the embassy moved to Abuja, and almost none of the employees there (mostly Yoruba and Ibo) had any desire to live in the middle belt of the country where Abuja was located. Finally the personnel office produced a staffing pattern with job descriptions for the office that would be built up in Abuja as Kaduna was closing down. I was pleased that all the FSN's in Kaduna who wanted to make the move—often difficult because of spouses' jobs and the lack of inexpensive housing and schooling in Abuja—were hired on.

As my departure became fixed, we also had to inform the owner of my house that we would not be renewing the lease. As at other posts, I was sorry to leave the house. Standing on four acres of land, it was unprepossessing from the outside except for beautiful

173

landscaping and a garden my predecessor had put in. He had also erected a thatched roof over the large patio. Maintaining this roof was difficult in a climate where termites thrive; at least one major reconstruction, as well as periodic thatching, had to be done just a few years after it had been built. Nevertheless, the patio was the site for almost all of my bigger parties—trade fair receptions for about 250 for example or large buffet suppers when people were seated at round tables all around the patio.

The interior of the house was very comfortable as well. There were double-sized living and dining rooms, with space to seat twenty-four for dinner, and each of the four bedrooms upstairs had its own bathroom, making it easy to house overnight guests. The security of the residence was another matter. There were sliding glass doors in several places, and the security officer from Lagos continually threatened on his periodic visits to install locking grills over them all. I could not imagine anything that would create a prison atmosphere faster, and I stoutly resisted to the end. All the doors and many of the windows had alarm sensors, so that a loud siren would go off if the perimeter were breached. This happened occasionally when the cook came on duty before I disarmed the system, and it always brought a call on the intercom from the guards at the front gate, checking to know why the alarm had sounded. I was usually in the shower when this occurred, so there was a good deal of rushing about wet and naked to calm everyone down.

During one visit from the security officer, he became concerned about the windows that could not be controlled with sensors because of the way they opened. He installed a bunch of motion detector sensors to watch those areas and put some batteries in existing ones. We retired for the night, only to have the system go off three times in the hours of darkness, for what reason I do not know. Perhaps the cockroaches so beloved by the cat Ruth were out for a nocturnal stroll. On each occasion the guards called from the gate; I instructed them to walk around the house checking all the doors and windows. Nothing was found, we all went back to bed, and then an hour or two later the cycle started all over. The next day, as soon as the security officer was on the plane for Lagos, I took all the batteries out of the motion sensors.

As the time drew near for my retirement and departure, people began to hold farewell parties for me. Although I am always pleased that people want to do something like this, I have a terrible tendency to become emotional and break down during the speechifying that goes with it. Even as early as the New Year party in 1994, which we held on my patio for all the employees and their children, I had gotten teary when I said this would be my last such gathering with them. Another big party took place on my patio a few days before my departure for all my Nigerian friends; this was a younger and more informal crowd than the usual official invitees and was a great deal of fun.

But the most emotional goodbye was the one to the consulate family. This party was held in the afternoon at the swimming pool owned by our office where much of our informal socializing went on. While we were enjoying our food and drink, the senior FSN working for USIS made a beautiful speech of appreciation and farewell, which I answered as best I could through my emotion. I was somewhat curious why a USIS employee had been chosen instead of the State Department protocol assistant who usually performed such duties. That man came over to me after the formal speeches and said he had, indeed, been asked to speak, but that he did not want to make me cry! I tried to tell him the crying was generally because I was touched and not because I was sad or upset. There were then some gifts to open; the FSN's had clubbed together to buy me a wall plaque that reads: "Sincere appreciation to Helen Weinland, U.S. Consulate General, Kaduna, Nigeria (1991-1994) From the FSNs. For the extra spice added to our career! Happy retirement." This precious memento hangs on my kitchen wall, the center of social life in rural Maine. Finally, after all the group pictures had been taken, the FSNs lined up in front of me and each said goodbye and wished me luck in his or her mother tongue. If I had been overcome with emotion before this simple ceremony, this was the icing on the cake. In addition to their wishes for me, I believed they were demonstrating their own diversity and unity.

Late Tuesday afternoon, March 29, I got into the consulate van with Adamu, and we started off for Kano airport. A friend from Kano came to the airport to say goodbye. Eventually, I had to start the tortuous job of going through customs and immigration and then wait in the VIP lounge until the wee hours of the morning when KLM stopped on its way from Accra to Amsterdam. The flight was called, and I headed out the door into the African night, carrying Ruth in her case; there, standing on the tarmac for a final farewell, was Adamu. Both of us broke down at that point.

Thirty hours later, I landed at Bangor, Maine, no longer a Foreign Service officer but ready for new adventures.

II: Thoughts

Dressing the Part

One of the stereotypes about diplomats that floats about in the public consciousness is that they are "striped-pants cookie-pushers." The stereotype is meant to conjure up days past when diplomats (always male) wore formal morning suits with frock coats and striped pants; these gentlemen purportedly spent all their time at receptions. I have never seen a diplomat in striped pants, except perhaps some males in seersucker suits. I never wore striped pants during my twenty years in the Foreign Service.

When I first joined the Foreign Service, I had been unemployed for a period of almost two years. I was paying my father back for a car-purchase loan, since the automobile I drove while unemployed threw a rod and was a total write-off. To compound my wardrobe problem and shortage of funds, I joined the service in 1974, just about the time when women's hemlines plunged from mini to maxi. My clothes were modified mini.

In Washington, in those days at least, women were relatively relaxed about the latest fashions, and my wardrobe was not a terrible problem. But the moment I arrived in Switzerland, it was clear to me that my relatively naked legs were conspicuous.

"Why don't you buy some new clothes?" asked a Swiss woman at our consulate in Zurich. "Your skirts are so short. No one is wearing them like that any more."

I responded, "Well, Marianne, I don't have any money at the moment."

This was not something she had considered, I think. Swiss women—indeed, European women—much more than Americans, consider staying abreast of the current fashion a necessity and not a choice. She was momentarily flustered, but I noted the extravagant compliments that came my way as I gradually purchased new clothing at prices that stunned me.

At least the stores carried Western clothing of good quality and taste. Sometimes fashionable taste in Europe did not coincide with mine. When I arrived in Berlin, all the women dressed in black and white; little else was displayed in the shops. The following year, black and white disappeared in favor of mustard, burgundy, and dark pea green, a palate calculated to make me look ready for a talented undertaker. Being in Europe was not always a solution to the clothing problem.

Most of the time when I was stationed abroad, even in Europe, I shopped through catalogues and received my purchases in the diplomatic pouch mail. This assured me of sizes I was familiar with and, more important, prices I could afford when I was in Europe.

A posting in Africa presented different challenges.

During my final posting to Kaduna, Nigeria, I turned increasingly to the local market. I was forced to replace most of my clothing while I was there. In my last extended residence in the United States I had hit a low weight during my lifetime seesawing attempts to control my waistline. Then, first in Berlin and, much more in Kaduna, I began the depressing and familiar blimping out process.

After a few months in Kaduna, I could no longer button and zip the summer clothes I brought with me. It was now fall, and I could not find anything in the American catalogues, which were flogging Polartec and down jackets.

Louanne Smith, one of the employees of the Kaduna consulate, married to a Nigerian and a long-time resident of Nigeria, helped start me on a career of buying locally made clothes. In Nigeria, most women do not buy off the rack. The process is much more fun.

First stop is the local market. In Kaduna, the market was in the center of town, a large structure with a cement floor surrounded by cement walls. Like most Nigerian and African markets, the commercial area had spread outside the market itself, first with booths constructed against the outer side of the wall, then with booths along the roads leading to the market, and finally hawkers who squatted along those roads with headloads of fruits, matches, cassette tapes—almost anything.

Usually, when I went to the Kaduna market, I parked in the lot at one of the Lebanese-owned stores, Leventis, which provided a fairly safe place to leave the car. From there I hiked the three or four block distance to the market entrance, dodging all kinds of taxis (the edge of the market was a drop spot for taxis traveling to other towns), hawkers, and beggars. The makeshift booths along the way, many of which were selling pirated cassette tapes, blared music at the passerby. Since the road was deeply ditched to carry the heavy rains in the rainy season, and since there were spots used for refuse dumps and other unspeakable purposes, I had to be careful where I placed my sandaled feet.

Within the market, merchants selling various kinds of products—cloth, housewares, children's toys—were generally grouped in the same place. If I was looking for cloth, I could wander at my heart's content once I got to the right area. In Kaduna, unlike the much more traditional market in the center of old Kano, the merchants included both Hausa men and women from groups like the Ibo and Yoruba in which mercantile activities are more often the bailiwick of females.

After a few visits conducted by people who knew the market and were familiar with the better merchants, I came to know who was selling cloth most to my taste. The only problem was that, even after a number of visits, I would get lost among the endless rows of similar booths. I knew that somewhere toward the upper part of the gradual slope on which the market was built there was a Yoruba trader who often had attractive tie-dye materials, but frequently I could not find the row of shops where he was located.

A common kind of cloth worn by northern Nigerians, men and women alike, was called "shedda." We would call it cotton damask, all one color woven with a repetitive pattern. Northern men have the elegant "baban riga" made from this fabric, embroidered by machine (relatively inexpensively) or by hand with raw silk thread (for much more money). Women buy the fabric for booboos, large, shapeless gowns, also embroidered, but also for more adventuresome clothing like pants with big tops and various kinds of suits with skirts.

Margaret Mama, an English woman long married to a Nigerian doctor in Kaduna, took me to her favorite shedda merchant. The introduction was all the more necessary since I was white and therefore, by definition, richer and easier to rip off than a Nigerian would be. The process of shopping in a Nigerian market is a delicate one—the buyer cannot immediately pay the first price asked, but also cannot insult the merchant by offering an unrealistically low price or accusing him outright of gouging. The price always has to be negotiated; once agreed on, it is firm.

This last principle was broken only once that I heard of. The second political officer who worked with me in Kaduna, Makila James, arrived at work one Monday morning still groaning over an encounter during the weekend with a visitor from the embassy in Lagos. Makila took her guest to the Kaduna market, where they shopped for cloth. The visitor wanted some linen to make a skirt. They found a fabric she liked, agreed on a price, and the length she

181

wanted was cut from the bolt. After the merchant cut the piece, the visitor insisted on paying much less. Makila begged with her to pay the price agreed (after all, when translated into dollars these prices were always very small), but the visitor refused. Makila was humiliated and angry, as well she should have been. However informal the system may seem to an American, there are rules that govern it.

Once introduced by Margaret Mama to her shedda merchant, I always returned to him when I wanted a piece of shedda for a new outfit. He carried a good quality (there were all gradations of quality, indicated by the number of stars printed along the selvage) and gave a good price, particularly to repeat customers like me. Of course, the price I paid was always higher than a Nigerian would pay, but that was to be expected.

You could laughingly tease the merchant, as I occasionally did, by saying, "Now, don't charge me that Baturi (white person) price; you know I know better than that." But there was always some kind of Baturi markup, and I was not that fierce a bargainer.

Having purchased the cloth, either at the market or at several retail stores like Madame Teru's (whose daughter Yemi was the nurse at the Peace Corps office), it was necessary to find someone to make up the garment. There were various solutions.

One was to go to someone with a small shop or home-based tailoring business like my friends Dupe Atoki, who is a lawyer but for a while ran a dressmaking business, or Lorraine Ekong, a doctor, who had a tailoring shop at her house. Both women were fun to work with, as they had good ideas about how to turn African cloth, especially tie-dyed or batik resist-printed local cloth or "wax print" factory-produced fabric, into clothes a Western diplomat could wear. Other times I went to a more anonymous business like "Beautyful" or "Queenie's."

And, to make up the shedda into booboos or pants outfits, I went to a building in downtown Kaduna where "Alhaji" ran a tailoring workshop of about twelve men seated at sewing machines. Here I chose a basic design from a catalogue of photos mounted in an album, was measured by the tailor, and then went back a week or so later to pick up the finished article.

As I have said, I turned to this activity first because I had become too fat to squeeze into my American clothes. In Africa, as well, I needed a great deal more summer clothing than I ever would in the northeastern United States or Europe, since I wore it all year long. And, of course, in Kaduna, I was often on show as the consul general, attending public events as an official visitor or sponsor or giving official receptions.

But I continued getting new items for my wardrobe in this way for two reasons. It was lots of fun, an enjoyable leisure activity. And I received an enormous amount of positive feedback from the Nigerians. They perceived my wearing of Nigerian cloth and clothes as a compliment to their culture and applauded a particularly successful effort. As I began to understand this, I began to insist on buying only Nigerian-made cloth.

This was much cheaper and poorer in quality than imported cloth. Once, after a tour of a textile factory in which I was given a selection of cloth as a gift, I offered a piece or two to my driver for his wife. He said, "My wife won't wear that kind of cloth!" I also learned that different groups in Nigeria prefer different designs and colors; the director of a northern cloth factory told me that blue and yellow printed cloth could be sold easily only to Ibo consumers, while greens and oranges were preferred by northern women.

One final observation about dress in Nigeria. In Kaduna, I was consul general in the district covering the entire northern two-thirds of Nigeria, an area inhabited largely by Moslems and much more traditional in its mores than the south. Although I was American and white, I still felt I would be able to conduct my business more easily if I conformed to the more conservative dress code of the northern woman, at least to the extent of wearing skirts that came well below my knee and avoiding dresses with straps or sleeveless tops. I simply felt it was unacceptable for a western diplomat to call on a traditional ruler in the north showing too much flesh, however normal that might be elsewhere.

But I never wore striped pants.

Feeding the Inner Diplomat

Unlike many people who have traveled all over the world, I am not a particularly adventuresome eater. I don't worry a lot about what I eat, but I don't go out of my way to find exotic dishes and learn how to cook them.

A good deal of my concern when I was overseas was the pure logistics of procuring enough food to eat. I have mentioned the difficulty of shop opening times in Berlin; when I was free to buy food, the stores were not open. This was true to some extent in Prague as well, but the problem there was compounded by the need to stand in line almost everywhere. Generally the lines at bread and dairy shops were fairly short, but produce stores often had long lines when the word went around that something good was available.

Just before Christmas in Prague, the government would arrange to import small quantities of oranges and bananas, tropical fruits that had to be paid for with hard currency. The lines at stores to purchase these rare treats could be tediously slow. A friend of mine in Prague, who was not a diplomat and had to shop on the local economy, told me of one time she was in line and a child behind her began to whine at its mother. The mother tried to hush the kid, saying, "They have bananas today!" to which the child responded, "What's that?" I often think of that as I cut up my daily banana on my bowl of granola.

In Africa, I turned the food shopping over almost entirely to the servants. They were, of course, much better bargainers than I was. They were also better judges of quality when purchasing things like rice that were sold in bulk. There were no brand names on which to depend, or descriptions like "long-grain carolina" or "basmati." They had to look at it, sift it through their fingers, and judge if it were relatively clean of sand before making a decision. Most important, the servants had the time to do the shopping,

184

stopping at one vendor or another. In Kaduna, whenever we decided to have fish for a dinner party, Sebastian mounted his motor bike and went to the best place in the city, far from the Central Market, to get the freshest specimens.

Although there was butchered meat for sale in the markets in Africa, it was not advisable to buy it. Instead most people who could afford meat purchased the animal or bird live and then butchered it at home. Prior to a large party at which I would be serving barbecued chicken, the outside sink ran red with blood. In Kigali, land of the thousand hills, we called the chickens "Olympic chickens," joking they became muscle bound from running up and down the hills all day. Most of the time, they were pretty stringy.

Traveling in the countryside in Kigali, it was not all that difficult to find food along the road, although the menu was pretty invariable. At the small roadside restaurants, I almost always spotted a fresh goat carcass hanging out back. As required, small pieces were cut off, and placed on skewers for roasting over an open fire. These brochettes were served with french fries and mayonnaise (the Belgian tradition). Since the meat had been slaughtered just hours before consumption with no time to hang and age, it was generally tough, but the eating experience was certainly better than what you get at McDonalds.

When I was in Kaduna, my friends in Kano sent me live turkeys every year for Christmas. These gifts were a mixed blessing. The first delivery was made at Christmas 1991, just as the consulate was closing on the Friday before the holiday. Literally a minute before I left the office bound for a wedding shower of one of the USIS employees, I was notified by the guards at the front gate that there were two turkeys for me. That year the solution was simply to take them to the party with me and use them for door prizes. The next two years, however, they were delivered to my home by an employee of my friend. I penned them up and tried to feed them for a few weeks, but in both cases at least one of them sickened and died. This unhappy outcome left me with a disposal problem, for I was unsure of the cause of death and I didn't want anyone eating the birds. I ordered them buried, but I don't know that my advice was taken.

On another occasion, the guards at the consulate called me at home on a Saturday to announce that a pickup truck full of yams had just arrived from the Emir of Minna for delivery to our political officer, who had recently visited the city. That officer was on vacation, and I had no idea how to deal with that number of yams. Yams, in Africa, are large tubers, perhaps a foot or a foot and a half long and weighing five pounds or more. They are a staple food in Nigeria and when I was in Kaduna they were expensive for the ordinary citizen. Had the consulate been open, I suppose we would simply have sent all the employees to the front gate to collect a share of the yams until the truck was empty, but I could not contemplate having a pile of yams in the driveway to deal with on Monday morning. I told the guards to accept a portion that could be piled up in their office, thank the drivers profusely, and not take the rest. I think in retrospect this decision was wrong. I probably insulted the Emir by not taking his gift, and we certainly could have distributed the yams by some means or other.

I never became fond of yams myself. Pounded yam is produced by boiling the vegetable and then pounding it in a large mortar and pestle. The finished product has virtually no food value except calories and is of a consistency of very sticky mashed potato. It is always eaten with some kind of spicy stew to give it taste. When the USIS director was about to leave Nigeria, friends said they expected he would miss a lot about Nigeria, for example, pounded yam. He allowed as how that was certainly one thing he would not miss at all.

In Kaduna, it was quite common for local businesses to send the consulate large gift baskets at Christmas. It was always a problem to decide how to deal with these. Returning them or refusing them, under strict application of United States government gift rules, would have been seen as impossibly rude. Although we got quite a number, there were not enough for every employee of the consulate to have one. So in the end we divided the contents into small plastic bags, making up enough for everyone to have one. Since each bag was different, we distributed them by drawing numbers, making the entire process a lot of fun for everyone. As some of the baskets contained bottles of wine or spirits, we distributed those through a separate lottery for non-Moslems.

The best African food is prepared and eaten in private homes. When I was traveling or entertaining in restaurants, I tried to find a good Chinese, Lebanese, or Indian restaurant. Most sizeable towns had one or two of these establishments. In Kigali, there was enormous excitement when a Chinese restaurant opened for business. The city already housed several fairly good French/Lebanese restaurants, but this would be our first crack at Chinese food. The venture was undertaken by a Rwandan diplomat and his wife, returning from a tour as Ambassador to China. They brought a Chinese cook home with them. The entire diplomatic corps was invited to the official opening of the restaurant, and most of us returned within the week with friends to sample its wares. The menu was incredibly ambitious. There must have been 150 dishes on it, representing some of the great delicacies of one of the world's most interesting cuisines. The only problem was that nearly none of them were available, nor could the Rwandan waiters explain very well what was available. We all continued to patronize the restaurant—after all, there wasn't all that wide a choice—but it folded after some time.

In Prague and Berlin, I ate in restaurants a good deal. I did most of my official entertaining in Berlin at lunch in restaurants, since I had no cook at home and I was far too busy to try to cook for company myself. In Prague, we ate in restaurants for fun. The food was almost always Czech, but Czech cuisine to my taste is good, although high in cholesterol. Eating out in Prague restaurants required reservations made through the embassy. Generally speaking, private citizens found it difficult to get into the restaurants that catered to the international crowd. An evening in a Prague restaurant was a leisurely and pleasant affair. Under Communism, there was no effort to maximize profit by having two or three parties per table each evening, so we never felt rushed to give up the table. One of my friends, learning I planned to eat one evening at the Opera Grill, said it was the only restaurant in which he suffered hunger pangs between the appetizer and main course—the service was that slow.

Many Foreign Service stories center on food—having to eat the bill of the duck in China, being offered the sheep's eyeball in the Middle East. Thank goodness I never had such things thrust upon me, for I could not have risen to the occasion. Nor have I retired to the Maine coast pining for African yams or Czech dumplings. I do just fine with my daily banana and granola.

Life Support

Shortly after I moved into my apartment in Zurich, I began to find it burdensome to clean it to the standards I like and to stay ahead of the piles of ironing. On the one hand, this was ludicrous, since it really does not take long to clean a two-room apartment with small kitchen and one bathroom. On the other, help was at hand in the form of a Spanish "guest-worker," Maria, who also worked for the political officer's wife. Maria came to work for me one morning a week.

I almost never saw Maria, since she worked at my apartment while I was up the hill issuing visas to the Zurich public. She was utterly reliable, honest, and hard working; her presence made my life a great deal more pleasurable. When there was a problem, however, we both became aware of a barrier between us—she spoke no German or English and I no Spanish. If there was something she could not understand or if I had a special job to ask her to do, we communicated over the telephone, through one of my visa assistants, who was living with an Italian boyfriend and could understand Spanish better than I could. Maria could generally make out from Janie what was what. An imperfect solution, but better than nothing.

One evening I arrived home after Maria had been there. On my bed was laid out a favorite blouse that Maria had ironed that day, with a note on top of it. I could tell the message was agitated, apologizing for something, but I could not tell what. The blouse appeared to me to be beautifully ironed as usual, ready to wear. No spots, no missing buttons. Finally I realized, turning it this way and that, that under the collar a good patch of fabric was missing— melted away by a too-hot iron Maria had placed there first. The location of the accident actually turned out to be lucky, since I assumed if it had taken me so long to find the hole, no one else would see it. I continued to wear the blouse for quite some time.

When I moved to Lagos, I moved from a once-a-week cleaning woman into the big time when I hired Innocent Ogbonna to join my household as cook-steward. In Nigeria it was the custom for servants to live in, and most houses of any size had free standing "quarters" behind the main building. At 4 Kingsway Close, where I lived, the quarters consisted of a cement building, divided into six rooms, one for each apartment, with shared toilet, shower, and cooking facilities. Innocent moved his furniture and belongings into the quarters assigned to him; his family remained in eastern Nigeria where his six children were in school.

An aside: the quarters inhabited by Innocent and the others who worked in our building were called "boys' quarters" in the colonial period. Male servants in those days were called boys, presumably to emphasize the dependence and childishness of incumbents. This terminology even carried over into Rwanda where the colonial language was French. Female house servants were called "boyesse," a feminized form of "boy" and the room in my house where servants could spend the night or take a siesta was the "boyerie." I found such words unbelievably offensive, and feigned incomprehension if anyone referred to the cook or steward this way.

The embassy administrative section in Lagos recommended that each employer negotiate a written contract with servants. This was not necessary but advisable so as to head off any disputes about holidays, working hours, and the like. In my case, I agreed to pay Innocent a fairly good wage. In addition, the contract spelled out that I was to provide him with both daytime and dress uniforms at certain intervals, one paid trip a year east to visit his family, a thirteenth month of pay at the end of each year (a kind of Christmas bonus), decently maintained quarters, and specified working hours. Any additional hours, say for dinner parties, had to be reimbursed as overtime. I felt comfortable with these arrangements, ones that few Nigerian employers and not all foreigners made with their servants.

Toward the end of my stay in Lagos, Innocent became quite ill. I found that I was his insurance policy, for health insurance, as we know it in the United States or in state-provided systems like those in Canada or Europe, is not found in Nigeria. I still do not know what the problem was—there was apparently some kind of terrible pain in his bones and joints. He visited a local doctor several times and, finally, left Lagos to travel home for treatment there. He returned only a few weeks before I myself left on transfer. Fortunately, he was able to find a new job with the military attaché at the British High Commission and, when I returned to Nigeria ten years later, was still working for the successor of that officer.

Innocent represented the first time I ever had anyone working full-time directly for me in my home. The relationship is one of both intimacy and distance, and for us egalitarian Americans it can be uncomfortable. Here was a person who knew everything about my private life, who washed and folded my underwear, who scoured my toilet, who, essentially, lived with me. Yet he also had his own life, and I exercised caution not to become involved very far in that. I had enormously greater means than he could ever hope to have; I had education beyond a college degree; I traveled the world and had a job that could occasionally bring me together with top political, business, and religious figures. These were advantages Innocent did not have and could not attain for himself, although when I saw him on my return to Nigeria several of his children were studying in universities and preparing for jobs in teaching, accountancy, and other professional pursuits.

I could express interest in his family, as he could in mine. I could bring some token gift back from a trip to the United States, for example. But it was important to make clear that there were limits in both directions. Innocent never asked for money beyond his salary, not even as a temporary loan against the next payment. I never felt guilty about not offering all kinds of assistance, which he could surely have used. This was a major benefit of the written contract, placing the relationship on a professional basis. And, for Innocent, the job was a good one—well paid by Nigerian standards, with some security even with the ever-changing diplomatic population since a well-recommended servant could always find a good job.

I did try to supplement Innocent's salary when I could. It was standard practice, when giving a large party, to hire the servants of colleagues as waiters and helpers, and I was happy to let Innocent know about such opportunities. He also took over a business from my boss's servant when she left Lagos. This was to bake desserts of all kinds for our embassy snack bar, using materials I supplied for him from the embassy commissary. For quite some time, this was a thriving operation, providing a good supplement to his wages, until the commissary management put two and two together. He was, of course, using cake mixes and raw materials I bought through the commissary, for which they were imported duty-free, intended for the use of American personnel only. Even though his sales were only to the embassy snack bar, at which both Americans and Nigerians ate, the commissary decided we were breaking the rules and he could no longer make money this way.

From Lagos to Prague; from Innocent to Blažena. Blažena was as different from Innocent as central Europe was from equatorial Lagos. Innocent was, for all the formal contract between us, a product of the colonial period. He inherited the deference toward the European employer built in to the employer-employee relationship. He would never have openly expressed opposition to me or any course of action I proposed. I was obviously aware of that, and on my part, tried never to do anything that would violate his pride or self-respect. When appropriate, I would ask his opinion about how to do things.

I didn't have to ask with Blažena. She told me what she was going to do, how something should be done, and what was what. If she wanted something from me, she asked. If I couldn't give it, fine. She worked for me three mornings a week (soft-coal-heated Prague mandated constant cleaning), and for other Americans at the embassy other days and times. Like Innocent, she found working for Americans a distinct advantage. In those days of Communist Prague, we actually paid for different services with three kinds of currency—regular Czech crowns (100 to a dollar as I recall); "Tuzex" crowns (10 to the dollar) which could be used only in special shops to purchase goods imported with hard currency; and "units," cigarettes and whisky.

Blažena received half her regular pay in Tuzex crowns, while being paid for extra work—serving at evening parties, sewing and mending, or, on one occasion, babysitting for my godson—in units. This alone gave her access to purchase and barter opportunities most Czechs did not have.

Blažena gave good value. She was, like Innocent and Maria before her, scrupulously honest and thoroughly reliable. She never missed work, and she never failed to meet expectations. Her advice was almost always worth taking, and her opinions were interesting. If she had to report on me to the secret police or let them in to the apartment, I don't think she did it gladly; for my part, I tried to make sure she would never have anything interesting to report or show them.

For one thing above all, I will always bless Blažena. One day, a woman who worked in our defense attaché office came into my work area and asked if I would like to have a cat. She and her husband had just adopted a kitten, but the husband was abusing the little thing. They were fighting about it, and she wanted to give it to someone who would treat it more kindly. I didn't agree at once, and I knew that Blažena was going to see a lot more of any pet and its mess than I would. I called home, where she was working that morning.

191

"Blažena," I said, "what would you think if I were to get a little kitten?" I knew she had been passionately attached to the dog of my predecessor, but dog people do not always like cats.

"Oh, Madame," she exclaimed, "oh yes, a little kitty. Yes, please take her. That would be great!"

And so, Ruth, or Rutka ("little Ruth") as Blažena called her, joined my household. Blažena loved Ruth as much as I did and took wonderful care of her. Sadly, not long after I left Prague, Blažena came down with cancer and has since died; but Ruth, who thrived on her love and care the first two years of her life, lived to the ripe age of eighteen before she was overtaken by renal failure.

From Prague, I was transferred directly to Kigali and, for the first time, inherited the servants of my predecessor. I served in Rwanda as deputy chief of mission; that meant the house was an "official residence," with two servants approved for the purpose of assisting me to entertain and keep a larger house going than I would normally have had assigned to me. At that time, there was a complicated formula for all ORE (official residence expenditures). Five percent of the incumbent's salary was deducted at origin, and the servants were paid from this amount; if salaries in the particular country came to more than five percent, the embassy budget covered the difference. That five percent was a deductible business expense on my income taxes. In addition to the salaries, I was also permitted to deduct anything I purchased for the house that was placed on the inventory (linens, cooking equipment) or used to support official overnight visitors (soap, toilet paper, and the like).

Thus, I was permitted to have two servants, one of whom, the cook, had worked for two or three previous DCMs. This was Jean, whose last name escapes me. Jean and I never really took to each other, although for almost a year we managed to struggle through. He was a competent cook, although not brilliant. Soon after my arrival, I hired a woman, Sopatra, to do the cleaning and laundry. It was not all that usual to have a man and woman working together on the staff of one house. I believe there may also have been tribal tensions. Jean was Tutsi, while Sopatra came originally from Burundi and may have been a Hutu refugee with permission to settle in Rwanda. I wasn't wild about her either, but, like Jean, she did her work competently enough.

Servants did not live on the compounds of employers as they did in Lagos. Their pay reflected the need for them to rent their own housing off campus, so to speak. Among other things this meant I had my main meal at noon, since on normal days, both Jean and Sopatra had to leave by 4 or 5 in the afternoon to get home before dark. After dark, moving around town could be dangerous. When I gave dinner parties in the evenings, my final task was to drive all the staff, both my own and temporary people hired from friends, to their homes. I always tried to hire people who lived more or less in the same direction, but all the same, I could find myself performing this chore at midnight in remote banana groves. It took me over a year to realize that one of the embassy drivers liked to work parties and, permitted to use an embassy vehicle, would take all the others to their homes.

One time, following a party given by the ambassador who had badly injured a knee, I offered to drive his cook and steward home. I dropped off the steward, and then found myself in the official ambassadorial vehicle (a Chevy sedan) with the cook flopping over in the front seat asking me somewhat incoherently why his flambéed bananas, the dessert that evening, had not flambéed properly. Most likely, I thought, because you seem to have consumed most of the brandy yourself.

Once Ruth joined the household in Prague, keeping her indoors was a major responsibility enforced on anyone in the house. I had made this clear to Jean when I arrived in Kigali, and the rule was that both interior doors to the kitchen were to be kept closed at all times except when actually moving through them, so that outside and indoor doors would never be open simultaneously. One noon I came home for lunch, however, to find both inside and outside doors wide open, leftovers heating in glass jars placed directly over the stove's flames, and Jean nowhere to be found. He finally came to my call and had no convincing explanation for these circumstances. I thought he was ill, possibly from malaria or something. Sopatra helped me get him down the steps and into the car, so I could drive him home. She was evasive when I asked her if she had any idea what was wrong. I believe he was drunk, but I had never spotted this problem before.

Not too long after this episode, I gave a dinner party. Jean was due to arrive at about 5:00 pm, to finish the cooking and help with table setting and other preparations. He came on duty well after that time, causing me great anxiety. I could smell liquor on his breath. Part of my preparation involved getting envelopes ready ahead of time with the payment for the casual help for the party. Earlier in the day, I had checked the cash in my wallet to make sure I had enough money in the correct denominations to take care of this obligation, and as I set up the envelopes in my bedroom, I found I was short a few notes. Thus, not only did I have a drunken cook, I also had a thief on my household staff. I knew both Sopatra and Jean had been in my bedroom as we collected chairs for the dinner tables.

The following day was confrontation time. I told Jean his turning up late and drunk the previous evening meant I could no longer have him on my staff. He protested, saying he was a good Christian and had not been drinking. I told him I would pay him the severance he was due, but that he would have to leave. His parting words were, "I could tell from the start you were an impossible woman to please," something he had probably wanted to say for ages. I also fired Sopatra, since I thought the circumstances pointed to her as the thief. She, too, protested, but ultimately left. I was now without servants altogether, and the situation was never resolved satisfactorily before I left Kigali.

Some weeks later, Jean and Sopatra came to the embassy cashier to collect their final severance payment. They arrived at the same time, and, according to the cashier, Sopatra went right for Jean, blaming him for her misfortune and accusing him of being the thief. I saw the tail end of this argument, and asked the cashier, whose judgment I trusted a long way, whether she thought Sopatra was innocent as she claimed. The cashier thought it more than possible, since Sopatra was so insistent so long after the event. I therefore agreed Sopatra could come back on the payroll.

Shortly before I left Kigali for good, I ran across a predecessor of mine in Washington. We chatted a bit and I told him I had fired Jean, originally hired by him and his wife, for drunkenness and theft. "Of course," was his only remark about these two behaviors, as if you could hardly expect anything else. I was furious, not so much that he condoned them, but that the cook had been passed on with not a single word about it. Fortunately, this was the only time I ever had anyone working in my private household whom I could not trust.

When I arrived in Berlin, I was determined to clean the house myself, since household help there earned astronomical amounts I could ill afford. This plan lasted about two or three months. By early fall, I realized I had hardly seen anything of the city or been able to enjoy exploring it, since my weekends were so taken up with cleaning the huge house I was assigned. Given my choice, I would have taken a two or three room apartment, since all my official entertaining took place in restaurants anyway. But I was burdened with a three-story, eight-room, two-and-a-half-bath house. The kitchen floor, perhaps fifteen by twenty feet of white tile that showed every mark, alone took an age to scrub. The master bathroom was two times the size of my current, very comfortable bedroom.

Reluctantly, I sought out and hired what I called the "Putzpaar." In Germany, a cleaning woman is a "Putzfrau," but I got a couple ("Paar"), Anna and Ivan Zeljko, who had originally come from Croatia twenty years before. Ivan was a carpenter/builder by trade, but health problems prevented his working at this job, and he enjoyed going out with Anna as a cleaner. She liked having him there for the heavier jobs, moving furniture and the like. The arrangement worked out fine for me, and for the others in the United States mission for whom they worked. The only bad part—for me, not for them—was the money, since wages for household help, as for anyone else in Germany, were pretty substantial.

Like Maria in Zurich, Anna and Ivan generally came when I was at work and I rarely saw them. Unlike Blažena in Prague, they did not have vibrant personalities; I remember mostly their underlying fear, probably shared by many foreign workers in Germany, that one day, suddenly, the rules governing their permission to stay in the country would change and they would be forced to leave. Although they obviously benefited from residence in Germany, presumably including good health care for Ivan's problems, they lived with an insecurity I would have found intolerable.

In spring of 1990, after they had worked for me some time, they asked me to accommodate a temporary shift in day or time. Ivan, Anna told me, was traveling to Croatia on a bus carrying a large number of expatriate Croatians to vote in the plebiscite about the future of Croatia. This was well into the post-Berlin Wall period when Yugoslavia was coming unstuck. I remarked to Ivan that I hoped the decision that would be made through the plebiscite would permit everyone in that area of the world to live together in relative peace and security.

"We don't want to live anymore with those people," he declared hotly about the Serbs. "They are Communists and not Christian."

I often thought of that exchange in the next couple of years, as Croatia was torn apart by civil war and involvement in the strife that then moved next door to Bosnia. At my departure, I had let Anna have the electric iron and ironing board that she said she wanted to take on their next trip home to visit her mother. When I listened to the BBC World Service during my morning shower in Kaduna in 1991—92, I wondered what had become of Anna's mother and my iron and whether Anna and Ivan were pleased with the results of the plebiscite he had taken such trouble to vote in.

In Kaduna, where I moved from Berlin, the household staff for my official residence included Sebastian Sossou and Saleh Moses Dawang. This was as good as it gets. Sebastian originally came from Benin, next door to Nigeria, and had been trained as a cook by, among others, the wife of a French employee of the local Peugeot assembly plant. Saleh came from Plateau State, close by Kaduna, and had worked for the American consulate in Kaduna for at least eighteen years. He started off as a garden worker but moved indoors

195

after some years. He worked for me as the steward, taking care of all the cleaning and laundry.

As in Lagos, both men lived on the compound of the house. Unlike Innocent, however, they had their families with them: Sebastian's five children, augmented by a baby girl born about a half year after my arrival, and Saleh's six children, two of them boys who left for university shortly after I got there and were home only for vacations. Sebastian also had a son who lived in Benin and visited occasionally; he was perhaps from an earlier marriage. So, on my four-acre compound, there were me, two families consisting of sixteen persons living in the quarters, and, during the day, five gardeners and five security men on the grounds. The gardeners and security guards were employees of a company that contracted with the consulate to provide these services, and I did not have to pay them. Saleh and Sebastian I paid directly under somewhat revised ORE rules. (Jesse Helms had decided to rule out the business-expense deductibility of the five percent. Those assigned to countries where the household wages came nowhere near five percent of our salaries had protested that it was unfair to charge the five percent when it was not fully used.)

Sebastian, of the two men, was more sophisticated. He spoke both French (Benin is a former French colony) and English quite well, while Saleh struggled in English. I soon discovered that to get accurate information from Salah, say about a telephone call or visitor in my absence, I had to ask simple yes/no questions. Either/or was impossible—he answered all such questions "yes."

Sebastian was also more demanding, looking for what he could get, but always in a non-confrontational way. He was upset that I paid them both the same wage, for he told me it was normal that the cook would be considered the senior of the two, with higher skills and responsibilities, and paid correspondingly higher wages. I countered that he had worked for an American employer only three years or so, and Saleh had been at the consul general's house for eighteen. I made it clear I valued each of them equally and I paid them exceedingly well, compared to wages in other Kaduna households. It was still a very modest amount in my budget.

With all the children on the compound, I was concerned to see them running around the grounds all day after I had been there a few months. The public schools in Kaduna State were closed, since the teachers were striking over non-payment of wages for several months. When this sorry state of affairs persisted beyond the Christmas break and into the new year, I took the bull by the horns. I told both men I would see what I could do to get their kids admitted to private elementary schools in town. This project was not so simple, as the educational standards of the public schools were dreadful and some of the kids, even around ten or twelve years old, could not write an English sentence or read a book. In the end, I got them into three or four different schools, after calling personally on the proprietors. One of the girls in particular was a difficulty. It was a relief finally to have her admitted to what was one of the most selective schools in Kaduna that happened to be run by an American woman willing to take a chance. The gamble paid off, for by the end of the year, Priscilla's performance was as good as her siblings'. The bill for the school fees fell on me as well, obviously, as neither Sebastian nor Saleh could pay private school fees; I left a kind of endowment fund when I retired from Kaduna that saw all of the children through elementary school.

Sebastian and Saleh met the acid test for my household help—they took good care of Ruth. Often, when Sebastian and I were discussing a menu for an upcoming party or an order to be placed with the commissary in Lagos, I would see him absent-mindedly stroking Ruth who would have climbed up on a chair next to him. When I traveled, I always came home to find her as fat and sassy as when I left. One memorable time, when I was on leave in the United States and had to call the house about some problem that could not wait, Saleh answered the phone out in Kaduna.

"Saleh," I started off.

"Hello, madame," he called down the wires. "The cat is fine!"

The cat had nothing to do with what I had called about, but the report, coming as it did before any more normal greetings and asking after family members, meant he knew my priorities.

With the one exception, in Kigali, I was extraordinarily lucky in the people who came to work in my home. They smoothed my life in ways that helped me concentrate on the work at the office and permitted me to enjoy my time away from it.

It was uncomfortable at first to have someone working in my home whose circumstances were so much less fortunate than mine. Giving directions about what I wanted done in this context didn't come easily, and asking that some procedure be changed was not all that easy. I have virtually never found a household worker who will use a vacuum cleaner to dust or clean upholstery, which galls me. At a certain point, I decided I preferred to live with what I believed were imperfectly cleaned sofa cushions than to fight over the issue. More demanding homemakers might not agree.

Ultimately, I believed the people who came to work in my home, whether they were day cleaners or full-time servants, were professionals who knew how to do the jobs assigned to them. In Africa I had to trust them to keep me healthy, for it was they who boiled and filtered the water I drank and purchased the food I ate. I treated them as people whose skills I respected and valued.

197

And I believe they found working for me advantageous as well. I always paid top wage and never quibbled about that. I might refuse to advance loans against salary and be hard headed in that way. But when there was a genuine need that I could meet, such as educating children or paying medical bills, I came through.

Staying Safe

When I was asked if I were afraid during my foreign assignments, I usually thought this question meant deep down, "Wasn't it frightening for a white woman to live in Africa among people who are always running amok and slaughtering each other?"

The short answer is No. A slightly longer answer is that living as a white woman in Africa is no more frightening than living as a white woman or indeed a woman in the United States or a lot of other places. The most hostile atmosphere in which I lived as a Foreign Service officer was Prague, Czechoslovakia, where I was under constant surveillance. As I was leaving Prague for Kigali, several of my Czech friends moaned, "Poor Helen, leaving civilization to go live in Africa." I snapped back, "I don't see what is all that civilized about your government." Most of them had spent various periods of time in prison for their dissident activities, and they saw my point.

Running amok is not an African specialty. A good Foreign Service friend, Bob Frasure, died in an accident in Sarajevo when an armed personnel carrier bringing him from the airport to the city over the only open road somewhat free of snipers slid off the road on the side of a mountain and killed all its occupants. He and the others who died in the accident were trying to negotiate an end to the carnage in Bosnia.

Occasionally, there were civil disturbances in places where I was serving. Shortly after my arrival in Kaduna, there were serious riots in Kano, a large city two hours to the north. The immediate spark that set off an orgy of killing was lit by the visit to Kano of an American-based German Christian evangelist, the Reverend Bonke. Most of my sources told me the real problem was caused when loudspeaker cars advertising the revival at which Bonke would speak

199

went into the old city of Kano, within the precincts of the traditional city walls, an area generally considered completely Moslem and off-limits to Bonke's evangelical zeal.

As the day for the revival came, tension flared and, without warning, Moslems began to attack Christians, particularly Ibo in the Sabon Gari market outside the walls along one of the city's major arteries. A number of businesses were burned out and looted. Several consulate personnel were in the city at the time the trouble started—a Peace Corps driver, the Peace Corps administrative officer, and the consulate cashier. The two Nigerians were Ibo, a group highly sensitized to outbreaks of communal violence, and one spotted the trouble almost instantly. The three got into their car and drove straight out of town, taking back roads and tracks through fields to avoid the main road.

It was just as well they did, for another consulate vehicle, the commercial office's car and driver, was on the main road just entering town when the trouble started. The car was stopped by the crowd, and the driver met with a Moslem greeting. Fortunately he was a northern Moslem and made the proper response, so was permitted to finish the U-turn he had begun and drive straight back to Kaduna. We had an anxious time until the Peace Corps car finally turned up, well after dark and some hours late.

I began to report to Lagos and to Washington that there was trouble in Kano. The consular officer tried, generally with little success, to get through by phone to the Americans in Kano who might be able to tell us what was going on. There was a group of several missionaries and their families resident in the town and, as we subsequently found out, they lived fairly close to the major corridor of trouble. Our best source was a British businessman who was reporting to the British Deputy High Commission by a telephone that worked; he was able to check on the missionaries and let us know they were all safe. We had a system of wardens in the town each of whom was supposed to contact a short list of other American citizens, and after about twelve hours we were fairly sure all the Americans were safe.

There were some specific problems, however. One was that the DCM, usually resident in Lagos, was traveling in northern Nigeria with his wife on an American defense attaché aircraft. They were in Maiduguri, in the far northeast of the country, and I had no way to get through to them on the telephone. I was not even fully certain they knew what was going on, for events of this kind were never covered in television news, at least until the military regime decided if they ought to be carried.

George and Sharon Trail, the couple in question, were due to fly in to Kano on Wednesday after the outbreak on Monday, and I planned to drive to Kano to pick them up. So I was headed for Kano. This was fortunate, for at about midnight the night before I had a telephone call from the Operations Center at the State Department asking what I knew about the detention of a group of Americans. It seemed that Pat Robertson's Christian organization in California had heard from the Bonke people that a group of Americans traveling with Bonke had been rounded up and were being held at the Kano airport. I was not able to provide the OpCenter any specific news, except to say I had spoken earlier in the evening with the British businessman. He had not told me of any difficulties experienced by American citizens. I told the State Department I was going to Kano the next day and would check on the story.

Consequently, I set off at dawn with my driver, Adamu Asuku. When we reached Kano two hours later, he decided to travel the long way around the city to bypass the area along the more direct route in which the greatest trouble had occurred. We arrived at the airport without any problem, and I sought out the office of the airport commander, an Air Force officer since Kano airport is a dual commercial/military field.

Enlightenment was not far off. Along the hallway leading to his office were a number of people who identified themselves as Americans and the Reverend Bonke's companions. The leader of the group of about twelve or fifteen people identified himself and said they had spent the entire night in the overstuffed armchairs in the corridor and in the commander's office. They had been collected at the Kano hotel, at which the group was staying, at the commander's request and moved to the airport to be out of the way of harm in the downtown area. The airport, as a military establishment, was considered a safe haven. Shortly before my arrival, the commander had been coordinating with the lead American to secure seats on the first flights leaving Kano for Lagos.

I introduced myself to the commander, a bright, capable person. He had understood from the start of the trouble the necessity to get Bonke first and the group accompanying him second out of Kano. The job was nearly complete. My arrival on the scene was close to superfluous, although it did reassure the Americans to learn that the State Department knew about them. I tried to be as honest as possible and not take credit either for having saved them from the troubles downtown or for speeding them on their way south, both these jobs having been accomplished by the airport commander. Nevertheless, I gained great credit in their eyes, and I was happy, to some extent, to have gained credit for the State Department with persons who had a direct line to Pat Robertson and the conservative right in American politics.

Shortly after the last American boarded a flight to Lagos, the United States defense attaché aircraft flew in from Maiduguri and offloaded my boss and his wife. They had indeed heard about the troubles in Kano and had been able to see from the plane before landing the extent of the damage along the riot corridor. In fact, some of the fires set by the mobs were still burning and could be seen from the air. By this time, the third day after the outbreak, order had been restored and the danger had passed.

Civil disorder broke out in Kaduna once during the time of my assignment there. The first I knew of it, however, was in the rental car I was driving from Washington to Baltimore-Washington airport where I was to board a flight to England, en route back home to Kaduna. "All Things Considered" on NPR carried a story that rioting had occurred in Kaduna and elsewhere in northern Nigeria; hundreds were feared dead.

I rushed to a phone at the airport and learned the report was true. I boarded my flight to London where I stayed in touch with the embassy there. One of the political officers was following events in Nigeria. By the time I was scheduled to return to Nigeria, the troubles had calmed down, and I flew into Kano where Adamu met me. Things had been pretty bad, he told me, although everyone who worked for the consulate and all their families were safe.

As we drove toward Kaduna, we encountered a military roadblock. The soldier waved us to a stop and asked through the window where I was going.

"To Kaduna," I replied. "That's where I live. I'm the American consul general there."

He considered this and then said, "Pray for Nigeria, Madam." I assured him I was praying and would go on doing so.

The trouble in Kaduna had arisen in Zangon Kataf, a village some distance away, inhabited by a small local ethnic group as well as a settlement of Hausa traders. This is a typical population mix throughout northern Nigeria, particularly in the Middle Belt where Kaduna State is located. The Hausa form the mobile commercial class of northern Nigeria; over past centuries they have settled in small pockets and conducted their trade in the village and town markets. In Zangon Kataf a dispute arose when plans for building a new market a short way outside town came into conflict with the local group who believed they should control the disposition of the land on which it was proposed to build.

The Hausa are generally Moslems; in the Middle Belt, the small ethnic groups are very often Christian. A dispute of this kind, therefore, almost immediately brings religious animosity into play. A further cause for complaint had to do with the authority delegated by the British colonial power to the Moslem power structure in northern Nigeria; having found a group of traditional rulers, Emirs, already in place, the British chose to rule through them. In Zangon Kataf, this meant the Emir of Zaria had a residual authority over the disposition of land that the Christian minority group believed should fall to them.

Trouble had been brewing for some months, and a commission had been delegated to report on the problems. As the report was about to be issued, violence erupted in the village. Later each group pointed the finger at the other. Lurid stories were told about atrocities on both sides. As news of the killing spread to Kaduna, the groups living in the big town chose up sides, based on ethnicity and religion, and the killing and looting quickly escalated.

Although no one at the consulate had been injured during the fighting, for some it had been a close call. Several lived in mixed ethnic neighborhoods. My own residence was only about a half mile from one of the centers of violence, where a Baptist pastor and his family had been slain and the church damaged. This was the church one of my servants attended, and he was deeply shaken by events. Close friends lived across the street from where this happened. Although their compound had a high wall and an iron gate, people fleeing the violence jumped over the wall to escape. For a day or two my friends had nearly a hundred people taking refuge on their property, requiring water and food.

One employee of the consulate apparently moved in with my servants while my driver also slept at the house, to be on call for the officer from Lagos who was acting in my absence.

So violence could come close. Foreign Service personnel do die overseas in these kinds of incidents, in war, and in terrorist attack. Fortunately, I never encountered violence up close. I don't think I would have behaved rationally if I had.

During the time I lived in Lagos, I was housed in a compound with no wall or gate at the entrance to the property. The servants' quarters were in back of the main building, along one corner of the lot. My apartment was on that end of the building. One night I became aware of a hullabaloo from the servants' quarters and looked out my bedroom window to see what was going on. Most of the servants and their families were looking on in horror, as a strange man was whirling about, threatening them with a machete. I realized something had to be done, so I rushed out the door of my apartment and down the stairs where I ran into Peggy Tracy whose apartment was on the other side on the ground floor.

Peggy asked me what was going on and I described the scene. I turned to go out the door, and she asked, sensibly enough, what I thought I was going to do about it. "Stop him," I replied. "And just how are you going to do that?" asked Peggy, who was a whole lot smaller than I am. She suggested that rather than rush weaponless into the fray, it might be better to telephone the embassy and get the security officer to come by. In fact, by the time help arrived, the man had left the compound and no one was hurt. But the incident made clear to me that my behavior in dangerous situations was likely not to be sensible.

The two times I was genuinely afraid of bodily injury actually occurred in crowds. The first was in Prague when I went to the Old Town Square with another embassy officer to observe a "spontaneous peace rally," one of those Communist-era events in which people were forced to demonstrate on behalf of the government's policy, in this case against American nuclear policy in 1983.

The rally was scheduled toward the end of the working day, and the workers of Prague were told they were to march from their offices and factories to Old Town Square for the rally. As my friend and I approached up one of the wider streets leading into the square, we realized that the workers of Prague were walking into the square and, just about as fast, walking out to get home for a beer and good dinner. There was two-way flow of humankind on Pařižská, and I suddenly found myself caught between the two, my body forced in one direction while the large camera bag on my shoulder went the other. I was certain I would fall to the cobblestones and have no way to regain my footing. Only the quick action of my colleague, who grabbed my arm and dragged me across the stream of people to safety next to a shop window, saved me from a good trampling.

A second time I feared being crushed was at the "turbanning" of the Sardauna of Sokoto, an officer at the court of the Sultan of Sokoto, the premier northern traditional ruler. This ceremony was a big event, and everyone who was anyone had turned up in Sokoto. The ceremony took place in a large throne room at the Sultan's palace, and for an hour or more before the principals arrived, the room filled with the Sultan's courtiers, businessmen, diplomats, and anyone else who could talk his or her way in.

There was also substantial representation from the press, but no provisions had been made for a press section from which they could take photos and see the ceremony. Instead, the press was packed in behind some of us diplomats, where we were all seated on the floor of the room in a wide semi-circle in front of the Sultan's throne.

Finally, the turbanning got underway. Alhaji Abubakar Alhaji (Triple-A) entered the room and advanced to the small space in front of the throne where he knelt in front of the Sultan. The Sultan made a gesture to two other members of his court who took a long, white cloth and began to wrap it around Triple-A's head in a turban, the symbol of his new title and authority. Behind me, the members of the press corps stood up and began to push forward, trying to get a clear photograph of events. Since Triple-A was kneeling down and all the action was taking place at floor level, it was nearly impossible to get a shot of him.

I realized that I was being pressed over by the reporters behind me. It was difficult to breathe, and, to save myself, I stood up along with a number of others who were directly in front of the press. This blocked their view, of course, and they shoved forward even harder. I took to punching backwards with my elbows to force them to back off.

"Ah, madame," complained the man behind me, "is that really fair?"

"As you are crushing me to death, I think it is completely fair," I countered. For the rest of the ceremony, the press pressed and I shoved, and a stalemate was achieved.

A few times overseas, we were alerted that trouble might be planned against Americans or American homes. One of those alerts was delivered in Berlin in the aftermath of the opening salvo of Desert Storm. The first day of the war there was a demonstration against American headquarters, and we were urged to take extra precautions at our homes and on the way to work. I consider German terrorists to be a far more frightening prospect than most. It was a genuine hassle, all the same. The ground floor of the houses on our compound had steel shutters that could be rolled down over all the windows. In my house, I had to keep my hand on the switch until the shutter was all the way down, so raising and lowering these blinds was amazingly time consuming. For the month or so after Desert Storm began, I simply left them down and lived in a twilight atmosphere on the first floor.

Prior to the outbreak of hostilities of Desert Storm, a phone-chain alert system had been established to permit rapid and complete transmission of news and instructions to all the staff. The bombing actually started in the middle of the night, Berlin time, and I was the first person on the political part of the chain called by a military communicator. She told me that the war had started, that all employees were to bring two pieces of photographic ID to work the following morning, that parking near the headquarters building would be restricted and we should not bring our cars to work, and that the American schools were closed. I wrote all this information down on the notepad next to my bed and called the next person in line. Of course I woke her up so I talked her into some coherence and suggested she write down everything I would tell her. When I finished that conversation, I went back to sleep. What took place in the next hour or two over the phone lines of Berlin strongly resembled the party game "Telephone." People turned up at work the next morning with no ID, photographic or not; people didn't come to work at all. Everyone had a different impression of what he or she was to do.

We were also cautioned as Desert Storm went on to be aware of strange vehicles in front of our houses. I noticed a closed wagon had been drawn up in front of the house next to our compound. It stayed there several days with no discernible activity around it. I reported this to the security officer who checked it out and reported it was a normal construction trailer for a renovation project about to begin at our neighbor's. So much for my fantasy of a band of terrorists huddling inside the wagon waiting for me to lower my guard.

Another incident in Berlin made me feel ridiculous. One summer day I was working in the garden and noticed a stranger looking over the wall into our compound. As it took some doing to see over the high wall, I wondered what on earth he was up to. I walked over and challenged him. He said he was the director or producer of some TV show that featured people and their pets. He noticed our houses and thought they would provide an attractive background for a segment of the show. Would we consider letting a film crew in to take footage of our sumptuous houses and our cats and dogs? No, I replied, and off he went. The story was so bizarre, it was hard to think he could have made it up, but then on the other hand...

Frequently, the alerts issued by the security office struck me as exaggerated. It is a fact of life, however, that American installations overseas are targets of attack. The 1998 bombings of the Embassies in Nairobi and Dar es Salaam proved that even in places where the threat appears to be low, terrible things happen. I was always torn, therefore, between taking alerts seriously or not. Being security conscious nearly always means inconvenience; not being security conscious can be fatal.

Staying Healthy

Speaking of health and medical care overseas is not the happiest subject for me. I became ill in Kigali. The treatment I received was motivated more by the wish of the State Department to avoid a lawsuit than by an interest in discovering what happened to me. An account of conflict between delivering good health care and saving the employer hassle and money is no surprise in these days of managed health care.

The State Department puts some energy and resources into the goal of keeping their personnel and families overseas in good health. Before traveling overseas, medical clearances must be brought up to date for all family members. Some people are not permitted assignment to some posts—say high altitude posts if a medical condition suggests they would be at risk. The clearance process is where the conflict between care and avoidance of lawsuit comes into play.

Besides the all-important clearance, we were required to have inoculations before traveling overseas, and the medical unit had a list of the shots required at each post. The list included not only the shots mandated by the receiving country, but also those the State Department judged prudent for residents there. Thus, traveling to Africa, I had not only the usual tetanus, smallpox, polio, and typhoid, but also cholera, yellow fever, meningitis, hepatitis B, and rabies pre-sensitization shots. I was given a supply of Aralen (chloroquine) for malaria suppression, to which was added paludrine when chloroquine-resistant malaria became common. We were also advised to have gamma globulin shots every few months to reduce the chances of getting hepatitis A.

Overseas posts have a Regional Medical Officer (RMO) assigned, responsible for the health of personnel at several posts in the area to which he or she travels on a fairly regular schedule. The

RMO's job is to check on the facilities at the post, particularly the nurse who provides day-to-day health care including keeping all the shots up to date. The nurse is usually a locally hired employee, except at large embassies where American nurses or family health practitioners may be assigned.

The visiting RMO also calls on local doctors and hospitals to evaluate the level of care available there. The purpose of these checks is to decide whether American personnel should be treated for various conditions locally or evacuated to the closest city where better facilities are available. In Africa, these judgments can be crucial. Decisions to evacuate or not are quite often the subject for heated debate and argument between RMOs and employees. Each post has a budget for medical evacuations, and an RMO who is evacuation-happy can come under pressure from Washington to keep costs down. In theory, of course, the health of the people at post is supposed to be paramount, but in practice these decisions cause quite a lot of second-guessing, particularly when the outcome is bad.

As in all of life, there were good, competent RMOs at the posts where I was assigned, and there were lazy, bad ones. I found the best policy was to take care of my own medical needs so far as possible, to keep enough money in the bank to evacuate myself if I had to, and to ignore the RMO as much as I could. I took the malaria suppressants as recommended, kept my shots up to date, and hoped for the best.

In Africa, the greatest health risks come from unsanitary water and food and from malaria. Since almost all of us had servants who prepared our food and took care of the drinking water supply, it was necessary to insure that these people fully understood the recommended methods for washing fruits and vegetables, boiling and filtering the water, and maintaining hygiene in the kitchen. It sounds incredible, but one of the necessary steps for preparing fruits and vegetables was to soak them for ten minutes in a solution of filtered water and household bleach, such as chlorox. This did not affect the texture or taste in any way I could discern, although a French gourmet probably could. Anything that was not peeled or cooked got this treatment in my kitchen.

Water had to be boiled for at least ten minutes and then filtered in a device fitted with ceramic candles. The filter systems sold popularly through travel catalogues do not do the trick, as they fail to trap quite a number of microscopic organisms. Every household in Africa has numerous bottles of drinking water prepared in this way, although commercially bottled water safe for drinking has also found its way into the markets there. Since ice cube preparation, water for cooking, and other water uses also depend on safe water, the boiling and filtering of water was an unending kitchen chore.

While I do not believe I ever became sick from water- and food-borne illnesses in my own home, eating out required care. I never drank water or an iced drink in a house where I was not sure of water preparation, nor did I eat salads or other uncooked foods in restaurants and hotels. In spite of all precautions, I did get a case of giardiasis while in Kaduna that I think I caught at the fanciest hotel in the country. Giardiasis, for anyone who has never had it, is an extremely common parasitical disease of the gut, very difficult to get rid of completely, and dreadful when in an active phase. I had to take the cure, rather massive doses of a drug, four times before I conquered it.

We had to be careful about all kinds of things in Africa. There were tumbu flies in Nigeria whose eggs could get under the skin and grow into larvae there, causing boil-like eruptions that were very painful. The flies laid their eggs in wet cloth for some reason. To avoid this plague, all laundry had to be dried completely in a drier or else ironed all over, since heat would kill the eggs. One American in Kaduna got tumbu fly eruptions just by sitting against her wet towel at the swimming pool. In Kigali we were warned about going barefoot outside, because there was some kind of worm that would lay eggs under toenails with results similar to the tumbu fly. In Rwanda, in the countryside, as well as elsewhere across a central African belt, there were tsetse flies that carried encephalitis or sleeping sickness. During one visit to the national game park there, tsetse flies invaded the car, and I received several painful bites on my ankle before we killed them all. Fortunately, none of the flies proved to be a carrier.

The greatest danger in Africa, however, was malaria. There is as yet no known inoculation that protects against malaria. The only thing that can be done is to take prophylactic drugs during the entire time of residence in a malarial area to suppress the development of the disease. For permanent residents of the area, this practice is not recommended, since the long-term effect of the drugs is worse than coping with the disease. Generally, Africans will have had malaria at some point during childhood and, if a person survives this first attack, immunity begins to build up. While subsequent attacks can be serious, even deadly, indigenous people count on their immunity and avoiding mosquito bites as the best defense.

For Westerners who come to Africa as adults with no immunity, malaria can be fatal. I knew several colleagues over the years who died or almost did of malaria. It was a threat I never underestimated. I tried to keep mosquitoes completely out of the house, which was made simpler with window screening and air conditioning. When the air conditioning was running and the temperature was cool, the mosquitoes did not bite. Occasionally I would wake in the night to realize the power was off and the mosquitoes were whining.

I also faithfully took the malaria suppressant recommended by the State Department at all times when I was stationed in Africa or traveling there. During my first tour in Nigeria, this was fairly easy, since chloroquine, a drug that had been used for some time, was still effective. By 1984 when I arrived in Rwanda, however, chloroquine-resistant malaria had arrived in East and Central Africa and caused great concern in the State Department medical division. The recommended prophylaxis was to add a relatively new drug, Fansidar, to the chloroquine. Fansidar is a drug in the sulfa family and was considered by the European doctors in Rwanda, mostly French or Belgian, to be much too strong for regular, prophylactic use. They used it only for treatment of the disease in active form, if then.

Nevertheless, I followed recommended State Department practice and took my Fansidar every week.

In summer 1985, I began to feel somewhat unwell, not acutely sick but just tired and dragged out. Since the ambassador left Kigali in July with no replacement in sight, and since we were also short of other personnel because of the usual summer changeover, I put it down at first to overwork. The RMO visited Kigali in late August or early September, and I asked him to check me over; he found nothing.

By early December, however, I was still feeling unwell, and a few more troubling symptoms appeared. I decided to travel back to Washington for a quick check by my own doctors and got permission to leave post—necessary because no Ambassador had yet appeared and I was in charge.

What turned up was a shock to my doctors as well as to me. My liver function tests were elevated well above normal. The State Department found out pretty quickly, since my doctor consulted with the best tropical disease specialist in the Washington area, who was also on the State Department payroll. I was taken off the malaria suppressants to see if the Fansidar was causing the problem, but the blood tests did not return to normal as quickly as they should have. Everything else came up negative as well. The State Department then said I could not return to Kigali unless I had a liver biopsy to see if that would reveal any problem.

The liver biopsy provided quite bad news—I had cirrhosis in my liver with some permanent scarring. Even worse, no one could clearly say why this had occurred, whether it was continuing, and what the long-term outcome might be.

The State Department finally agreed I could return to Kigali, but only for three weeks, long enough to welcome the new Ambassador and turn over the baton, pack up my house, collect my cat, and leave.

Over the next year, the liver function tests that I had every month and then every two months gradually returned to normal ranges. No one knew for certain what had happened, but my own G-I doctor took the position that I was as safe abroad as I was in the United States. He saw no reason why I could not be sent back overseas. The medical division saw it somewhat differently and continued to withhold a full medical clearance.

After two years, when I was getting ready to bid for a new job and wanted freedom to go anywhere in the world, I had a new medical examination, performed by my personal physician, and then requested a review of my medical clearance status. I was furious when it came back limited and went to see the doctor in charge of the clearance process.

This man can only be described as a sadist. He thoroughly enjoyed his power over me. At one point he asked me, "Who do you think decides, Miss Weinland, where you are assigned overseas?" When I replied that the Personnel Division made the assignments, he replied, "No, Miss Weinland. I decide where you can go." He denigrated my personal doctor who had written a letter in support of a worldwide medical clearance ("these local doctors think they know everything") and he refused to reconsider the decision. I was in tears, and he enjoyed every minute of it.

When I returned to my office and had a chance to calm down, I telephoned the G-I specialist and told him the State Department doctor had, among other things, asked me why I cared whether I had a full medical clearance or not; I could still go overseas, but just not to a large number of posts, particularly African ones. The G-I man, bless him, understood immediately what the issue was—"You won't feel completely well without a world-wide clearance, obviously," he said.

The G-I doctor undertook to telephone the State Department man and discuss the whole question with him. Sometime later, I had a call from the State Department doctor who announced, "I have decided, after my phone call with Dr. Gelfand, to restore a class 1 [worldwide] clearance." I think I was supposed to thank him, but I could not.

During this entire saga, the State Department had been completely uninterested in looking into the question of what had caused my hepatitis and cirrhosis in the first place. I knew instinctively it had to be related to something—the Fansidar, a tropical microbe—in Rwanda and my residence there, but the medical folks appeared not to care at all. And, happily, over the next years, my liver function tests remained normal, I was cleared to go overseas, I served again in Africa, and all was fine. There were whole families of drugs I was not able to take, and of course my drinking days were over. But, generally, I enjoyed good health up to my retirement.

Just about ten years after this incident, however, the liver function tests began to go slightly out of normal ranges again, throwing me into complete panic. The problem proved to be gall bladder disease, which is relatively simply dealt with in these days of laparoscopic surgery. While he was at it, the surgeon took some liver tissue for a follow-up biopsy that was read by one of the country's leading experts on drug-toxic hepatitis, who had also looked at the 1986 slides. It has now been pretty firmly established that the cause of my trouble was, in fact, the Fansidar I was taking for malaria suppression.

I have no idea if the State Department would be interested in this information. They ought to be, since a large number of its employees was taking Fansidar at the time I became ill. Because of other side effects, the use of the drug was discontinued after only a few years, so I had the bad luck to fall into just the period when it was used. It is certainly possible others had a similar, but less acute, hepatic reaction to the drug and may be carrying around cirrhosed livers.

Forcing the State Department medical division to act in such a situation generally requires a large group of extremely angry people who publicize their anger in a way that ultimately has to be dealt with. In this way, a number of families that had been stationed in Moscow in the 1970s and subjected to microwave radiation finally got the State Department to do an epidemiological study on the adverse health effects many of them thought they had suffered. Cooperation from the medical people is, however, unusual.

While I was still battling to get my medical clearance back, I found there was no way to challenge a decision from the medical division. In this way, the sadist controlling clearances was correct. The American Foreign Service Association, the employees' union, was specifically exempted from questioning a medical decision. The Personnel Division had no authority to counter a clearance decision. An individual like me is completely without support, even if outside doctors state an opinion counter to the State Department's.

What the Medical Division is afraid of is that a person will be granted a clearance to go to a post, become ill, and then sue the Department for having failed to inform him or her of the medical risks of that assignment. There are, in fact, cases of just such a thing happening, even cases in which the individual signed a waiver and still claimed the Department should have prevented the assignment. The entire medical clearance process is designed to avoid such a suit, and, in my opinion, is more skewed toward this defense than providing carefully considered, individual medical care.

Thus, in response to the question, "What happened when you got sick?" I would respond, most of the time help was available locally and we got better. Occasionally, someone had to be sent somewhere else for evaluation or treatment, and usually this process worked fairly smoothly. But every once in a while, the medical division handled a case officiously and inefficiently. In the end, I found I had to take responsibility for my own health and deal with the risks, considerable at some places, myself.

Getting a Job and Getting Ahead

The Foreign Service resembles the Armed Forces more than the Civil Service in its personnel practices, most especially in its "up or out" principle, although it has wrinkles that are particular to it alone. Like the Armed Forces, its officers are commissioned by the President and serve at the will of the President. Their promotions are confirmed by the Senate. Failing promotion at certain fixed intervals, they are retired against their wills. They move from one assignment to another quite frequently, serving a good deal of their careers outside the United States. It is not exaggerating to point out that it can be equally or more dangerous to serve in the Foreign Service than in the Armed Forces, as the wall tablets inside the diplomatic entrance of the Department of State attest. I lost friends in the Foreign Service to tropical disease (Margaret Tracy in Tanzania) and to armed violence (Robert Frasure in Sarajevo). Another friend was held hostage for fifteen months in Tehran (Ann Swift). I know others who were present at embassy bombings in Beirut and Nairobi.

Promotion depends on evaluation, and the evaluation process itself evolved fitfully over the time I was in the Foreign Service. When I joined the Department of State in 1974, the Foreign Service was in the midst of a painful transition from being an old boys club to a service run on apparently modern lines of management. It had just lost the first of two court challenges from Alison Palmer who claimed the Department had discriminated against her because of her gender. The Department had also recently, in face of challenges from women who had been forced to resign upon marriage, reinstated a large number of women who had suffered from that policy. It was trying to increase the percentages of minority and female members through various means.

My first performance evaluation was written by the deputy director of the Philippines Desk in late summer 1974. I quickly learned that what was written on the form was carefully doctored, not so much to create total fiction as to shape the comments to the intended outcome. At that time one page of the evaluation form contained a long list of qualities on which the person was rated from "outstanding" to "poor" or "not applicable." In order to assure some form of honesty, the rating officer was required to check at least three traits as "needing improvement" or some such thing. Elmer Hulen, my evaluator, explained that he had chosen three qualities for low rating, not because those were my most obvious deficiencies, but because they were the three least likely to be negative for a junior officer.

For the rest of my time in the service, the form changed but the calculations did not. The rating officer was asked to mention two areas in which the person needed improvement, but the effort was always to find areas that would not be damaging. One of my evaluators mentioned the fact that I did not like to use a dictating machine, hardly a reason to deny a promotion. Sometimes the same negative trait would be split and discussed as if it were two qualities rather than one. Once I became a rating officer, of course, I indulged in the same fiction writing.

By the end of my service, a rating officer was required to discuss performance at least three times during the year with the subordinate and put the dates on the form. Sometimes the dates were made up; sometimes the conferences really took place. Fairly often, in interviews I convened, I would tell my subordinate something like, "I would never actually put this on the form, but what you really have to work on improving is" and then I would mention real deficiencies like missing deadlines or sloppy drafting.

When the time approached to write the Efficiency Evaluation Reports (EER's), we were all asked by our rating officers to produce a list of the achievements over the past year we wanted mentioned. Quite often my superior asked me to suggest areas for improvement as well, but I did this only once. I was too honest and did myself no favors. After that I always forced my superior to write the fictional account. We were permitted to discuss the draft and ask to have comments strengthened or softened. Occasionally I did this.

One of the secrets of the Foreign Service was that, however much the management people tried to make the evaluation system work equally to the advantage of all, it didn't. Who wrote the report weighed heavily with the promotion panel; where I was stationed at the time the report was written was equally important. However hard I worked at a difficult post in Africa, my evaluation was not taken as seriously as it would have been coming from China or a major

215

European post. In this way, the assignments part of managing my career was as significant as the evaluation. To people like me, who were somewhat marginalized in both processes, it appeared that people who worked only moderately hard in major posts and under well known supervisors got ahead faster than those willing to take more adventuresome jobs under less prominent bosses.

Once I became senior enough to write efficiency reports myself, I realized that I had to start from what should have been the conclusion of the process—deciding if the person should be promoted or not. In most cases the answer was yes, and so I wrote the necessary fiction on the form while trying, in conferences and other conversations, to counsel the person how to improve performance. In a few cases the answer was no, and I saw no reason to avoid writing a franker report. Promotion opportunities were limited in the Foreign Service, and they became more so after a major change in the management of the system after 1978. If that was the case, and a person's performance was genuinely mediocre, I didn't see any reason to shape the report to get him or her promoted.

In one instance, I was assigned to a job in which my predecessor had been quite ineffective. Both the ambassador and the DCM told me this as I arrived to take over. Nevertheless, the ambassador had directed the DCM to write a good report for my predecessor. Even more galling from my perspective, the ambassador directed the DCM to nominate my predecessor for a Superior Honor Award, the highest award given within the department and one for which I was never nominated. My predecessor gained both promotion and the award. I am sure the ambassador's reasoning was that he himself gained because he took care of his troops, but the cynicism produced by such manipulation was, in my mind, destructive of morale. Another odd discrepancy in the evaluation system was the recognition for rating officers who wrote particularly good reports. A letter of commendation was placed in their files for consideration by their promotion panels. Yet, strangely, only those officers who wrote reports that got people promoted were commended, even though reports on mediocre officers were just as difficult, if not more so, to write well.

Like the military, the Foreign Service produces one promotion list a year. The day it comes out is anticipated with excitement and dread, and in each embassy or office as it is distributed from the communications and message centers, there are audible comments on the quality of the list. One year, I would see the names of a number of hard-working, deserving friends and feel good about life; other years, all the duds I knew throughout my career were gathered together. The most important consideration, of course, was whether my name appeared on it, whoever else might be there alongside. I spent one promotion list day crying in the ladies' room.

My own promotion history was strange indeed. I was first promoted within ten months of joining the Foreign Service, ahead of anyone else in my entering class. (This promotion came on the basis of Elmer Hulen's EER.) My second promotion came rapidly as well, along with others in the class; my third also placed me in the vanguard. At that point, although I did not know it at the time, my promotions simply stopped for the next ten years, and I slipped all the way to the back of the class. My evaluations were good, my supervisors told me they could not understand why I was not being promoted, and the union representative on whom I called for help was baffled.

Everything being equal, I should have been promoted at the conclusion of my tour as DCM in Rwanda, but several things happened: the ambassador left post, and my report was written by a desk officer who was junior to me; I had left post for medical reasons, the discussion of which was inadmissible although the fact my tour was cut short was not; and, because of having to leave on short notice, I was unfortunate enough to take a new assignment that didn't have much content to it. So there I sat, while all my peers passed me on their way up. Only in 1991, when I happened to be in Berlin when the Wall opened up and when I finally stated in my section of the evaluation report exactly why I had left Rwanda and what I had achieved there and in the interim, did I gain my next promotion.

The energy expended on promotion is equaled by the effort spent at lining up the next job. I am frequently asked if Foreign Service officers are able to pick their assignments. The answer is that we can influence the assignment and reject ones we don't want for the most part. When I first joined, the process was relatively informal and greatly influenced by the old boy network. Ambassadors could request people they wanted and get their way. Gradually, under pressure from equal employment directives, assignments were freed up from personal influence and inside manipulation, at least in theory. As is normal in such a change, however, the procedures became infinitely more bureaucratic. Like the American election cycle, the assignment cycle expanded to fill a large percentage of time between one assignment and the next.

Embassies are organized, as I have said, into political, economic, consular, and administrative sections. Personnel in the Foreign Service are organized into comparable "cones." I entered the Foreign Service in the consular cone, but, about five years later, was "re-coned" as a political officer. Assignments were supposed to go, in the first instance, to a person in the cone for the job and also to a person at the same grade as the job—that is, a grade 3 political job in Tokyo was to be assigned to a political officer at grade 3. Unlike the Civil Service, the Foreign Service separates the grade of the job from the grade of the person. If we were assigned to a job above our grade, this was a "stretch," and generally speaking a stretch assignment was only made if no one actually at that grade bid on that job. Logic tells us the chances of a stretch assignment were much greater at posts that weren't too popular, and the only one I ever got was in Lagos. Sometimes, people were assigned to "down-stretches," that is, to jobs graded below their personal grade; this happened generally with tandem couples, two married Foreign Service people who wanted to be assigned to the same post. Theoretically it was possible to be assigned out-of-cone as well, although again the chances of that were greater in unpopular places.

There were multi-functional assignments as well. These could either be jobs at smaller posts with double duties (political and consular) or, at more senior levels, jobs requiring more management than specialist skill (deputy chief of mission). Multi-functional assignments were desirable, because they increased the chances of promotion. When I was DCM in Rwanda, for example, I was considered for promotion by the political panel (because I was a political officer) and by the multi-functional panel (because my job was multifunctional). I got a double pass at it.

About a year before reassignment, the personnel bureau circulated lists showing which jobs were going to be open, their grade, and any required language ability. Since quite a number of languages required a year's training, we had to bid for those jobs two years in advance. We had to submit a list of between six and twelve assignments we would accept, in priority order. Again this was delicate, for if we bid, even at a low priority, for a job no one else bid for, we could be slotted into that job without even being considered for a job we wanted more. Drawing up the assignments bid list was even more delicate than applying to college.

Although the process was supposed to be impersonal, the way it worked out was far from that. It paid off to pound the corridors, calling on office directors of the countries where our preferred jobs were. If we learned the relevant ambassador was visiting Washington, we tried to get an appointment to see him or her. I know for certain that my having taken the trouble to see Ambassador Blane when he was on consultation in Washington is what got me the job as his DCM. The two jobs ambassadors did have control over were the DCMs and their personal secretaries, and he picked me from the list given him because he had met me. I lobbied hard as well to get my job in Berlin. Every time I bid in the last ten years I was in the Foreign Service, I went to see people and wrote people I knew who were assigned to places I wanted to go, asking for a good word from them. Every two to three years we had to go through this process. Relying on the personnel system alone to place us in desirable jobs was foolish indeed.

Each person had an assignments counselor, who was delegated to look out for our personal interests. Some were better than others; an energetic person who respected my ambitions and would go to bat for me was a boon. The ones I had ran the gamut from bone idle (the woman who lifted no finger as I was job hunting from Zurich) to well plugged in. At the time I was prying myself loose from the UN desk job, my assignments counselor was a personal friend and tried to give me careful advice based on his own personal experience with two of the characters involved.

In the end, each assignment was the result of my own preferences, hard work, and luck. The only time I had assignments I really disliked were the ones in the Department after I left Kigali. The first was the UN affairs job. But even there, I worked for a short spell under a supervisor who was assigned to Berlin when I was bidding on that job and to whom I turned for a good word during that assignment process. Following UN affairs, I took a job in the intelligence bureau that was represented to me as something much more interesting than it turned out to be. Finally, during that three and a half year hiatus, I took a job on the Zimbabwe desk in the Office of Southern Africa Affairs. By this time, the job was well beneath my capabilities, but my failure to get promotion limited what I could ask for. That office was also badly managed at the time, and it was not a happy place to work. I'm sure my own frustrations over failure to get promotion didn't improve office morale.

With the exception of that time, however, I enjoyed all my assignments, all of which I requested. Nevertheless, the period of stagnating promotions and uninteresting assignments was key in my decision to retire as soon as I was eligible for a pension. By the time I left for Berlin, I had made up my mind that unless something miraculous happened I would leave in 1994.

Telling the Truth

Over three centuries ago, Sir Henry Wotton said, "An ambassador is an honest man sent to lie abroad for the commonwealth." Diplomatic staffing and practice have changed in the intervening years, but the public often perceives diplomats this way, particularly when it hears what was a knock-down, drag-out, fruitless set of discussions officially described as a "full and frank exchange of views." The perception is strengthened by the conspiracy-loving disposition of the current generation to assume anyone claiming to work for the State Department is really an undercover CIA agent. Although I am not allowed to discuss CIA work in any detail, I may state unequivocally that many persons, the large majority in fact, who claim to work for the State Department actually do just that. They are bona-fide Foreign Service officers.

Did I have to lie for my country? I can remember only one time I told an outright lie in its service. It happened this way. During my tour in Lagos, when I was covering the legislature, I was invited by a member of the Nigerian House of Representatives to attend the installation of a chief in his home village near the capital. I had not seen such a ceremony before, and although my host was to be the same Fola who chased me around the kitchen, I decided not to pass up the opportunity to experience some local culture. I reasoned he could hardly chase me around the village in full view of his chief.

Everything started off fine. We got to the place after a bone-jarring trip up a dirt road in a Volkswagen beetle. We called on members of Fola's family who lived there, and I sampled my first palm wine. Luckily it was still morning, since palm wine ferments relentlessly over the course of a day and by evening is lethal; in the morning it is still a refreshing, mildly alcoholic beverage. After an hour or so of this arrival activity, Fola informed me there was a reporter from the local state radio station who was eager to interview

220

me. As a member of the National Assembly, Fola was trying to get some publicity for his hometown; a diplomat from the American embassy had obviously been used as a drawing card.

I was a fairly junior member of the embassy team and generally not permitted to speak with the press. I tried to wriggle out, but I was between a rock and a hard place. I was Fola's guest, after all. We reached a compromise: the reporter would tell me his questions before he switched on the recorder, and I could rule out anything sensitive. We began the interview with some easy ones: how long have you been in Nigeria? do you like it here? do you like Nigerian food? The reporter had told me he wished to ask a final question about the boycott of the 1980 Olympics the United States was trying to organize; the interview came after the invasion of Afghanistan, and this was a hot topic. Since I knew the official guidance, I agreed and delivered my answer, stating the United States government thought it inappropriate to participate in games meant to celebrate peace when the host country was brutally occupying a neighbor. The reporter then asked a follow-up question: "That is your country's policy; do you support it?"

I didn't actually support the boycott. With a few exceptions, I find sanctions and boycotts counterproductive. I was, however, standing in a Nigerian village with a live tape recorder running and an invitation to renounce a foreign policy initiative of my country. I took a deep breath and said slowly and clearly, "That is the policy of my government and I support it." The reporter turned off the tape. He had no idea how close he had come to a scoop for his station's evening broadcast. Lucky for me I had told the lie, for later in Lagos another member of the embassy staff told me he had actually heard the interview on the radio.

We were not often called on to lie so straightforwardly. It was much more common to be required to blur the outlines of the truth. Anyone who follows the news and hears a press spokesperson deliver the officially cleared guidance on some subject sees this process at work. Lying outright is inadvisable, because it will always come out and erode credibility the next time around. Instead, the goal is to convey as much information as can be made public without endangering the outcome of policy deliberations or negotiations and then waffle on the rest. If a question gets right to the nub of what we cannot comment on, we answer some other related question or say, "I don't have anything on that for you."

As I became more senior, there were times when I had to deal with the press. At first I was nervous, for in some ways the goals of the diplomat and the journalist are quite opposed. They do coincide at points, most importantly on the aim of creating a public well informed on foreign policy issues. It can be helpful to a journalist to

221

discuss an issue or event with an experienced and knowledgeable diplomat, who often has a much fuller and more informed understanding of a place or event that has blown up out of nowhere. Most foreign journalists have to cover many countries other than the one in which they live, and experienced ones generally touch base with resident diplomats when they arrive for a week of reporting.

I discovered this first when I was posted in Czechoslovakia, and a *New York Times* reporter arrived from Bonn to do a series of stories on the dissident community. I had numerous contacts among the dissidents, and he asked me to go to lunch with him for a background discussion. The reporter, Jim Markham, was experienced and entirely trustworthy; I knew that if I told him something on background, he would use it just that way, to fill in his own observations, to help him with context and interpretation. I was not going to be quoted. After this baptism, I found it easier to work with journalists. I never would have lied to them, and they knew that. They also respected it if we arrived at a point where I could not help them.

Not all journalists can be trusted. A colleague working in the Office of Southern African Affairs learned this the hard way. He was Mozambique desk officer during the time the right wing of the Republican Party was trying to force the Reagan administration to recognize the rebel group RENAMO, which was terrorizing the Mozambique countryside, as the legitimate supporter of democracy and Western values. Asked by the conservative daily, *The Washington Times*, to comment on a story, my colleague had asked to go on background; this meant he should have been identified in the story only as a "State Department official," but the paper gave his name and full title right on the front page. His comment was franker than it would have been had he spoken on the record. After that, none of us trusted *The Washington Times* to respect the guidelines. If we were unable to speak on the record, we simply replied, "I can't help you on that" to anything its reporters might ask us. That is, assuming they got us on the telephone; we never answered their calls if we could help it. We didn't lie; we stonewalled.

Dealing with reporters was one thing; explaining American foreign policy to host governments was a different process. When we were formally required to explain a policy to the host government and, often, ask for their support in the form of a UN vote or a public statement, we received a cable from the Department of State with an explanation of the policy or decision and a series of talking points. We would type up the talking points in the form of something called a "non-paper," a lovely diplomatic term. A non-paper is a piece of white bond on which is typed a title and the talking points but no other information. Officially it does not exist: it is not on letterhead, it is not signed—it is a non-paper.

Armed with the non-paper, we would head for the office of the appropriate official in the Foreign Ministry to make our *démarche*. Sometimes the person we spoke with simply listened, accepted the paper, and made sympathetic noises. Other times, the issue could provoke a thorough discussion, either because the host government disagreed with the course the United States government was proposing or because it agreed and wanted to learn more about what the United States was intending to do. I can remember one time my boss, the political counselor in Lagos, was asked to make a *démarche* about something our government was planning to do. She had the non-paper prepared and sailed off to the Foreign Ministry. About an hour later she was back, upset. Her interlocutor at the Ministry was a smart guy and had listened to the talking points with amusement; at the end of her presentation, the Nigerian had demolished them with convincing logic. "If the Department is going to send me off to do this," my boss complained, "at least they could give me some intellectually convincing arguments!"

Another time I was in Prague. From our own press clips, we were aware of grumblings in the bowels of the Reagan administration about the government on Grenada. The Prague press began to carry alarming articles about how the American behemoth was intending to fall with all its military might on this tiny little island. One morning, *Rudé Pravo*, the official Communist daily, had a front-page photo of a United States warship; the caption stated the ship was steaming toward Grenada. My boss and I laughed as we read the caption; what an exaggeration of our Caribbean policy! Two hours later, my boss arrived in my office with a cable in his hand. "Look at that," he remarked. "I have just been told to go up to the Foreign Ministry to deliver this in a *démarche!*" It was the announcement that United States troops had just invaded Grenada; the appended talking points explained the necessity of the step.

We could, therefore, find ourselves in the office of a host country official or, less formally, at a reception or dinner party, trying to explain some action the United States government had taken. Under relatively friendly circumstances, with a fellow diplomat we trusted, we could let down our hair and admit we thought some policy was a little over the top. We could, for example, explain the domestic political considerations that had driven the decision. With close friends we might be willing to discuss our own political predilections. In general, however, when we were overseas, we were representatives of the United States government, and not the Republican or Democratic members of that government. The job was a twenty-four-hour a day one. I believed if I were not in complete sympathy with the government in office, I had to inhabit a public persona that consistently supported it.

Such impartial behavior was particularly important at times of United States national elections. I was in Lagos at the time of the 1980 presidential campaign and election. I am a registered Democrat. The thought of a Reagan victory sent cold chills down my spine. Nevertheless, in Lagos I had to keep these opinions to myself and to discussions only with American citizen colleagues at the embassy.

Jimmy Carter was overwhelmingly popular in Nigeria, a country he visited two years before the election. In addition, it was a strange concept in Nigeria that an incumbent leader could be voted out of office; it ran counter to the African tradition of unquestioning respect for the leader. Perhaps, in a more cynical frame of mind, it would also be fair to say the Nigerians could not understand how an incumbent could fail to use every tool at his disposal to crush the opposition.

A few weeks before the election, I was in the office of a special advisor to President Shagari. He brought up the election, and I informed him the polling was showing gathering momentum behind Ronald Reagan and the Republicans. He questioned my conclusion and accused me of being a Republican. I answered, "My political opinions are not relevant here and I'm not going to tell you which party I support. But I do think the Nigerian government should be prepared for a Reagan victory." I was nervous the Nigerians would take it so for granted that Carter would win a second term they would be badly placed to reach out to Republican officials.

We threw a big election night party at the embassy. All the legislators were invited, as well as the Nigerian press and other friends from the community. Our friends arrived and assured those of us standing at the door they knew Jimmy Carter was going to win. With the six-hour time differential, returns did not begin to come in until after midnight. In those days long ago, before CNN and the Internet, the USIS office had established a primitive radio relay with Voice of America. The end came decisively and quickly—Ronald Reagan was winning a convincing victory. Our Nigerian friends were stunned. Some of us closet Democrats snuck upstairs to the political section to indulge in a consolatory Scotch before we rejoined the crowd for mop-up news of Senate and House races. We hoped the evening provided a hands-on lesson on the peaceful and orderly transfer of power in a democracy.

While it was obligatory to support United States policies when serving abroad, it was also important to maintain a public stance of support for all the personnel at the embassy. It would have been reprehensible, in my view, to criticize the ambassador or other colleagues to fellow diplomats or officials in the host country. I had the normal opinions about all the colleagues with whom I served, ranging from admiration and deep respect to complete contempt. Happily, most of the time my opinions were toward the positive end of the scale. But when they fell below it, I was able to share them only with like-minded Americans at the embassy.

In Zurich, we faced a problem that is not unknown throughout American society—one of the Americans posted there was an alcoholic. This affliction is, of course, a deeply distressing one for everyone concerned. The Department had clear procedures for handling such cases that involved confidential medical consultations, evacuation to a residential treatment program, and if absolutely necessary, return to Washington. These discussions and decisions were the province of the consul general and none of my business.

What was my business were the questions I got from the Swiss employees in the office and, as the problem became more severe, from the public. One Swiss woman who worked under the direction of the man concerned was upset by his behavior and occasionally questioned me about it. I had to allay her frustrations while, at the same time, not discuss what was going on behind the scenes. At another time, one of the local TWA people who frequently visited the consulate remarked to me that he had found the man incoherent in his office. It was very difficult to ignore those times when I would come upon the person hiding his bottle in the pocket of a coat hung on his coat rack or slamming shut a desk drawer after a furtive fill-up. I didn't feel I could tell on him to the boss, but occasionally the atmosphere became very tense.

At the end of an extended period of remission, the behavior started up again after the suicide of an AA buddy. One evening I was leaving the office after closing time; the only other person still there was this man. He was in his office and, apparently, quite drunk. We had no Marine guard in Zurich and were responsible for locking up the office and maintaining the security procedures at the end of the day. My colleague said he was staying on for a while, but as I walked home I realized I feared for both the security of the office and the safety of the friend who would, at some point, have to make his way home through the Zurich tram system. So in the end, I became the whistle-blower; I was unable to reach his wife by telephone from my apartment, and I called the consul general.

The necessity to avoid criticisms of American colleagues while abroad is not merely one of professional etiquette. We had to be aware that hostile intelligence services might be working to vacuum up stray bits of information that could be used, if they chose, to turn an American diplomat. If such a service sensed disgruntlement, or heard from us that a colleague had a weakness such as drink or sexual appetite, these openings were an invitation to exploitation. In a place like Czechoslovakia under the Communists, we were particularly vigilant. But there were Soviet embassies and consulates in every country where I served.

Berlin was the scene where this kind of danger became most apparent to me. There were many German employees of the mission, most of whom were friendly, intelligent, well-educated people. It was natural that they would become friends we would entertain in our homes or go to concerts and movies with. One in particular, an employee in the information and press side of the USIS office, became close friends with several colleagues in the political section. Early on, he transcended the barrier that I always felt had to exist even in these friendships. I had become acting head of the political section only about two weeks after my arrival and well before I felt any assurance about my grasp of the Berlin essentials. Sitting around the open area of the political section office at the end of the day on Friday, we were all chatting and joking as we prepared to leave for the weekend. This person, the only German in the group, asked me, "Well, Helen, you're in charge. Do you think you can handle it?"

There was a degree of familiarity in the question that seemed to me inappropriate. I would have laughed it off if an American had said it, but somehow it wasn't right coming from him. I answered frostily that I had been in charge of an entire embassy and I thought I could handle a political section. After that, I never trusted him. Following a supper with friends, a year or so later, when this person was again the only German present, and again when we had been speaking in fairly unrestrained ways about others in the mission, one of my American colleagues said, "I think you don't like Steve much." I agreed.

A few months later, I came to work and was stunned, like everyone else, to learn the German authorities had arrested Steve for his activities as a KGB agent. The arrest was over a year after the opening of the wall, when access to all kinds of intelligence information about spies planted in the West was becoming available. Prior to his employment at the United States mission, Steve had worked for the Berlin city government, and it was for his spying at that time that he had been arrested. I felt shock but also vindication, since my sensors had worked well in his case. Those who had genuinely befriended him felt the complete betrayal of trust that such people leave in their wake.

When I was abroad, therefore, there was always the need to keep some kind of barrier erected. Except when speaking with American colleagues, I always felt a built-in time delay between what was in my head and what came out my mouth. I had to assume the telephone was tapped. If I had household help, I had to consider the possibility they gossiped about me or even reported to the security forces. I always assumed my trash was searched. It wasn't just a question of supporting policy or mouthing official press guidance when dealing formally with host country officials. The built-in censor was part of the mental process involved in any communication. Along with considering whether what I was about to say was intelligent, funny, or appropriate, I had to think whether it ought to be said at all.

A process like this becomes second nature after some time. It is also, obviously, not lying but rather considering how much of the truth to tell, how that much should be packaged, and who besides the person in front of me might be hearing it.

One major reason I periodically looked for an assignment to Washington and a year or two of residence in the United States was the need to lay down this invisible shield I had to keep installed around what I said about my work, my colleagues, and my life. Like other aspects of Foreign Service life, I perhaps found it more burdensome than did others. As a single person, without a spouse to whom to gossip about office matters, I had to bottle up a lot. In Kaduna, when I was boss, it was even more difficult; I fell into a pattern of leaving the post for at least two or three weeks twice a year to decompress. On those short breaks, I was relieved at being able to say what was on my mind without the invisible protective shield. My family and friends in the United States weren't all that interested anyway in consulate general problems in Kaduna.

Moving Around

One of the questions I was asked most often when I was in the Foreign Service, a perennial in those little notes at the bottom of Christmas cards for example, was whether I enjoyed all the traveling I did. I always read this question with a sense that few understood my life, because living abroad for extended periods of time is quite different from *traveling*.

I did travel quite a bit, either going to or from an overseas post, or within the country to which I was assigned. They were two entirely separate activities, and both differed considerably from the kind of travel most people think about when the word comes up—going to some place either to relax from work or to look at new and often exotic things. Most business travel also is different. My father traveled a lot on business when I was young, but he did not take us with him, nor did he ever consider that he lived anywhere but with us.

Traveling to or from a post involved more than getting on an airplane. The first step was to collect the necessary documentation to call in movers, arrange dates for packing out, and plan how to break up one household to set up another somewhere else. Moving from Washington to an overseas post meant that a portion of my possessions was to be placed in storage in Washington. Except for my first overseas assignment in Zurich, I occupied government leased and furnished housing, so all my furniture was left behind. This was the easy part.

Over the years I accumulated a large number of books. Books are heavy, our shipments had weight limits, and bookshelves in government furnished housing are rare. Most of my books, therefore, went into storage—but which ones? Overseas I always wanted to have reference books like a dictionary and atlas. I needed to have the full run of Jane Austen novels which I reread every couple of years or so. It was useful to have books about American history and culture. Packing meant a careful combing through of books, records, pictures for the wall, and all the other personal possessions that make my house my home. What went into storage was going to stay there as long as I was overseas, so if I slipped up I was going to have to do without for a long time.

Moving overseas also involved correspondence with someone at my future post about the living quarters I would occupy, since sizes of beds, numbers of rooms, color schemes in bathrooms and so on affected my shopping. Many of the places I was assigned did not have department stores where I could buy sheets and towels. In Berlin, I found that German bed sizes are just that much different from American beds that sheets from one place are not usable in the other. Because the Berlin housing was furnished with German furniture, it was fortunate that Berlin department stores were as good as they were. I learned from Prague before my move there that the bathroom in my future apartment was orange and brown (yes, really!), and the only towels I owned at this point were lilac and pink.

How big was the dining room table in my new home? What shape? Again, what was the color scheme in the dining room? These were all questions I learned with experience to ask prior to the actual move.

After twenty years of this peripatetic home making, much of which was driven by the taste of a previous occupant, I owned towels of wondrously varied color schemes. I owned bed sheets for single, double, and queen-sized beds. I owned square and oblong tablecloths, sized for tables that seated eight, ten, and twelve persons. Some of this I sold or gave away even before leaving a post. (Good American bed sheets move quickly in Nigeria.) Other stuff I have given to the church rummage sale since moving to Maine. My linen closet is still bursting, and I suspect I will not wear out all the towels I accumulated overseas before I die.

Packing up and moving out are stressful activities, as anyone knows who has done it. During my twenty years in the Foreign Service, I moved ten times. I never did figure out how best to supervise the packers—whether just to go off in a corner and let them get on with it or to watch their every move. In Zurich, one lone man came and spent two or three days wrapping each item and placing it in boxes. The entire apartment smelled of cardboard. I hid from him as much as possible, huddling in the bedroom, the last place he hit, reading all the old issues of *The New Yorker* I was dumping. Periodically he came to find me and show me a chipped glass or a broken bowl, to make certain I knew it was damaged prior to his packing. At the end of that pack-out I remarked to the wife of the political officer, "This must get easier the more you do it." She

229

looked at me with the sad face of experience; I remembered that look with every subsequent move.

As I was moving from Prague, the packers had been and gone. The day of the actual move the burly men arrived to hump all the stuff down the five flights of stairs. The elevator in my apartment building would hold only three humans, assuming they were trim and quite friendly with each other. Cartons filled with china and books were another matter, and were carried on the men's backs. It was hot work. After the apartment had been emptied of all my possessions, I offered the four sweaty men something to drink; three of them accepted pint-size bottles of Pilsner beer, the export variety they could not buy locally. The van driver said he would have a Coke. The four of them stood in the kitchen, chatting amiably and resting a bit. Then the crew chief said, "Okay, guys, let's drink up." This was the sign for them to upend the beer bottles and drink down the entire contents without pause. I was flabbergasted, certain that Czech genes bred a special valve into the throat that permitted one to drink down a pint of beer without drowning.

Once my Czech cat, Ruth, joined my household, moving became more complicated and traumatic. With each move, Ruth traveled with me, in the cabin of the airplane in a small carrying case under the seat in front of me. Making the reservation for her was often more difficult and harder to confirm, particularly if there were an intermediate stop, than the seat for me. I always carried along a much larger, rigid carrying case as well as her under-the-seat one on the off chance she would have to travel in the hold.

Anyone who thinks this kind of traveling is fun can think again!

Travel within the various host countries where I served was often enjoyable. This kind of trip was undertaken with a purpose— getting to know the country outside the capital city, calling on regional officials, businessmen, and cultural figures, and hoisting the American flag away from the embassy. Such trips were always followed by a trip report, recounting opinions and attitudes that might differ from those in the capital. If I visited businesses or trade fairs, I might mention possible American trade opportunities. When I was in Kigali or Kaduna, travel outside the capital was often occasioned by the launching of a project funded by American assistance.

I only began serious in-country travel in Nigeria. Since it was expensive to cover the costs of the vehicle and driver, we nearly always included at least two officers on any trip. I realized as early as my familiarization tour in Nigeria in 1978 how important the right travel companion was. At various times on that trip, three different officers went with me. The petroleum officer, with whom I spent the longest time, combined the best and worst traits. He was fascinated with Nigerian culture and was constantly poking into local weaving or pottery studios, looking for an out of the way adventure. On the other hand, he simply could not keep to an agreed-on schedule. If we decided at the end of the day we would be up, checked out and ready to go by 8:30, he might appear in the hotel lobby at 9:30 and still have to eat breakfast. I wore down my molars dealing with this behavior. I traveled as well with a political officer, whom I replaced a year later, and his wife. What I remember most about that part of the trip is being caught in one of Nigeria's famous "go-slows," out on the open highway between Ife and Ibadan in the southwest. (In fact, a "go-slow" is essentially a "go-not-at-all," when traffic is halted often for no apparent reason.) Both of them were relaxed and funny about the frustrating experience. My third travel companion was the stuff of William Boyd novels—the consul general in Kaduna. He had injured his knee somehow and occupied the entire back seat of the sedan in which we traveled to Sokoto, a trip of five or six hours. Packed in with him was a cooler full of canned beer. The entire journey was punctuated with popping beer can tops as he pointed out various irrigation projects and other sights along the route.

While it is fun to travel with someone eager to taste the local culture, it can occasionally get out of hand. Once I was permanently assigned to Lagos, I was asked at the last minute to take a trip planned by a fellow political officer, who was suddenly transferred from Lagos. My companion was his closest friend at the embassy, an economic officer. The political officer in particular was an over-the-top culture nut, and between them they had concocted the idea of traveling from Maiduguri in the far northeast of the country by a kind of back-country track they could see on a map that might or might not be accurate to Zinder in the Niger Republic, the country to the north of Nigeria. This route was presented to me only when we were in Maiduguri, although I knew all along there was a plan to spend the weekend in Zinder. I resisted the idea of leaving the paved road in a Chevy Carry-All van in none too great repair, operated by a Yoruba driver who spoke no Hausa in an area where that was the *lingua franca*. The driver didn't have much say in the matter, but I sensed he, too, was not eager to risk life and limb trying to get that unwieldy vehicle to Zinder on a country track. In the end, I won, mostly because I had no intention at all of losing.

We proceeded to Zinder by the tarred road, the long way around. At 4:00 pm, we reached the border between Nigeria and Niger and cleared the Nigerian border post. We had visas for Niger. The entry border post, a few miles down the road, was staffed by a portly gentleman in an immigration service uniform. We presented our passports, which were taken into a shed; a short time later

231

another person left the shed and headed on a motorcycle back the way we had come. The portly gentleman reseated himself in a wooden chair under a tree at the side of the road. Some minutes later, I inquired, in French, whether we could have our passports back and be on our way. He informed me that his colleague was checking with Niamey by radio. He could not say how long this would take—sometimes it was a few minutes, sometimes hours.

I explained to him that we needed to get to Zinder before dark, and he explained to me that we could not go on until Niamey, the capital city, was raised on the radio. We said in that case we would like to have our passports back, and we would return to Nigeria. No dice. To all my further protestations, he replied only, "Ce n'est pas ma faute (It's not my fault)." After increasingly frustrating conversation along these lines, and after trying in vain to find someone at the army radio shack where our passports had been taken, we had no alternative but to sit and wait by the side of the road in no-man's-land. In all, we were there about an hour and a half. I was furious at Stuart, my companion, and his sidekick, now on the way to Bangkok on transfer, for having decided on this little weekend excursion to Zinder, even though our objective was reputed to be a very interesting trade center in the old Hausa culture of the region. I was the only person who spoke any useful language, and the burden of getting us away from the portly gentleman and on our way fell to me.

Once we were cleared for travel, we made tracks for Zinder, though night was falling. About halfway there, Stuart suddenly called for a halt; it seemed he was hit by a ferocious gut bug. We limped up to the hotel, where they fortunately did have rooms, although they had never heard of us. Stuart was miserable and in no shape to go out for the fabulous French meal he had been longing for all day (another reason for the detour to Zinder). I had to get the driver settled in his hotel, since he spoke no local language to negotiate for a room. Meanwhile our rooms were made up, lights on, with the doors wide open to a courtyard. As I found when I finally locked myself in to dine on the snack food we had packed, this procedure meant the room had plenty of time to fill up with mosquitoes, which whined and bit all night long.

In the morning, I joined Stuart in the courtyard. He was feeling pretty chipper. My eyes were swollen shut with mosquito bites. In addition, I had just gotten my menstrual period and had bad cramps. I glared at him over breakfast and said, "You wanted to come look at this town. When the car gets here, you go and look at it. Take as long as you want. Then come back here and get me and we will go back to Nigeria."

Now, of course, twenty years later, I regret I did not go look at Zinder with Stuart. By all accounts, it is an interesting place and well worth a visit. But I was so angry, in such discomfort, after a sleepless night, that I didn't. You really do have to be in the mood to be a tourist.

With the right companions, cross-country adventure could be fun. A few months before the Zinder expedition, I traveled in the Middle Belt, with a friend from the embassy and the Kaduna consul general who had replaced the beer-popping Africa hand. I had a map that was just as unreliable as Stuart's, and it showed there was a direct route from Jos to Makurdi, a town along the Benue River where we were bound, that cut off miles of the route proposed by Haruna, the driver. On the map, it appeared to be in better condition than the longer road as well. We conferred with Haruna and found when we got to the turnoff that the short route was a well-graded laterite road. Off we went. The road, which quickly deteriorated in quality, led through fascinating countryside, on the east side of the central plateau in Nigeria. Funny-looking volcanic hills popped up throughout the landscape, and as the rainy season had just ended, the black earth on their sides was covered with intensely green vegetation. We stopped at noon for a pleasant picnic and set off again. A short time later, we came to a stream, some twenty feet or so wide. A group of young boys were standing in it, marking the line of the ford. Haruna spoke with them and asked them to stand all the way across, showing the water was eighteen inches or two feet deep. We were now about an hour and a half from where we had turned off the tarred road, and none of us wanted to retrace our steps all the way back and take the long way around to Makurdi. Finally, Haruna told his boss, the consul general, he thought we could get across and he stepped on the gas. There was one heart-stopping point when we could all feel the van lift a little off the bottom of the stream and begin to slip sideways, but then the wheels caught again and we climbed the bank on the other side. Fortunately, that was the only river we had to cross, and we arrived in Makurdi after an interesting trip through countryside we did not often see, safe and sound. I'm not sure I would do it again.

During my time in the Foreign Service, I found that I loved visiting factories most. Perhaps this was a throwback to my father who worked all his life for a manufacturing concern and shared stories about new processes and products. At any rate, with the exception of a tannery, I cannot recall a factory visit I did not find absorbing in some way or other. In Nigeria, I visited a cigarette factory, a paper mill, a pump manufacturer, and many others. The only time I tried to draw a line, I was unsuccessful. This was when I was in Kaduna and Ambassador Swing was coming to the north. The

233

officials arranging his visit in Bauchi, a state capital with not much going for it, told the political officer arranging the trip that they wanted the ambassador to visit the modern abattoir and meat-canning factory the state had established. "No slaughtering during the ambassador's visit," said the political officer. She reported back to me that the officials' assent to her stipulation appeared half-hearted, and indeed this proved to be the case. As we pulled up at the Bauchi canning concern, we could hear a cow bellowing back behind the office building. "No slaughtering," we repeated. "The ambassador is not going to want to watch a cow being killed." As it finally developed, the ambassador did not actually watch the killing, but the cow was killed during his visit. I sat in the car.

In Czechoslovakia, traveling turned out to be as much fun for the security forces in the provincial towns as it was for us embassy officers. On one particular trip to northern Moravia and Bohemia with a newly-arrived economic officer, the surveillance was intense. These secret police did not get much practice on foreign diplomats. When we did turn up, they had much technique to brush up on. I noticed them the evening of our first day on the road. The next morning, we set off in our embassy car. My colleague was driving, going slowly enough on the fairly open roads to make me grind my teeth. We came to a fork in the road and turned toward the next town on our itinerary when he was waved over to the side of the road. A policeman approached the car and requested my colleague's documents, informing him he had been speeding. The police officer walked off, and my colleague turned to me. "Was I really speeding?" he asked worriedly. "No way," I answered. "I don't know what this is about." Some time later, the policeman came back to our car and returned the driver's license and registration, telling us we could go on. The answer to the riddle came a mile or so down the road, as a bright-red Škoda (the Czech-made car for the average citizen) pulled away from the side of the road behind us. I could see from the clothes on the occupants of the Škoda that it was the same car that had followed us all morning, but it now had new license plates, issued from the district we had just entered. I don't know whom they thought they were fooling, but it wasn't me.

As a diplomat, my colleague could not in any case have been fined for speeding. An incident occurred during another trip I took with his predecessor and the Czech employee in the economic section. At a certain point on the trip, the Czech employee, who of course did not enjoy any immunities, was pulled over inside a town for speeding. He had been driving 90 kilometers an hour (about 50 mph) and continued at that speed when the limit had dropped to 60 kph (about 35). I began to reach for my diplomatic ID card when the policeman leaned in the window. "Do you speak Czech?" he asked in

Czech very, very slowly to our Czech employee. Our guy put on a contrite face and nodded, hesitantly. Still very slowly and clearly, the policeman said to him, "The speed limit inside Czech towns is 60, and you were driving faster than that. As foreign diplomats, you should be bound by honor to observe our laws and speed limits. Please drive at the proper speed." Having finished his tortuously slow speech to us, he waved us on. After going around the next curve, all three of us burst into uncontrolled laughter. Our Czech driver had escaped a serious fine by playing dumb and pretending to be linguistically challenged.

I discovered to my chagrin another hazard of in-country travel in Czechoslovakia when I accompanied our new ambassador on his first official calls in Slovakia, at that time still unified with the Czech lands but with fairly extensive autonomy. We began at 8 am, shortly after we rose for the day, with a call on the premier of Slovakia. The meetings went on all morning, an hour for each government official. Each encounter provoked the offer of hospitality, which in Slovakia involves little glasses of *slivovice* or the local *borovička*, highly alcoholic firewaters. Obviously, one cannot refuse such hospitality, and we dutifully downed the stuff; we then went to lunch where we washed down a delicious, cholesterol-laden meal with the local wines.

In the afternoon, there was yet another call, this one at the Education Ministry. We were greeted at the front door of the building and then escorted to the back of the foyer from which, on a conveyance called a "Paternoster," a kind of perpetually moving elevator, we were to ride to the top floor. The name of this contraption is Latin for "Our Father," presumably the prayer we were meant to utter as we leapt into the slowly moving open cabin. I had to time my move for when the floor of the cabin was exactly opposite the floor on which I was standing. I did okay on the entry part of the trip; it was at the arrival upstairs that I over-anticipated my exit from the cabin to terra firma, jumped a fraction too soon, stumbled on the inch or two rise, and, in full *slivovice*-befuddled glory careened all over the upper hallway while trying to catch my balance. I believe I also uttered some blasphemies. During the subsequent meeting, when I was note-taker for the ambassador's discussions, I found my pen wandering off the steno-pad. I did not write my most brilliant Memorandum of Conversation.

After the ambassador's calls, the USIS director and I, who had accompanied him, stayed on for another day's business in Bratislava. Before supper, we met for a drink in the hotel bar where we were thoroughly photographed by an innocent looking "businessman" with a little button camera in his jacket lapel. After this man had a chance to test his equipment for a time, Bill, the

235

USIS man, and I set off to look for a restaurant. Bill thought he knew roughly where a good one was, but he went down the wrong side street. As we turned around to return to the main drag, we encountered a man in a parka wearing a wool tweed deerstalker cap, à la Sherlock Holmes. It proved difficult to locate the restaurant, and we met more and more deerstalker-capped men on the street, each walking behind us. The entire town was crawling with deerstalkers. It was the newest look for the secret cop in Bratislava, straight from nineteenth-century Scotland.

Occasionally when I was assigned overseas, I went on short private trips for a little R&R. I made one such excursion to London during my assignment to Prague. The embassy motor pool offered a ride to the airport well in advance of my departure time, so my trip could be combined with a communicator meeting a plane with the diplomatic pouch. I checked in over an hour before my flight and went through the customs and passport formalities immediately. This proved to be a mistake. When I disembarked in London, I found the lock on my suitcase had been forced. Inside, the suitcase looked as though it had been run through with an eggbeater—everything was stirred up, shifted around, and out of place, although nothing had been taken. I have no idea what the security people at the airport thought I might be carrying in a checked-through bag, but they didn't find anything.

Traveling was often enjoyable. It was a break in the routine of office work. It expanded my understanding of the culture and history of the places where I was living, which I had to interpret to the State Department. I visited factories, launched projects, made speeches, met a lot of folks who lived outside the Beltway in their own countries, and deepened my affection for the places I served. I experienced some good laughs with my American and foreign travel companions.

The image that comes most readily to mind when I think of traveling in the Foreign Service is from my time in Rwanda. Compared to Nigeria, it was easier and safer there to travel by myself, and I took a number of trips alone in my ivory-colored Peugeot 504. One time I was driving to the northeastern part of the country, to visit one of the Peace Corps volunteers or discuss a development project. I was on a deserted road in the middle of Africa. The sun shone brightly on the red dirt. All around were the flat-topped acacia trees characteristic of the eastern African savannah country. I was struck by the sense of being in a place I never imagined myself visiting. I grew up in a thoroughly conventional, middle-class, 1950s suburban setting. I had not dreamt of traveling in Africa. And yet here I was, driving through a landscape that seemed familiar and homelike to me, under the big sky of the African grasslands. I loved that countryside, and I realized at the same time the impossibility of fully explaining to any friends back home what it felt like to be there. It was not the sensation of the tourist, looking for the exotic. Rather, it was a sense of being in a place where I belonged that was completely different from where I came from.

Visitors

Classic political science theory tells us that the executive branch of the American government, to which the Department of State belongs, carries out policy determined by higher reaches of that branch, acting in collaboration with the Congress. Theoretically, again, that policy is determined by what public opinion tells the government, through the elected president and through the elected members of Congress who must not only legislate on certain aspects of foreign policy, approving treaties and passing trade and immigration bills for example, but also appropriate the money to carry out that policy. The power of the purse and all that.

Nowadays, the Congress so micro-manages foreign policy that it comes close to determining staffing levels at every overseas post and signing every USAID contract. Ever more sophisticated polling also gives at least the appearance of serious public opinion on foreign policy issues. When I first joined the Foreign Service in 1974, congressional control over foreign policy was closer to the classic theory than to the current nickel-and-dime process that has nearly strangled the articulation of our policy overseas.

It cannot be overlooked that Henry Kissinger was Secretary of State in 1974. Whatever judgment is made about the policies he pursued, his success owed a great debt to his ability to woo the Congress and the press. He presented himself as a man with an overarching concept who required only the respect and resources necessary to put it in place. In large part, he got what he asked for, with little of the second-guessing and tinkering with policy that goes on now. Whether he should have been given such a free hand is beyond my subject here. Fair to say that no Secretary of State since, whatever President he or she served, had such wide and unquestioned support.

238

Periodically, members of Congress travel to overseas posts to see for themselves how the people's interests are being served. Congressional delegations, or "Codels" as they are known to the Foreign Service, are usually made up of members of a particular committee that wants to look into a particular aspect of policy: trade barriers, or drug trade interdiction, or defense cooperation, for example. The trip is meant to serve the committee and its staff members in much the same way that hearings in Washington do—provide first-hand information and impressions to permit better legislation and oversight.

As I say, that is the theory.

During my twenty years in the Foreign Service, I experienced a few Codels that actually did the job they advertised. The senators or congressmen called on relevant host government officials, participated in embassy briefings with good questions, and left the post having given the impression that a serious and substantive event had taken place. In a few cases, these Codels consisted of just one member of the Congress and a staff member—Senator Paul Tsongas who visited Lagos, Senator Richard Lugar who stopped briefly in Berlin. Another Codel I remember was headed by Congressman Barber Conable and concentrated on trade issues during a series of calls in Prague. That Codel was also unique in my experience in including one wife, Elinor Conable, who requested her own substantive meetings with Czechoslovak women leaders.

Most Codels, however, demanded unbelievable amounts of protocolary work, usually over a weekend, with very little substance to show for it. Some involved nothing more than a congressman or two showing up and requiring a lot of handholding and stroking during an entirely private trip taken at taxpayer's expense. Almost always, embassy personnel were required to put together a separate program for the wives, who wanted only to go shopping, using embassy vehicles and accompanied by embassy personnel as translators and freight forwarding specialists.

The first genuine Codel I saw was a visit of about six members of the House Armed Services Committee to Lagos. The chairman of the committee at that time was Melvin Price, an Illinois Democrat who was getting along in years. My job in the embassy political section involved liaison to the National Assembly of Nigeria. In the year prior to the Codel visit, Nigeria completed a transition from military to civilian government including multiparty elections. The National Assembly, and indeed the entire Nigerian government, was a young institution, modeled to a great extent on that of the United States. In my capacity as the officer reporting on legislative matters, the ambassador asked me to participate in briefing the

Codel on the recent political transition and the operations of the legislature.

The Codel assembled in the embassy conference room, and the dogs and ponies of the embassy, including me, trotted in and sat at the table, speaking in turn. I gave as succinct a summary as I could, describing with my genuine enthusiasm the political events of the past year, the building of a democracy and the peaceful exit of the military government. At the end of my little lecture, I invited questions, and Chairman Price opened with a classic: "Is Nigeria a democracy?" he wanted to know.

Had I still been in my college classroom, I would have snapped back, "Clean out your ears, Price, and listen up!" but, of course, Foreign Service officers cannot speak to congressmen that way. So I smiled patiently, and said, "Yes, congressman, Nigeria has a democratic government."

I might have thought this was an aberration, except for the fact that pretty much the same delegation showed up about three years later when I was in Prague. I can well imagine that congressmen enjoyed being on the Armed Services Committee, for Chairman Price certainly liked to travel. By the time he came to Prague, however, he was visibly old and frail, and must also have been tired, since the Codel arrived after several days in Paris attending the Paris Air Show.

The ambassador gave a dinner party for the delegation, to which a number of Czechoslovak officials were invited. Ambassador Matlock sat at the head table with Price and the ranking Czechoslovak official, and as we finished the main part of the meal, he introduced Chairman Price. The chairman stood and delivered himself of a stream of remarks, the burden of which was that he and his delegation were pleased beyond all understanding to be in Prague, capital of one of the finest countries in the world, home to some of the greatest friends the United States had.

At the table where I was seated with at least a few thoroughly Communist and officially fairly hostile Czechoslovak officials who were the ambassador's guests, it was difficult to see whether the Americans or the Czechs were more astounded at the chairman's statement.

In some posts I served in, we had no Codel visits at all. In Berlin, during the year after the opening of the wall, we had endless, overlapping Codels. Every committee in both houses of the United States Congress thought up a reason to visit Berlin. We noted that one senator came four times to Berlin with different Codels. Trying to put together a meaningful program after a while became embarrassing, because so many of the delegations wished to call on the same list of people in the Berlin government. There are only so many times you can request a person to receive a group of American congressmen without feeling a little apologetic about it.

In Berlin, we were lucky in a way, since some of the visitors were more interested in the military aspects of our presence there, and the Army could take the lead role in planning the visit and providing the logistics. Even there we could get called in. One night, when I was duty officer on the diplomatic side of the house, I had a call from the Army officer controlling the visit of a lone congressman. He had a problem. The congressman had flown into Berlin on United States military transport and had therefore been able to enter the city without a passport or travel document of any kind. He wished to cross to East Berlin, an excursion that still required passports for any Americans not actually stationed at the United States mission. The Army control officer wanted to know if I would issue the congressman a passport. Quite apart from the legalities of the question, there was no way I could do this, nor was any consular officer willing to do it. For obvious reasons, an American passport has so many built-in security features, the materials for which are properly locked up in safes during non-working hours, that it is impossible to issue one just on a whim of the duty officer. The congressman was not to be denied, however, and I later learned he had somehow been taken to East Berlin without a passport. Apparently, his only interest was in shopping for some kind of specialized product, most likely wooden nutcrackers or blue onion china from the Dresden china factory, perennial favorites.

Many Foreign Service officers who serve at posts where Codels are a continuing plague develop a deep and abiding contempt for the Congress after seeing a parade of ill-informed representatives of the people pass through. The trips are very costly, since Congress is exempt from the restrictions on travel budgets under which executive branch members live. Congressmen also do not feel the need to abide by legislative requirements they place on the executive branch. A "Fly America" principle on international travel has long been in place, requiring government employees to travel on United States flag carriers when at all possible. Frequently this requirement put onerous demands on travelers. Nevertheless, I spent an entire day in Zurich changing a ticket for a senator who decided he would rather travel on Swissair than TWA. The ticket had to be endorsed at the TWA office, at which the employee told me she was not supposed to issue an endorsement for that kind of ticket. I finally said, "If the Congress legislates the rules under which you are working, I guess a senator has the right to break them."

I was fortunate over the years to be stationed in only two posts visited by a Secretary of State. In Zurich, Henry Kissinger dropped in three times; in Berlin, James Baker came twice. The contrast between the two experiences gave rise to a reflection that the staff surrounding the Secretary never dropped a requirement but only added more. A Kissinger visit in the mid-1970s was a traveling circus, but the Baker visit in December 1989 was beyond belief. The Kissinger visits were preceded by the arrival of an advance staff of a few officers and security people who had already laid the groundwork through cables. They worked cooperatively with the staff at the consulate and embassy in Bern and treated us like colleagues. Their arrival preceded Kissinger's by perhaps two or three days.

Baker's visit on the other hand was presaged by the arrival of a staff support team at least a week ahead of the Secretary. Their attitude toward the mission staff was oppositional and hostile; they appeared to assume we were inexperienced and incompetent. While the security people went off to huddle with German police and security types, the head of the advance team demanded increasingly complicated scenarios from those of us working on the visit. It was impossible to talk them out of anything. They would not discuss or negotiate requirements; they would only demand absolute, unquestioning compliance. I often wonder if the Secretary of State knows the idiotic and repetitive work that precedes any visit overseas.

If Kissinger traveled with, say, a hundred people, including a massive press corps, Baker traveled with twice that. Vice Presidential visits (of which I saw two) involved several hundreds, and I hesitate to guess what a Presidential visit involves. There are relatively few places in the world with hotel and communications facilities in which such a visit can take place without calling on all kinds of expensive backup solutions. By the time the traveler arrives, all spontaneity has been wrung out of the process. Every minute is choreographed; every step is counted and marked with tape.

I have difficulty judging whether these visits, on which a good deal of time and money are spent, accomplish anything. Much of the time, the purpose of the visit is domestic political gain rather than any foreign policy objective. This was certainly the case of the Vice Presidential visits to Nigeria, both of which occurred shortly before the President for whom they worked (Carter and Bush I) ran for reelection. The idea was to curry favor among African-American voters. Visits from Secretaries of State are more likely to involve substantive meetings. Kissinger's stops in Zurich involved in one case a meeting with the Shah of Iran and, in the other two, negotiations for a settlement of the conflict in southern Africa. One of Baker's two visits to Berlin was made to finalize the treaty that officially ended the wartime allies' control over Germany and Berlin. The fact that the most public event of that visit was the

242

decommissioning of Checkpoint Charlie was a serendipitous accident, even if it was the lead on the evening news.

My Scotch-Irish soul is troubled by the enormous waste of human and financial resources that goes into these events. But the cheeseparing that is instinctive to me is not going to be adopted any time soon by either the Congress or the executive branch.

Being Female

A woman's experience in the Foreign Service is probably like that in most large organizations; it includes much that is neutral and more than enough that ranges from irritating to awful.

I arrived at my first overseas post with the Foreign Service just before Christmas 1974. I had been a Foreign Service officer nine months and had just completed ten weeks of intensive German language training. Although I was posted to Zurich, where the language spoken on the streets is Swiss German, I had been taught Hochdeutsch, the standard German spoken in Germany.

I entered the Foreign Service with a partial knowledge of written and spoken German, so I was placed in a class already in progress at the Foreign Service Institute, locus of all language training for Americans about to be posted overseas. The class I joined consisted of five males who had been wrestling with the language full-time for ten weeks when I showed up. They were the fast class, with fairly good ability to master a foreign language, and they had bonded tightly.

"Hello," I said, as I took my place at the table in the first classroom of the day. "I'm Helen Weinland." There was total silence until I spoke directly to each and asked his name and where he was posted. Total silence was what I encountered from my fellow students for the next ten weeks.

They had been told the previous week that I was to join them. Apparently, they resented the fact that I was to dilute their little male club. They were all ambitious—one at least rose to become the Commercial Counselor at our embassy in Bonn some years later—and I would divert attention they felt they deserved from the teachers. At least, that is what I infer from the fact that they would not speak to me, that they interrupted every attempt I made in the

244

next weeks to speak in German in the class, and that they ignored all my efforts to exchange friendly conversation with them. Since none of them would speak to me, I was unable to ask why they were so unfriendly.

Foreign Service friends to whom I told this story in later years do not believe that fellow officers could have sent me to Coventry in this way. It is certainly not usual among Foreign Service colleagues. But when I encountered one member of the class later, while I was in Zurich and he had been detailed there to work on a Kissinger visit, he still stared straight through me when I greeted him.

Toward the end of my miserable ten weeks of German instruction, we were in the hour in which we participated in free discussion, in German, of some issue raised at the start. That particular day we were joined by the supervisor of the training who dropped in from time to time to see how we were progressing. The teacher of that particular hour was the head of the German department, Frau Plischke.

One of the students, the future Commercial Counselor, suggested that we discuss some question of economic relations, and so we did for most of the class. I attempted a few times to put in my oar, starting off, "Ich denke dass...(I think that)," a construction that requires the following clause to be arranged with the verb at the end after everything else. Before this becomes second nature, it requires a lot of mental gymnastics, and during those flips in my head, some other member of the class would jump in and cut me off.

With five minutes to go, I had yet to utter a complete sentence. Frau Plischke then said, "So, Frau Weinland, jetzt sind Sie in der Reihe (Okay, Miss Weinland, now it's your turn)."

In my best German, I answered, "These people aren't interested in my opinions," to which the teacher responded, "Do you think they are male chauvinists?"

"I know all about that," I replied. "I taught women's history at Ohio State University."

Frau Plischke persisted. "That's very interesting," she said. "You must tell us about that tomorrow in this class."

"I wouldn't dream of talking about such things with these people," I said, as I gathered up my books. Thus ended my only overt rebellion during my German training.

However awful those ten weeks were, it was unofficial male chauvinism and not officially directed discrimination. I encountered enough of the latter during my twenty years in the Foreign Service to make me deeply cynical about the State Department's efforts to confront it.

In fact, my assignment to Zurich, my first overseas post, resulted from the first episode of gender discrimination I encountered. The normal assignment process at that time for new officers was to meet after a few weeks in the entry course with the personnel officer responsible for junior officer placement. At that meeting, I rank-ordered the five geographic areas (placing Europe first, as I recall, and Asia second). Subsequently my counselor told me there were no available postings in Europe, and he offered me a choice of three Asian consulates at which there were jobs for a junior officer in the consular section: Cebu, Philippines; Medan, Indonesia; and Udorn, Thailand.

I spoke with a number of people who had been in Asia and discussed the choice with them. They were unanimous—Medan would be the most interesting post of the three. Medan is a city on the island of Sumatra in north-western Indonesia. I would be the only consular officer in a staff of five Americans and thus fairly independent. I would have a wide range of duties that I would not enjoy at a larger embassy. So I told my counselor that Medan was the place I wanted to go, and he agreed to pursue the assignment through the rest of the process.

This meant going to "panel," i.e. a meeting between the personnel counselor for the officer concerned, the personnel officer who dealt with all the posts in a particular geographic region, and the officer from the executive office of that geographic bureau who dealt with personnel issues. My assignment to Medan went to panel and I was rejected. No explanation was given to me; I was simply told I could not go to Medan. Instead I was assigned to go to Manila, a huge embassy, but not for a year. During that year I would be detailed to the Philippines Desk at the Department of State on which they needed an extra hand for a number of jobs looming on the horizon.

While I was at the Philippines Desk (which turned out to be a fascinating job for a new officer), I came to know another woman officer who had been in the Foreign Service eight or ten years and had served in both Indonesia and the Philippines. She had the inevitable network of connections in the State Department, one of which was the personnel officer for Asia who had sat on the panel that considered me for Medan. He told her the reason I had been rejected for the post was that I was a female; Medan was a Moslem part of a Moslem country, and it was thought (in 1974) that a woman could not be effective in the post. He was unwilling to be quoted as having told me this (panel deliberations were supposed to be confidential), but that was what had happened. This decision occurred in the immediate aftermath of Alison Palmer's successful suit against the Department of State for its sex discrimination.

Not much more than ten years later, a female Foreign Service officer was named as the consul general (i.e. head of the post) in

Medan. Since Harriet Isom, the woman in question, has subsequently been ambassador in two embassies, she must have done a creditable job there.

In 1974, as a three-month old FSO, I decided not to fight the system, make waves, or raise a protest to my having been denied the post on the grounds of my gender. I merely went to work to cancel my assignment to Manila, where I would have been a little ant in one of the largest visa mills in the world. I managed to do this by accident, running into my personnel counselor one night on the bus and finding out, as we climbed the hill toward Washington Cathedral, that there was an opening at the consulate in Zurich. I was successful in breaking the Manila posting and getting the job in Zurich.

After running the gauntlet of German language training, I arrived in Zurich. Male chauvinism there came largely from the Swiss. Many of them could not believe I was the vice-consul; many could not believe I could make decisions (that is, negative ones) about visas that would stick. There was also the ponderous man who was the head of an organization known as SFUSA (Swiss Friends of the United States of America) who periodically dropped in to the consulate to call on the consul general. Every time he was introduced to me, this gentleman forgot he had ever laid eyes on me before and then informed me that SFUSA had dealt with the question whether to admit women and had decided (little chuckle here) not. "Heh, heh," I responded with a diplomatic counter chuckle.

Not getting the job in Medan was not the last time I encountered gender discrimination in Foreign Service assignments. When I was due to leave Zurich in 1976, it began to get close to the time for my departure and I had not received any onward assignment. I had been proposed for a staff assistant job and was pushed by a senior officer who knew my work, but I lost out to another (female) young officer. Thus September came, three months before I was due out, and there was nothing definite on the horizon.

I flew home to Washington on my own nickel and met my assignments counselor. She was brand new in the job. At our first encounter, she languidly consumed a yogurt as a delayed breakfast while I explained my dilemma. She made it clear no one had ever done her a favor in the assignments process and she did not intend to exert herself for me. She asked that I let her know, after pounding the corridors for a few days, what I found out.

From her office, I went to call on a friend I had met during a Kissinger visit to Zurich. He worked in the office that provided staff support for the Secretary of State and knew the staff people in all the major offices in the Department. He knew there was an opening for a junior staff officer in the office of the Under Secretary for Political Affairs, at that time Philip Habib, the third ranking position in the State Department.

Cliff called the senior staffer in Habib's office and told him I was job hunting. I listened to Cliff's side of the conversation, and it was clear I was not going to get a toe in the door. When he hung up the phone, he told me the senior staffer had said, "We had a woman in that job before and it didn't work out." End of conversation—if one woman had flubbed the assignment given to her, no others need apply.

In those days of the mid-1970s, it was still more or less legal to discriminate in this way. Certainly this was before the opposite phenomenon set in, and office directors and placement officers sought to diversify their staffs. It was, nevertheless, after the Palmer lawsuit against the Department over its discrimination in assignments and promotions. Palmer successfully proved that the discrimination she suffered was based on her gender; she won a substantial amount of money in settlement that she had already decided by 1976 to use in a subsequent class action suit on behalf of all the women officers in the State Department.

To my everlasting shame, I opted out of that class and its suit against the Department of State. I honestly thought, in the late 1970s, that I did not suffer from gender discrimination and that the suit did not reflect my experience. I can be somewhat dim at times. I had already lost out for sure on one job and had been refused consideration for another because of my sex, but somehow I did not see this as proof of a consistent pattern of discrimination.

Even without me, Palmer and the other women who led the class action won their case in the early 1980s. The State Department was found to have discriminated against women in recruitment, promotion, assignments, and many other ways. The orders for remedial action took a long time to work their way down from the court, which found that the initial proposals from the Department were not adequate. By the 1980s, too, there were many government regulations covering what was and was not legal for managers to do and say in hiring, promoting, evaluating, and assigning women. Certainly the experiences I had in my early years in the Department could no longer happen, at least as explicitly as they had—or could they?

In 1988, I was again set to look for a new assignment. By this time the process had changed a lot from my early days and began a lot earlier in the cycle. A year before the time when the transition would occur was not too early to begin making contacts, telling people I would be available and was interested in a position in their office or at their embassy. One difficulty, however, was that this process began well before the publication of the yearly promotion list that came out in mid-October. I therefore found myself in September talking with people who controlled positions graded a rank above the one I actually had, on the premise that an overdue promotion would come my way in October.

One job that interested me was the chief of the political section at the embassy in Nairobi, Kenya. The ambassador at the time was Elinor Constable, and I wrote to her, expressing my interest in the job and outlining my experience both in Africa and as a political officer. A few weeks later I had a phone call from her DCM, who was back in the Department on consultation and had been passed the letter by Ambassador Constable. He wanted to meet with me, so I went upstairs to his borrowed office.

Almost the first words out of his mouth were, "I hope you didn't write to the ambassador and ask for this job because she is a woman and you thought that would give you preference." I was flabbergasted, but managed to reply, "No, I applied for this job because I think I would do it well."

We talked a bit longer, about my experience and credentials, and then he said, "All things being equal, we probably would prefer to have a man in this job. There are already too many women in the embassy." The current incumbent of the position was a woman.

While his first warning about hoping for preference was merely offensive, his second statement was blatantly illegal under State Department regulations. I felt as if I had been kicked in the stomach. Looking back, I realize what I should have done—opened the door of the office and asked another woman to step in to listen to him repeat what he had just said to me. But I do not think clearly under these circumstances and, of course, I wanted something—a desirable job—from him. We finished the conversation, and I crawled back to my office.

I reported this conversation to several people: my assignments counselor ("that must have been an upsetting thing to have said to you"); the deputy assistant secretary for African Affairs who oversaw the assignments process to African posts ("I was surprised when George told me he had said that to you"); and a female deputy assistant secretary for African Affairs whose reaction I can no longer remember. It was clear that none of these persons intended to do anything about what had happened, and, unless I were willing to bring a suit, nothing would be done.

A few weeks later the promotion list came out and I was not on it. At that point, I decided there was no hope in making a fuss about getting the job, since I was not at the right grade for it and there would be legitimate reasons for not considering me. I have to say I experienced some *Schadenfreude* a year later when I heard that the DCM had been "selected out" of the Foreign Service (that is, let go) for his lack of promotion and expiration of his senior officer contract. Couldn't have happened to a nicer guy.

If gender discrimination continued in the Foreign Service almost until I retired, what about sexual harassment?

In January of 1978 I joined the Nigeria desk in the State Department. In those days of fatter staffing and great attention to this giant of Africa, there were three full-time officers who concentrated on matters Nigerian, the officer-in-charge (a man who had served one tour in Nigeria and another elsewhere in West Africa) and two more junior officers who handled economic/commercial and political/consular questions. I had the latter job.

The officer-in-charge was one of the best I worked with during my twenty years. He was bright; he didn't let his ego get in the way of training more junior officers; he was ambitious, fair, and hard working.

My rank-mate who handled the economic and commercial portfolio was a different matter. He was about my age and married with one child. I have no idea what was going on in his head, but he was fascinated by the fact I was single. "Where do you go to meet men?" was one of his recurring questions over cafeteria lunches. He could not comprehend the idea that a single woman in her thirties did not make meeting men the sole activity of her life after working hours.

He continued to pester me about my social life, what bars I hung out in to pick up or get picked up, and what I did for sex. I know well what Anita Hill went through. During the Hill-Thomas confrontation twelve years later, I instantly believed her account of the harassment she received from Clarence Thomas. I was unable to convince my colleague that I had no information to give him that would satisfy his curiosity and, even more, that I did not wish to be quizzed on this point. But I didn't want to be hostile; I had been raised to be nice, friendly, and conciliatory.

After a year or so of our joint service on the Nigeria desk, my colleague's wife went out of town to visit her family. We Nigerian desk officers were at a reception at the Nigerian ambassador's house. During the party, my horny colleague sidled up, put his arm around my waist, and said, "Want to screw?" I honestly thought he was joking, so I laughed out loud and said, "Of course not!" After all, I had been a guest in his home with his wife; they had both come to my house for dinner. Call me naive, but I simply did not think that people under those circumstances had casual one-night stands. My brush-off hurt his feelings.

Again, not too many days later, my colleague appeared in the door of my office, following my having asked him for some information or advice about a work problem. He said, "What you really need, besides a good screw, is..."—whatever he was suggesting to deal with my problem. That was the revelation, a long time coming but nevertheless a solid one. After that I was careful not to agree to cafeteria lunches *à deux*, and I no longer engaged in friendly banter in the office.

When it came time for the annual performance evaluation, I was criticized for a lapse in performance at that time; I countered by stating I had been upset by the harassment of my colleague but that my actual work had not suffered. Some time later my assignments counselor warned me not to get any more negative work ratings that might suggest I was difficult to get along with, thus falling into the classic pattern of blaming the victim of sexual harassment for the problem.

What was the most baffling of all, however, were the strange contortions male colleagues went through when they thought they were being supportive of women officers. Their attitudes pointed to their inability to think of women officers as anything other than that, a kind of graft on the body of the real Foreign Service. On the one hand, I appreciated the fact they were trying; on the other I was irritated by their not getting it.

I encountered this attitude most obviously in Berlin. I was assigned to the American mission in the western part of the city in July 1989. I joined the political section, along with three other women officers who arrived more or less at the same time. Our assignments came immediately after the Social Democratic Party (SDP) had won the Berlin elections after a long spell of Christian Democratic Union (CDU) domination. The SDP, in coalition with the Alternative Liste/Green Party, named a *Senat* (the executive part of the city government) with a majority of women members (7 out of 13).

The coincidence of a United States mission political section with a majority of female members at just the time the "Red-Green" city government coalition formed was the subject of comment by male members of the mission staff. At first it provided a kind of amusing lead-in to discussion with elected members of the *Senat* and legislature, but after a few introductory weeks, it became tedious. I found myself using the same "heh-heh" laugh I used fifteen years before in Zurich with the president of SFUSA when one of my bosses (particularly the deputy minister or the head of the political section) raised it in conversation with city officials. "Come *on*, guys," I was thinking, "let's get off it."

I finally let it out, after about a year, when we were hosting a visit from the State Department's Senior Seminar, a group of senior Foreign Service officers assigned to a year of advanced training in foreign policy formulation and management. The leader of the group was a man who had held my job a number of years earlier.

At a cocktail reception for the group, at the Minister's residence, my immediate boss, the head of the political section, introduced me to the Senior Seminar leader and made the now standard comment about the women of the political section. The head of the seminar then told me with pride that there was a certain percentage of women in the seminar that year and, what was more, they were performing with great ability, adding to the work of the seminar.

I replied something to the effect that it was welcome news that women were doing so well, and that sometimes we might even outperform the men. My boss was furious with me, feeling I had undercut him with someone he was trying to impress. I was just tired.

From start to finish in the Foreign Service, I was, at a minimum, made to feel like an exotic. Almost at the time of my retirement, the personnel system at State was wrestling with the problem of evaluating officers' performances without having the officer's gender creep into consideration. A telegram was sent to all offices overseas, outlining some suggestions and inviting others. Among the strangest was a suggestion that officers be referred to in the evaluation narratives by number, rather than name and that all gender-specific pronouns be excised. Writing evaluations was already an artificial and peculiar operation, in which the drafter had to balance carefully the truth against his or her real intentions, whether the person evaluated really ought to be promoted or not. To add to this careful sculpting of prose (which also had to fit into a rigidly short space on the form) a system of numbering the employee and referring to him/her as "the subject" or "007" seemed calculated to take any remaining spontaneity out of the process altogether.

Another suggestion in the circular telegram was to remove, particularly from women's evaluations, discussion of qualities that were considered feminine and, therefore, by assumption ones that did not work actively to get the officer promoted. Such things as charm or agreeableness were to be ruled out in favor of discussing the officer's drive or effectiveness in achieving goals.

I cabled back to the personnel system a suggestion that male officers might usefully be rated on those feminine qualities. Over my years in the service, I had observed a number of my male colleagues, considered go-getters and success stories, exhibiting cultural insensitivity in ways that impeded their ability to establish close contacts among host-country nationals. A little more charm would have helped them greatly in their effort to explain American interests in particular instances.

I never received any acknowledgment for my telegram, nor did my suggestion figure in the summary of suggestions later circulated by the State Department. I retired about a month later, so I do not know whether the personnel system has shifted to the "007" mode of evaluation.

I do know that the first draft of my final State Department evaluation, sent to me about forty-eight hours before my retirement had a statement that went roughly, "Ms. Weinland has excellent contacts, even though she serves in the conservative Moslem north of Nigeria." I had to point out to the DCM in Lagos who wrote this that what he had written was illegal and inadmissible. He is now at his second ambassadorial post.

Making Friends

Being in the Foreign Service is similar to being in the military service, moving through a succession of assignments, always putting down roots and pulling them up. With each move, I left behind people I cared about and moved on to a new group. In some sense there was a pool of ready-made friends among the new work colleagues, and this was quite naturally where I started forming new friendships. But there were limitations in this process.

Foreign Service posts are smaller than nearly any military installation, and at many of them the available pool is little more than a puddle. While the consciousness of rank and the separation of officers and support staff are less obvious and certainly not enforced by regulation, there is all the same a command structure. Jealousies can grow up if the boss is seen as too friendly with a lower-ranked employee.

Additionally, there are the normal questions of compatibility, shared interests, and congruent lifestyle. People who are raising small children will generally be involved in different activities from people who have finished that or people who are not doing it at all. Overseas, people who can speak the local language with facility may want to go to theatre or other entertainments that people without the language will not enjoy.

With every move, therefore, I felt lucky to find one or two people who liked doing what I liked, were comfortable in the country where we were assigned, and wanted to hang out from time to time. In Prague, there were several people who fit this bill. The hostility of the host government also threw us inevitably in with other diplomats, American or "friendlies," for our circle of friendship. There was a significant element of chance that filled the embassy at that

254

time with a group that generally got along well and enjoyed each other's company.

At the other end of the scale was Lagos. I arrived at the end of the tenure of an ambassador who had fostered dissension by the great importance he placed on tennis. Those who played tennis well and wanted to hang out on the court at the ambassador's residence were in the golden circle, while those who did not felt left out and discriminated against. Some of this sense of grievance persisted well into the new ambassador's tenure.

From my perspective, the social relationships at the Lagos embassy were made much worse by an inordinate amount of marital discord and wife swapping. Additionally, many of the wives in particular were nervous about the increasing incidence of violent crime in the city (which has only gotten worse in the intervening twenty years). So much fear mongering took place at gathering spots like the embassy pool that I stopped going there.

In former colonial Africa, a great deal of racism persists even years after independence. I found this attitude particularly rampant among embassy wives who tended to form friendships among the westerners employed not only at other embassies but also as managers at foreign firms. This was a group of people I usually did not find attractive; I didn't want to associate with them much at all. I had to look elsewhere for friendships, and in some cases did not find very many.

Ideally, during a foreign assignment a diplomat should form some friendships among the host-country population. There are limits on this possibility, however. Unless people in the local population are accustomed to socializing with embassy or consulate employees, it is not a usual place for them to look for acquaintances, let alone friends. Business executives might approach a member of the embassy for some service or a speaker and then become friendly, but this is not a normal occurrence. Occasionally when I was moving to a new post, a friend at home might give me a name of someone there to look up, but this was not all that frequent. How many Americans after all had friends in Kigali or in Prague before the end of Communism in 1989? If I were lucky, my predecessor or another member of the embassy staff would introduce me to acquaintances of theirs at a social event. But generally speaking, embassy-hosted social events were regarded as business and not pleasure. In quite a number of places, local citizens were not particularly eager to become friendly with people stationed at the American embassy.

In Prague, an extreme case, friendly social contacts between Czechs and American embassy officials were discouraged on both sides. The Czech internal security police carefully monitored their citizens' relationships with foreigners, and the ordinary Czech was hardly likely to look for trouble in the form of friendship with an American diplomat. From our side, the security regulations required that we file a report on contacts with Czech citizens. This was as much an ass-covering exercise as anything; if the relationship were on record we could not be accused later of concealing it if it turned out to be less than above-board. We Americans were also strictly forbidden to have any kind of friendship with an intimate component with Warsaw Pact citizens.

In spite of all these regulations, however, I did form friendships in Prague that have endured the separations of time and space. One or two were with people who eventually emigrated and left the Communist regime behind. Another was with a couple of which the wife was an American citizen. Following the Velvet Revolution, the peaceful end to Communism, it was possible to look up some people whom I had not stayed in touch with after I left in 1984, and I exchange occasional messages with them.

In Lagos, too, I formed friendships outside the embassy, although most of them were based in the first instance on professional contact. It was difficult in those cases to become very close, since the men quite often (although not always) had a sexual interest as well as a social one in mind. Witness Fola. But at least there were people with whom to socialize, go to parties and so on, although I suspect in many cases the nature of the relationship was misunderstood by others who probably thought I was a girl friend rather than just friend, period.

Kaduna was more comfortable, since there were some couples I came to know in which, like my Czech friends, the wife was from somewhere else. Although in these marriages, the wife had assimilated to Nigerian life, there was more openness to friendship with an American than might otherwise have existed. Generally, the husbands had extensive education and residence abroad and were more familiar with the Western style of friendship.

One happy exception to the pattern was a family in Kano, a city two hours to the north of Kaduna. The husband was one of several brothers who owned an extensive group of businesses. I became acquainted with him, first at the Kaduna Polo Tournament and subsequently when I visited Kano and toured a textile factory owned by the company. He invited me to visit his home to meet his wife, and she and I became friends. I spent a fair amount of down time there, talking with the wife, meeting the children, and relaxing in what was a large and extremely comfortable home. Although the family was cosmopolitan in the sense of having homes in London and Atlanta, it was not at all westernized. The women were not in purdah in a strict sense, but the wife did not socialize with her husband's male friends. My friendship with them was important to me not only for the usual benefits of friendship but also because it provided an invaluable window into traditional northern Moslem culture.

Underlying everything, however, was the reality that I was an American diplomat and, in most cases, responsible for reporting on opinions, attitudes, and policies of the host country. Conversations with its citizens, even when they were friends, were grist for my mill. Usually, I did not identify them by name in the reporting, but by profession or interest group. My reporting was almost always classified, although not in any sense "covert" the way CIA reporting is.

The constant uprootedness meant for me an increased dependence on contact with old friends in the United States and Europe. I was scrupulous about keeping people informed of my frequent changes of address; I tried always to send Christmas cards with long personal notes to friends who dated from all eras of my life—college, graduate school, and beyond. Everyone sheds friends throughout life, of course, and I was no exception. A lot of old friends were lousy correspondents, or else just decided not to stay in touch. But in general I have been blessed with close and enduring friendships that span the period of my life in the Foreign Service. I collected a number of precious new ones during my twenty years with the State Department as well.

And Where Are They Now?

When I left the Foreign Service, I retired to Penobscot, Maine, where I have lived for going on ten years. I began planning this move some years before, in the aftermath of the illness that caused my early departure from Kigali and the frustration I felt at the jobs I was assigned in Washington. A lot of decisions about finances, location, and possible post-retirement jobs go into such a move, and on balance I would say that most of them turned out well for me. By 2001, however, I had found the winters too difficult to cope with on my own, and I began a pattern of spending the six cold months in Boston—still cold but provided with urban transportation and amusements.

While I was in Berlin, I purchased a modular, cape-style house in Penobscot. During my years in Kaduna, I added a garage. The house and garage stand on roughly five acres in what is called The New Subdivision, six building lots strung along a third-of-a-mile-long road. Surrounding these lots is a wooded area of over eight hundred acres, all owned by the same family that created the new subdivision. Such a large area in this part of the world is full of wildlife of which we see a small fraction—moose, bear, porcupines, deer, Northern hare, and ruffed grouse all feed on my lawn or wander across from time to time. I believe there are probably a whole lot more species "back there."

Penobscot is on the Blue Hill Peninsula, an interesting area of Maine, one to which traditionally artists, writers, musicians, and crafts people have migrated over the past century. The Haystack Mountain School of Crafts on Deer Isle is a world-renowned center for all kinds of weavers, potters, carvers, and others who teach or attend the classes that run all summer long. Kneisel Hall in Blue Hill, also a summer center, has attracted string players and pianists for nearly a century. The presence of these two institutions is a magnet bringing others who enjoy what they have to offer and want to live in a community that combines these cultural pleasures with some of the most beautiful and still unspoiled landscape in America.

Those like me who move in "from away" receive a somewhat wary welcome from those who have been here all along, or at least in the two hundred plus years since permanent farm settlement in this area began to pick up. Penobscot, like all the other towns in western Hancock County, has many residents who can trace their roots back to the first families who sailed up the coast from southern Maine or northeastern Massachusetts to stake out farms and began clearing the rocky soil. A good number of our residents work in "the mill," a paper mill owned by Champion International about twenty minutes' drive away in Bucksport. Others earn their livings at trades such as building, plumbing and electrical work, or vehicle maintenance and repair. Some work at the nursing home, and a good number live off the proceeds of combining a number of seasonal occupations— fishing and lobstering, woodcutting, wreathmaking (for Christmas), blueberry raking, and caretaking for the "summer people."

A natural tension exists between those whose roots were sunk here long ago and those who have yet to put down a very long taproot. Those of us from away are apt to ask for services or ordinances the more local people resent and either don't want to or can't pay for—zoning regulations, music programs in the schools, public libraries, and sidewalks. Every town in this area has seen full-fledged battles over land use; the person from away wants to preserve the value of what he or she has, possibly enhance it, while the Mainer is scared to death rising values will put property tax beyond his or her ability to pay. This is not a frivolous tension. Those from away are also more used to the sacrifices in individual liberty involved in living in communities, while the Mainer is ready to defend to the death his right to use what is his any way he wishes.

Every March each town holds its town meeting, one of the few remnants of direct democracy left in America. In Penobscot, the meeting opens the first Monday of March when we elect the moderator of the town meeting and vote on all the local offices to be filled—selectman, school board, or road commissioner. The public part of the meeting begins the next evening with the consideration of all the non-school matters, while the school budget and related decisions come up a week later. Some people find town meeting unbelievably boring and refuse to go. This attitude is not totally unreasonable, but as someone who has lived under both Communism and military dictatorship, I am incapable of turning my back on freely exercised civic duty.

There is absolutely no predicting what will set someone off. One year it was an item of $600 for some new rugs at the school.

Occasionally we will wrangle for a half hour about an expenditure of $300 and blithely pass without a word of comment a line for $75,000 to run our dump or transfer station, as it is called. A few years ago, the five residents on our little road petitioned the town to take over ownership of our road, meaning the town would then be responsible for plowing and repair. I could not believe this item would pass. It came up as one of the last municipal articles at the end of a four-hour meeting; we had already discussed, at length, a new fire engine and the long-range plan for the town. The only objection expressed to the road article was to the road's name, an objection from one of the Mainers in the crowd who thought the name belonged to another, now vestigial, road he had played on as a boy eighty years earlier. The article passed, that night it snowed, and it was music to my ears to hear the town plow going up the road at 6 am the next morning.

For a short time, I took a paid job as a reporter on one of the little weekly papers published in this end of the county, all owned by the same publisher. I realized then that I approached the job much as I had my reporting assignments overseas. I was living in a culture I needed to understand. The political dynamic of my new home was as strange to me, after Washington, D.C., and suburban Maryland, as that of Berlin or Kigali. The same skills I had used to interpret those cultures and political systems were focused on Penobscot and Castine, with the one difference that here, I had to learn to be part of it. I was no longer the disinterested observer; my taxes and energies were part of what was going to make my town work.

With the possible exception of Switzerland, none of the five countries I lived in overseas is today as it was when I left. One has split in two and another has united two pieces into one. And even Switzerland has had some rude shocks since twenty years ago. When I lived there, I was often irritated by the smug, self-satisfied attitude with which the ordinary Swiss citizen navigated through life. Our political officer and his wife were both Jewish, and there were elements of this smugness which got even farther under their skins. One day, the wife, Helen, burst out to me that, much as she liked her closest friend in Zurich, she got tired of hearing the Swiss woman complain of the shortages and other deprivations of World War II. Helen spoke of the scenes at the train station in Basel when Jews, hoping to leave Germany and the Nazi regime behind, were turned back, literally yards from safe ground. Although Helen and Harvey had been born in the United States, there were various distant cousins who had perished in the Holocaust, as is probably true of almost all American Jews, and Helen could not bear to hear her friend complain that there had been food shortages during the war in Switzerland.

I often thought of that conversation with Helen when watching the Swiss Ambassador to the United States on TV and his baffled incomprehension as he fended off attacks on his government and the Swiss banks for their unwillingness to account for wartime Jewish deposits and assets. The Swiss have so seldom been criticized, loudly and publicly, for their behavior as a nation, that when the group of determined survivors and heirs made clear they could not be turned away with simple assurances that every effort had been made to trace account holders, the Swiss were flummoxed. Whatever most of us think of former Senator d'Amato, he became a demon to the Swiss. His Senate Banking Committee may have gone a little over the top on tactics, but essentially he had justice on his side and the Swiss could not stand it.

Changes in Czechoslovakia are so vast and dramatic since I left in June 1984 they hardly need to be discussed. I visited Switzerland once after I left my job there, and found it and the friends I looked up essentially unchanged. When I first traveled back to Czechoslovakia in November 1990, almost a year after the Velvet Revolution, I experienced constant shocks. The first was right at the border—I needed no visa. I just handed in my passport, and after a short while, the smiling immigration officer handed it back and waved me through.

My closest friends, with whom I could have stayed, were not in Prague; they had emigrated just a month after the big change, traveling to a job in the United States already lined up for them. I stayed, therefore, in a private apartment whose owners had vacated it and made it available to me for hard-currency payment. This arrangement would have been unthinkable under the Communists. For about three days I wandered around town mostly on my own and close to tears almost the entire time. Books written by friends from six years before and only published in the West, often from *samizdat* manuscripts, were now openly on sale at all the bookstores. I was able to telephone former friends to whom I would never have spoken on the telephone before, and meeting them openly in restaurants was completely normal now.

Because I had no telephone number for the Catholic priest, Václav Malý, who had been a frequent movie-goer at my house, I took the tram out to his neighborhood and walked up the hill to the house where he had a one-room apartment. He invited me in for coffee and we chatted for an hour, roaring with laughter as we recounted the surveillance stories of the bad, now ended, times when I lived in Prague. All was not completely sweetness and light, however. Malý was at that time recovering from a badly broken arm and elbow he suffered when struck by a car on the streets of Bratislava the previous June. He had been engaged in political

261

activity and had attended a rally. Whether the accident was truly an accident had never been fully determined; even the suspicion it had not been was a reminder that there were some people who were coming out losers in the transition to democracy and were fighting to prevent it.

To me the most surreal change in Czechoslovakia was the list of the new government in 1990. Beginning with President Václav Havel, and moving down through Foreign Minister Jiří Dienstbier, my former video evening guests included the Deputy Foreign Minister, the Defense Minister, the ambassadors to the United States and Poland, and the wife of the director of the Czech News Service (he had been in jail the entire time I was in Prague). Malý himself, denied permission to work as a priest under the Communists, had celebrated Christmas Mass in St. Vitus Cathedral, on national television, about a week after the Velvet Revolution succeeded. When I returned to Prague in spring 1991, just before leaving Berlin for Kaduna, Malý was back at work in a beautiful, large Romanesque-revival church. He is now a bishop.

I remarked to a friend when I was in Prague that Czechoslovakia would perhaps find the transition difficult without a rich western uncle such as East Germany had in the Federal Republic. Her answer was that she was glad the Czechs were being forced to see the transition through on their own. Years after that conversation, I see in hindsight that there were a lot of roadblocks in that process. Among other things, the country itself split in two, a development that perhaps could have been prevented. The re-division into the Czech Republic and Slovakia did, at least, take place without violence, more than can be said for Yugoslavia.

The same friend also pointed out what is true for her entire generation in eastern Europe, those now in their sixties and seventies. "It's too late for us," she said. She was glad for the change for her children and grandchildren. It is sobering, I would think, to look back and see the political enthusiasms of one's youth turned into the repressive evils of Communism. Too late to acquire the skills for life in democracy and market capitalism, this generation in eastern Europe can only hope the next will build a more just community.

The close friends who emigrated to the United States after the Velvet Revolution are now back in Prague. He is a theologian and was offered the opportunity to chair a department at the theological faculty, now reintegrated in Charles University. She teaches at the much enlarged International School in Prague. I visited them in 2000 and asked after various friends we had in common when I lived there. It is now completely normal to say, "Well, he has become very radical in his views; we don't support his party at the elections." Her political opinions about people are the ones any normal, free people have about one another. Former dissidents from different traditions—Christian, reformed Communists, traditional liberalism—do not now agree very often, whereas they presented a united front under the Communist regime. The entire framework in which life is lived and discussed and carried out has changed so entirely since the two years I spent in Prague that the previous one seems like a nightmare.

When I returned to Nigeria, ten years after my earlier tour in Lagos, there had been regression. The political system had reverted to military rule from the civilian regime I reported on from Lagos. Many of the friends from Lagos days had spent time in prison, some under rather harsh conditions. The economy was in a mess and headed for much worse. The two and a half years I spent in Kaduna were a roller-coaster ride of hopes and disappointments about turning both trends around; when I left, a far more repressive military regime had taken office and the level of official looting reached ever more deplorable levels.

About a year and a half after my departure, General Abacha and his governing council announced that a coup plot had been uncovered. Quite a number of people were arrested, including the former head of state who had mid-wifed the only successful transition to civilian rule from military government, Olusegun Obasanjo, and his deputy, Shehu Musa Yar'Adua. Their death sentences were commuted to life in prison after an international outcry. Those arrested, as well as a number of journalists who tried to report honestly on events, disappeared into various prisons around the country.

I often thought of Yar'Adua after that. He had lived around the corner from me in Kaduna, and his peacocks frequently yelled their heads off in my garden. I occasionally called on him. He had hoped to run for the presidency when Babangida was supposedly leaving office, but he was one of those banned from political activity. Nevertheless, he remained active behind the scenes. Yar'Adua would most likely never have won a national election. His home power base was weak, and there were very likely skeletons in his closet I knew nothing about. He was friendly to me, but guarded in what he said. I never could decide if his reserve was a pronounced form of the normal northern Nigerian manner or a wily face he put on for me as a western diplomat. Nevertheless, I found his understanding of what democratic thinking and behavior really were as good as that of any Nigerian I met. I believed he had an internal understanding that democratic behavior really did mean he couldn't win all the time and that his party, when out of power, had to work so far as possible on measures for the common good with the party in power and plan for the days ahead. He had a well-developed ironic sense of humor. He exercised it when I called on him not long after Abacha had seized power and detained Yar'Adua for some days. Following the "coup plot," which, frankly, I did not believe ever existed, I hoped Yar'Adua was maintaining his sense of humor. Unfortunately, he died in prison in December 1997, about six months before Abacha himself suffered his final heart attack. Yar'Adua's death was, from all I have been able to learn, the direct result of illness from the poor prison conditions, followed by the withholding of medical assistance until it was far too late. He was not as well known in the west as Mashood Abiola, who suffered the same fate seven months later, but I believe his death was as great a loss to the nation as Abiola's. I mourn his loss.

It is shocking to hear of the death of a personal acquaintance under a repressive regime. The events in Rwanda following my departure cause me a despair I can hardly express. The troubles in that country started before the massacres that so shocked the world. In 1990 an invasion of largely Tutsi refugees crossed the border in the north with Uganda. The history of these people and the goals of their invasion go back to pre-independence Rwanda and are the subject of a number of excellent books by journalists who covered the troubles. Whatever the wrongs the invading force sought to right (and they were real), the effects after the Rwandan Army failed to repel them, as they had on previous occasions in the past thirty years, were also real and nasty. The fighting took place mostly in northern Rwanda, where for about three and a half years there was the kind of killing and small-scale, bloody fighting that characterizes a guerilla war in which neither side can gain the upper hand. The national political arrangements that had maintained the surface appearance of calm when I lived in Rwanda had hardened prior to the outbreak of hostilities and became more polarized afterwards. President Habyarimana found himself increasingly squeezed by Hutu extremists in his own government on the one hand and by American and other international mediators on the other, who were urging him to establish a multi-party democratic regime. In early April 1994, when Habayarimana was returning from a negotiating session in Arusha, Tanzania, his plane was shot down and he was killed.

Immediately afterward, within hours, wholesale killing broke out in Rwanda and went on for the next three or four months at a rate the world has rarely seen. No one will ever know how many perished, but the number is probably well over half a million. The horror has been covered in the Western press, reporting to the international community that reacted much too weakly, much too late, and with far too little understanding of what to do.

Among the early targets of the killers were the moderate Hutus and token Tutsis who were in the government and positions of power in Rwanda. During the time I was in Kigali, a married couple—he Tutsi and she Canadian by birth—worked for USIS. By 1994, Lando, as we called him, had left the USIS office and become active in politics. He was Tutsi and eventually joined the Habyarimana cabinet as a token Tutsi minister. He and his entire family were among the first slaughtered, wife, two children, and himself. I have heard conflicting reports of exactly how the murder took place. My intractable, thieving cook Jean, after I dismissed him, had gone to work for Lando and his wife who ran two restaurants in Kigali. As Jean, too, was Tutsi, I suspect at some point he was killed in the carnage.

One of the senior Rwandan members of our embassy staff was the assistant in the consular and political section, Rusimbi. He worked directly for me, as well as for the political/consular officer, as my assistant for Peace Corps matters. He was an intelligent and loyal member of our staff. He was, I was told, "called out" during the massacres. I interpret this to mean he had taken shelter, most likely with his family, in some place where large groups of people thought they would find sanctuary, usually church compounds. These areas were no safer than anywhere else, because the Hutu *Interinhamwe* (gangs of thugs) came to these places with lists of persons whom they "called out" of the crowd and then hacked to death.

In March 1997 I traveled to Washington to attend a memorial service for Gene Chiavaroli, the USAID director in Kigali during my time there. Gene had been much loved and respected by all who worked for him, and a large number of us who had known him in Kigali turned up to mourn his sudden death from a heart attack. At the service, I was happy to see again Bernadette, our cashier at the embassy, the woman who advised me to take Sopatra back on the payroll. Bernadette married an American employee of Africare, and they are now living in Washington. During our greetings I asked, as one does, after her family in Rwanda. "They are all dead," she answered me, "and I cannot talk about it."

I felt the same despair and hopelessness with Bernadette as I had felt in Prague speaking with my friend who survived Auschwitz about her life and survival; what can you say to a person who has lost an entire family to this kind of brutality? It is impossible to contemplate this kind of end for someone you have known and worked with daily, joking, conferring, taking and giving advice. I simply cannot think about Rusimbi's death, or the murder of Lando's entire family. And yet, I believe it is our responsibility to think about it and remember it, to honor those who died in this terrible way and try to create conditions in which such a thing will never again come to pass.

My friend Rosamond Carr, owner of the flower plantation in northern Rwanda, was evacuated from Rwanda at the height of the troubles. A lot of local people had taken refuge in the buildings on her farm, and prior to her departure many were hacked to death in her front garden. As soon as she heard it was safe to do so, Roz returned to her plantation. Her house had been thoroughly looted but gradually all the people who had worked for her made their way back. Some had suffered harrowing experiences; a couple had to escape from the refugee camps across the border that were under the iron control of Hutu thugs. Roz and her senior Rwandan employee, Sembagare, established an orphanage for children whose families had been killed in the slaughter and whose more remote relatives cannot be traced. (Compounding the difficulty is the fact that Rwandans do not have "family names." They carry a Rwandan name, given at the naming eight days after birth, and a Christian name, conferred at baptism.)

For a while the orphanage carried on at Roz's compound, although the house is quite close to the border with Congo and bands of infiltrating Hutu thugs from the camps across the border created constant trouble. In 1998, this problem became so severe that Roz, her staff, and the orphanage had to move to Gisenyi, where there is a more settled atmosphere. At last word, there were over a hundred children being cared for in the orphanage. Four years after the worst of the killing, extended family members can still not be traced. Roz has written an account of her life in Rwanda in a memoir, *Land of a Thousand Hills,* published in 1999.

Every once in a while, my phone or e-mail springs to life and reconnects me to the twenty years I spent in the Foreign Service. Within the last three months of 1999, I had a visit with a couple who served with me in Prague. These occasions are a great chance for insiders' gossip, and we went at it with abandon at a restaurant in Boston. Another reunion was with my theological friend from Prague, in the United States on an exchange teaching stint. After catching up on family news, we talked about how a nation can bring reconciliation at the end of a repressive regime and how well Czechoslovakia had done on that score. And there are the more fleeting phone visits—the Peace Corps cashier from Kaduna just passing through, the neighbor on the corner in Lagos who has just retired from his post as Nigeria's ambassador to the UN and, most recently, the private secretary to the Emir of Zaria. I may have retired but I have not fallen off the edge of the earth.

When I was overseas or in Washington, burrowing away in my small office, I often thought my life was a lot duller than my friends believed. Setting it down like this in black and white, I have changed my mind. I'm glad I got to live it.

About the Author

Helen Weinland served as a Foreign Service officer in the United States Department of State for twenty years, from 1974 to 1994. During that time, she was assigned overseas to Zurich, Lagos, Prague, Kigali, Berlin, and Kaduna. She also held assignments in Washington, D.C., from time to time.

Prior to her entry in the Foreign Service, Weinland taught history at Indiana University as a teaching assistant and as an instructor at Ohio State University.

She was educated at Mount Holyoke College, Edinburgh University and Indiana University, where she worked as a graduate student assistant on the staff of *Victorian Studies*.

Since her retirement from the Foreign Service, Weinland has divided her life equally between the coast of Maine and Boston.

Printed in the United States
17548LVS00002B/52-132